THE TRANSFORMATIONAL SELF

THE TRANSFORMATIONAL SELF
Attachment and the End of the Adolescent Phase

Harold K. Bendicsen

KARNAC

First published in 2013 by
Karnac Books Ltd
118 Finchley Road, London NW3 5HT

British Library Cataloguing in Publication Data

A C.I.P. for this book is available from the British Library

  ISBN 978-1-78049-142-4

Edited, designed and produced by The Studio Publishing Services Ltd
www.publishingservicesuk.co.uk
e-mail: studio@publishingservicesuk.co.uk

Printed in Great Britain

www.karnacbooks.com

CONTENTS

ACKNOWLEDGEMENTS

I want to thank early readers Joseph Walsh, Craig Hjorth, Colin Pereira-Webber, Barry Childress, William Gieseke, Adele Kaufman, and my son Michael Bendicsen for their interest in this topic, recommendations with respect to content and consistency, and encouragement to share it with a wider audience. Modifications of this version were also read by Samuel Abrams and Robert A. King. The thoughtful assessments of both Samuel Abrams and Robert A. King with respect to scope and content are appreciated; their input was quite helpful and led directly to the second version.

My study group consisting of Kirk Alley, Bernadette Berardi-Coletta, Susan G. Burland, Debra A. Carioti, John Colby Martin, Rosalie Price, and Kathleen M. O'Connor provided support for my hypothesis along with unvarnished criticism and encouraged me to adopt a "finish it and submit it" attitude.

In particular, I want to thank Joseph Palombo, Co-Founding Dean of the Chicago Institute for Clinical Social Work, and Barrie Richmond, Faculty member of the Chicago Institute for Psychoanalysis (CIP), for giving me so much of their tightly scheduled time to offer critical organising suggestions and ideas about framework. The erudite contribution of Joseph Palombo sensitised me to the neo-positivist perspective in current trends in mental health research, led me to expand the section on the neurobiological self, cautioned me about the potential for conceptual confusion in mixing metaphors, and helped me to recognise how important this dimension is to more fully understand the transformational self.

The scholarly participation of Barrie Richmond was motivational and is unquestionably one of the cornerstones of this paper. His enthusiasm for the nature of adolescent dynamics and his curiosity about the process of adolescence validated my hypotheses and made the weariness of revision more enjoyable than tedious. His knowledge about the intersection of metaphor theory and psychoanalysis was particularly relevant. His patient, tolerant approach allowed me to move at my own pace, make mistakes, and learn from them. Without his persistent encouragement this monograph would not exist.

With respect to the second version, I want to thank Aileen Philips Schloerb, a psychotherapist in the Child and Adolescent Psychotherapy Clinic at the CIP, my daughter-in-law, Elizabeth Bendicsen, and William Gieseke (in particular once again), for their careful proof reading and overall assessment as to goodness of fit with the elements of this theoretical composite. In the Child and Adolescent Psychoanalytic Psychotherapy Program at the CIP I want to thank Co-Director Ed Kaufman for encouraging me to access second year students: Jean Rounds, Teresa Fitzgerald, Renee Raap, Harriet Berlin, Camila Bassi Peschanski, and fourth year students: Audra Bowie, Claudia Benitez, Andrea Fouchia, Stephanie Halpern, Monica Buttafava Trotta, Kevin McMahon, and Charlotte Mallon (visiting student) who asked those supremely difficult questions that only students can ask, further clarifying my thinking.

Again, my study group of Debbie Barrett, Bernadette Berardi-Coletta, Debra A. Carioti, John Colby Martin, Kathleen M. O'Connor, and Rosalie Price read earlier and later copies and were, consequently, able to compare and contrast both versions of this material. They stressed the need for conceptual clarity and consistency in order to avoid confusion and ambiguity.

The second and present version owes its existence to Barrie Richmond and to Joe Palombo. They have been insightful partners and valuable collaborators in this long journey. Barrie encouraged me to deepen my understanding of the transformational self from the standpoint of Kohut's seminal paper on the transformations of narcissism. In addition, Barrie explained the nature of the paragraph in some detail as a means to strengthen and focus my otherwise wandering writing style.

Joe Palombo has been most generous with his time and sharing of his scholarly knowledge. His many contributions to this second version are too numerous to mention. However, a few are poignant and most significant. Joe's encouragement to reorganise the monograph to improve flow and readability was of great importance. His suggestions to expand the sections on neurobiology, attachment theory, and non-linear dynamic systems theory considerably strengthened this project.

I am grateful to Dorothy Valintis who brought her considerable grammarian skills to bear as one of the proof readers for the last edition of this work. Also, my family deserves special mention, especially my wife Kathleen, who has been most patient during the long hours of rewriting and editing.

In addition, I want to recognise the assistance of Ellen Fechner and Maureen Hansen for supplying formatting assistance for the chart entitled, "Modern and postmodern philosophical paradigms in clinical social work from a developmental model perspective". Kate Schechter provided valuable guidance on the display of variables and on reconfiguring the chart to fit the specific purposes of this monograph. Rita Sussman offered suggestions on positioning pieces of data which improved readability and further clarified my thoughts on the subject.

Last, I want to thank Rod Tweedy (Editorial Assistant), and Catherine Harwood (Production Manager), at Karnac Books; as well as the production team at The Studio Publishing Services, for their reliable support and patient guidance through the entire process of preparing this manuscript for publication.

Harold K. Bendicsen, LCSW, BCD, is a clinical social worker who maintains a private practice in Elmhurst, Illinois. He holds a certificate in Child and Adolescent Psychoanalytic Psychotherapy from the Chicago Institute for Psychoanalysis. He has held clinical, supervisory, and administrative positions in child welfare agencies, residential treatment centres, and social service agencies. He is Adjunct Professor at Loyola University Chicago School of Social Work and a member of the faculty of the Child and Adolescent Psychoanalytic Psychotherapy Training Program at the Chicago Institute for Psychoanalysis.

To my grandchildren:
Jayden, Jack, Audrey, James, Willem, Sophia, Alexander, and Joseph
And to my brother: Norman

PREFACE

The journey to complete this monograph has been long and adventurous. The first version of this monograph was presented at the
Association of Child Psychotherapists' workshop series entitled
*Difficulties in Attachment Across the Life Cycle: Infancy, Adolescence and
Adulthood* in Chicago, Illinois on June 26, 2001. This version was
framed in an ego psychology context. Ego psychology, grounded in
traditional positivist philosophy, while offering many explanatory
advantages, had to be abandoned because of its poor conceptual fit
with contemporary, postmodern thinking. Once the limitations inherent in subordinating the conceptual elements to an overarching framework were appreciated, a better fit was found in allowing the pieces to
come together as the process unfolded. The solution was found in
weaving together concepts from modern metaphor theory, attachment
theory, self psychology, neurobiological research findings, contemporary psychoanalytic developmental psychology, and complexity
theory in the context of two psychotherapies of adolescent girls to
create a tighter fitting composite and a more coherent understanding
of the processes. I now label this weave regulation theory (see the
Synopsis for clarification).

The sources of creativity are many. For those engaged in clinical work of a psychological nature, engagements with clients provide boundless opportunities to stimulate imagination. Erik Erikson credits such work with enabling him to complete his signature conceptualisation: the nature of the identity crisis (stage five in the Ages of Man) attendant to the transition into young adulthood. This work directly paved the way to additional theorising in the widely acclaimed *Young Man Luther* (1958) (Friedman, 1999, pp. 260–286).

The immediate sources for the transformational self are data derived from two psychotherapies conducted by me. Well into their treatment these clients spontaneously generated the self-referencing metaphors that got me thinking about the usefulness of this material for clarifying the often turbid transition from late adolescence into young adulthood.

A second source of creativity is the stimulation provided by my colleagues who helped me refine scattered notions and concepts into a coherent narrative of ideas. They provided an invaluable sounding board for assuring the viable interconnectedness of diverse ideas. They challenged the coherence of my argument and in so doing contributed immeasurably to the logical readability of my argument.

The third creative source came from my own late adolescent—young adulthood experience. I have often wondered how it is that I became a psychotherapist. In college I read *Young Man Luther* and wondered if I too was destined to experience a moratorium. I now see the *Transformational Self* monograph as an extension of the work I did on this developmental subject in my personal psychoanalysis. So perhaps I too demonstrate a creative principle that I believe was articulated by Nietzsche among others, that theory building is to some degree autobiography, that is, motivated by a quest for personal understanding.

I am suggesting that client data, input from colleagues, and personal experience can combine in fortuitous ways to form a creative synergy. This is my understanding of the converging creative forces that led to the unfolding of this monograph.

To give us yet another perspective on the creative impulse, it is helpful to know that during the first phase of psychoanalysis, that of drive theory between approximately 1885 and 1905, an astounding hotbed of intellectual and scientific crosscurrents existed on the nature of the human psyche and human sexuality. The dominant conceptualisations involved German biophysics and psychophysics, French psychopathology, and sexology. Makari (2008, pp. 118–225) informs us that by 1905 Freud had weighed in on these matters and had formulated two monumental intellectual syntheses. The first was propounded in the *Interpretation of Dreams* (1900a) and was known as "the model of the mind". The second was articulated in *Three Essays on the Theory of Sexuality* (1905d). It was absorbed into the first and was known as the "psychosexual" synthesis. Respectively, both syntheses were unified psychologically by the dynamic unconscious and biologically by libido theory. These remarkable syntheses served to integrate and otherwise reformulate the sometimes contradictory extant hypotheses by replacing them with "a commanding explanatory framework that includes mental health, mental illness and human sexuality" (Palombo, Bendicsen, & Koch, 2009, pp. 13–14).

Over one hundred years later we find ourselves in yet another intellectual whirlpool, this one can be thought of as an extension of the traditional nature *vs.* nurture controversy in human development. Can new knowledge from diverse fields contribute data to help form a contemporary synthesis that can answer today's questions posed about human development? For example, is development best understood by positivist or social constructivist philosophies, by linear or non-linear dynamic systems theory? Are the processes best understood as continuous, as in a stage-like progression, or does growth occur in discontinuous bursts? An opportunity presents itself to reformulate these and other vital questions by employing regulation theory. Toward that end I am proposing a hypothesis labelled the transformational self synthesis.

The overarching framework utilised in this monograph is emerging regulation theory. Regulation theory is an inter-disciplinary concept originating in the notion of affect regulation as the primary regulating force in human development (Hill, 2010; Schore, 1994). Is there one regulator or are there multiple regulating forces acting in concert? Are they unified in some yet not fully understood way? (Polan & Hofer, 1999). These questions are considered in the Synopsis. Elements are taken from relevant disciplines that comprise regulation theory and I consider each as follows.

I have tried to avoid mixing the terms "ego" and "self" to maintain conceptual clarity. This has not always been possible because of the entrenched theoretical hegemony that aspects of ego psychology still enjoy. See Chapter Three for a discussion of the difficulty separating ego from self. In addition, consistency has been maintained in the use of the gender pronoun she. This stance facilitates the discussion of the case illustrations which are of adolescent girls and, furthermore, emphasises that the transformational self is a gender neutral concept.

The organisation of this monograph into twelve chapters grouped into five parts is designed to lead the reader systematically through the evolution in thinking that led to the transformational self. In Part I, I pose the question, "When does adolescence end?" and discuss the problems in conceptualising the transition from late adolescence into young adulthood. I establish the context for these problems and suggest that an answer may be found in contemporary psychoanalytic developmental psychology. The concept of the transformational self is introduced and I lay out my general thesis. Also philosophical and methodological assumptions are presented.

In Part II, the transformational self is discussed from micro, meso, and macro system perspectives. The transformational self is embedded in a developmental context and so needs to find a comfortable conceptual home.

In Part III, the transformational self's constituent parts are discussed from metaphor theory, attachment theory, neurobiology, non-linear dynamic systems theory, and cognition dimensions. These interlocking, interactive domains of knowledge comprise a new overarching perspective called regulation theory. These contributions combine to act as a bio-psycho-social-spiritual three dimensional gyroscope that manages and stabilises the ever changing self-state over time.

In Part IV, I apply the transformational self to explain the turning point in the courses of psychotherapies of two adolescent girls. I detail the vicissitudes of treatment by illustrating the dynamics associated with the unfolding of the transformational self.

In Part V, I summarise the elements in my argument and leave it to the reader to evaluate its coherence and usefulness. With respect to the core issue, "When does adolescence end?" I suggest an answer can be found in the mobilisation of the transformational self during the course of an individual's development.

INTRODUCTION

This monograph is an attempt to add to the theoretical discussion regarding the nature of the intrapsychic and interpersonal transformational changes associated with the transition from adolescence to young adulthood. I will introduce the concept of the transformational self, a phase specific dimension of the neural self, and demonstrate the enhanced explanatory power that it offers in attempting to examine the sometimes dramatic shifting self-states accompanying the metamorphosis from adolescence into young adulthood. A necessary precondition for the emergence of the transformational self is the maturation of the pre-frontal cortex and its enhanced neural connectivity. With this biological achievement, executive functioning, a strengthened ego/self capacity, can arrive at a mature level of external stabilisation and internal, intrapsychic structuralisation. Conceptualised in self-referencing metaphor and expressed and reinforced through long term potentiation (repeated firing patterns of synchronous neural assemblies), the late adolescent reconfigured self-state becomes a true developmental potentiality evidenced by the use of different self (and other) representations. In other words, self-referencing metaphor becomes the pathway to personal metamorphosis. The psychotherapies of two mid-adolescent girls will illustrate the application of the transformational self concept.

Regarding the title, *The Transformational Self: Attachment and the End of the Adoplescent Phase,* even though the word "end" is used, I do not propose to discuss the literal "end" of adolescence. I am not concerned with questions of task completion or reaching certain developmental end points. Rather let us consider "end" to mean a metaphoric device representing a developmental transition that is obtained through which the individual moves from late adolescence to young adulthood. I am concerned with uncovering those benchmark dynamics that suggest that the individual is making developmental progress (A. Freud, 1965) in terms of achieving an enhanced level of adaptation and moving to more mature levels of functioning. Put differently, "Personal development moves forward in the direction of increased mastery and a sense of integrity along socially defined paths that often facilitate and sometimes impede this development". Problems arise when the search for the essential other "fails or when the essential other found cannot be satisfactorily integrated into the rest of the person's psychological life" (Galatzer-Levy & Cohler, 1993, pp. 341, 346).

PART I
CONTEXT AND PROBLEM FORMULATION

CHAPTER ONE

Introductory considerations

When does adolescence end?

The questions of "When does adolescence end?" and "When does adulthood begin?" are no longer a matter of anthropological and sociological rite of passage speculation. Clearly there is no consensus. In its entirety, there probably never was. We need only think of courts and legislatures wrestling with the question of maturity; when does an adolescent attain the age of legal responsibility for drinking, marrying, entering into contracts, and driving? Parents, too, struggle with the responsibility question while wondering, "When will this teenage phase ever end?" The armed services assess the optimal time for conscription and recruiters ask, "Should a high school degree always be necessary?" Researchers studying human development struggle with defining criteria that would clarify the nature of this critical life cycle transition. Psychotherapists in patient assessments always consider the issue of developmental lags and study the discrepancies between a patient's developmental age *vs.* chronological age. The authoritative Hall (1904), at the beginning of the 1900s, set in motion the idea (building on the developmental trajectory of Rousseau's *Emile Or On Education*, 1762) that prolongation of the adolescent phase was culturally necessary and therefore normative. He considered prolongation desirable because "Child-labor laws kept children under 16 out of the work force, and universal education laws kept them in secondary school, thus prolonging the period of dependence" (Henig, *New York Times*, 2010, p. 4). Psychological tasks became associated with this period of dependence, among them the need to properly sublimate sexuality (in particular masturbatory expression), which has ever since been taken as natural verisimilitude (Esman, 1993; Ross, 1972).

The seeming need for our occidental culture to elongate adolescence is a fascinating subject. Social commentators reflect the most recent observations that the adolescent phase is being extended from ten to twenty years and more. The timeliness of this topic is reinforced by lay publications: "It's taking a lot longer to reach adulthood, study says" (Cholo, *Chicago Tribune*, 2003). MacArthur Foundation researchers quoted in this article suggest that the interval between adolescence and adulthood be formally labelled the pre-adult period. Yet another article describes an emerging group moratorium (Erikson, 1958) phenomenon consisting of eighteen to twenty-eight year olds deferring tasks associated with accepting adult responsibility. "Meet the Twixters, young adults who live off their parents, bounce from job to job and hop from mate to mate. They're not just lazy . . . they just won't grow up" (Grossman, *Time*, 2005). "Back to the Nest: Millions of fledgling adults are returning to mom and dad". The situation has grown so pervasive not just in the US, where twenty-five per cent of Americans between the ages of eighteen and thirty-four now live with parents according to the 2000 US Census, but also in England and Canada where similar trends are taking place (Levine, *Chicago Tribune*, 2005). "We offered a safe port in a stormy economy that has battered many a 20-something. The toxic mix of college and credit-card debt, stratospheric rents and uncertain career prospects had left [our daughter and her husband] scrambling from pay-check to pay-check. By moving into our guest room and paying us a modest rent, they figured they could regain their footing" (Graham, *Wall Street Journal*, 2005).

This social/cultural phenomenon has been cinematically portrayed in the 2006 romantic comedy, *Failure to Launch*. In this movie the adolescent/adult central character, rather than return home, never leaves, prompting his parents to employ an attractive interventionist with rather predictable results (Common Sense Media, 2012).

The economic recession crisis of 2008 and beyond plays a central role. "In recession, no place like home: Parents see young adults 'boomerang' back into their houses because of job loss and debt" (Mack, *Chicago Tribune*, 2010). "Recession's effects haunt a generation: Without strong career starts, young adults are set up badly to propel nation's prosperity". "Unemployment for 20-24 year olds hit a record high of more than 17% earlier this year" (Lee, *Chicago Tribune*, 2010).

But the children and parents caught up in these boomerang dynamics need not result in dysfunctional family outcomes. "More than three-quarters of young adults ages 25 to 34 who have moved back home with their families during the Great Recession and the troublesome economic years that followed say they're satisfied with their living arrangements and upbeat about their future finances". "Those arrangements have benefited their parents as well: almost half of boomerang children say they have paid rent and almost nine-in-ten have helped with household expenses" (Parker, 2012).

The most recent scholarly enumeration of the elongation of adolescence issue is articulated by Robin M. Henig (*New York Times*, 2010) in "What Is It About 20-Somethings? Why are so many people in their 20s taking so long to grow up?"

> We're in the thick of what one sociologist calls "the changing timetable for adulthood". Sociologists traditionally define the "transition to adulthood" as marked by five milestones: completing school, leaving home, becoming financially independent, marrying and having a child. In 1960, 77 per cent of women and 65 per cent of men had, by the time they reached 30, passed all five milestones. Among 30-year olds in 2000, according to data from the United States Census Bureau, fewer than half of the women and one-third of the men had done so. A Canadian study reported that a typical 30-year old in 2001 had completed the same number of milestones as a 25 year old in the early 70s.

Henig continues citing psychology professor, Jeffrey J. Arnett (2004), who proposes a new distinct developmental stage, the 20s, that he calls "emerging adulthood".

> Just as adolescence had its particular psychological profile, [Arnett says] so does emerging adulthood: identity exploration, instability, self-focus, feeling in-between and a rather poetic characteristic he calls

a "sense of possibilities". A few of these, especially identity exploration, are part of adolescence too, but they take on a new depth and
urgency in the 20s. The stakes are higher when people are approach-
ing the age when options tend to close off and lifelong commitments
must be made.

So the controversy continues unabated. Can psychoanalysis, and in
particular psychoanalytic developmental psychology, make a fresh
contribution to understanding the dynamics of individual functioning
in the midst of this expanding cultural phenomenon?

Towards a definition of the transformational self

The transformational self is a self-organisation, a state of mind, that
emerges at the developmental transition out of the adolescent phase.
At this emergence the adolescent begins to imagine different possibilities for her self-concept, or identity, if you will and therefore, signals
readiness to assume mature status in adult society. It is a cluster of
reconfigured self-state potentialities and beliefs about those potentialities, competencies, and capabilities, which have been and are being
tempered by the "adaptation to reality" (Hartmann, 1939).

Incidentally, the ideas of transcendence and transformation in late
adolescence are familiar. Jaffe states that despite wide diversity on the
nature of adolescence, "there is general agreement that a central issue
in adolescence is the shift toward guiding one's own experience
(Richmond & Sklansky, 1984). This shift variously termed reorganization, transformation, or integration occurs along a number of trajectories" (Jaffe, 2000, p. 19). Another example comes from Loewald (1962):

> This ideal ego . . . gradually becomes an ego-ideal . . . seen in a much
> more differentiated and elaborated form than previously in parental
> figures . . .. The future state of the ego (ideal) is to be attained by merg-
> ing with the magical object. No stable internal structure representative
> of the ego's self-transcending, exists as yet; the self-transcending is
> dependent on a magical communion with an ideal authority . . . taking
> an intermediate position between external and internal. (p. 266)

In the trajectory of treatment of adolescent males, Lucente (1986,
p. 173) refers to the adolescent as "self-transcending" with a more

mature ego-ideal, more autonomous functioning, and "greater responsivity to his own internalized core competencies". Yet another example comes from Blos (here using "self" in a subordinate way): "The mental representation of the self at the close of adolescence is a qualitatively new formation, and reflects as an organized whole the various transformations which are specific to the phase of late adolescence" (1962, p. 147).

It is useful to think about the transformational self as a developmental extension of the transformational object (Bollas, 1987) in that having had an "average expectable" infant–mother attachment followed by "average expectable experiences" the adolescent is identified with the potential to metamorphose the self. The existence of the transformational self is inferred by the (re)organisation of a set of processes understood as reconfigured self-representations reinforced through long term potentiation (repeated firing patterns of synchronous neural assemblies) that significantly contribute to reshaping one's personality.

Christopher Bollas' concept of the transformational object (1987) was strongly influenced by Winnicott's ideas. Bollas conceptualised the transformational object as the infant's first subjective experience of the object as transformational. This potential becomes an "unthought known", to use Bollas' phrase. The "unthought known" is unconscious, having come into being during a non-verbal state of early differentiation, not subject to contemplation and more existential than philosophical. It is "remembered" through the recapturing of "echoes" of affective states associated with cumulative transformational experiences of the early self. It is a state of being that can be re-experienced through the recreation of an attunement rapprochement that mimics the earlier condition. This is similar to Modell's (2000, p. 141) metaphoric mind. Drawing parallels between the dyads of infant–mother and patient–therapist, Modell maintains that the metaphoric mind originally characterises the "complex infant state of multilayered consciousness that accepts the simultaneity of sameness and difference" from care-taker/therapist. In addition, Stern's (1985, pp. 97–99) phrase, "Representations of Interactions which have been Generalized (RIGS)", refers to infant–mother interpersonal interactions that are averaged and represented preverbally, conveys the sense of the transformational object. Transformation in this sense refers to affectively organised states of intersubjective relatedness,

that shape the ensuing attachment process and facilitate differentiation. See David Wallin's use of the "unthought known" in attachment
informed psychotherapy (2007, pp. 115–132).

General thesis

New criteria need to be formulated to account for the varieties of
developmental processes encountered in the transition from late
adolescence to young adulthood. Traditional ego psychology explanatory frameworks such as the developmental tasks of Blos (1962) and
Colarusso (1992) are no longer adequate. (These traditional tasks are
reviewed in Chapter Ten in the context of the ending of adolescence.)
I intend to shift the discussion from the rather static review of developmental tasks to the dynamic analysis of interactional processes. My
working hypothesis is: an integration of neurobiological research findings, non-linear dynamic systems theory, linguistic metaphor theory,
contemporary psychoanalytic developmental theory, attachment
theory, self psychology, cognition, and relational dynamics work
together to transform the sense of self and bring some measure of
closure to, and movement through, the adolescent phase. I have
decided to label this integrative process regulation theory. (See the
Synopsis for an elaboration of this position.) The process of transformation is understood through a systems approach combined with an
intra-psychic perspective in which the appearance of idiosyncratic
metaphors contribute to the adolescent's enhanced self-representation. With even a minor self-referencing metaphoric input an identity
synergy is created through repeated firing of specific neural networks
that manifests in a disproportional outcome—the transformational
self. Empirical data gathering in the clinical office setting, set in the
context of a single case research design methodology, shapes interpretations understood as hermeneutic inferences regarding the possible significance of the unique self-referencing metaphoric phenomena.
This paper then is an exercise in inductive reasoning where data from
a few sample subjects is generalised to the overall cohort of late
adolescents.

I am proposing a two pronged effort. First, I create a new, unitary
framework of interdisciplinary processes that I label regulation theory
that accounts for the structural and functional aspects of transitioning

from late adolescence to young adulthood. Second, I will apply regulation theory to two psychotherapy cases to demonstrate its operational usefulness from both diagnostic and treatment perspectives and, in so doing, illustrate its enhanced explanatory power for describing dynamic processes.

CHAPTER TWO

Theoretical considerations

This chapter takes the position that there must be an integration of informed data collection and rigorous theorising about that data in order to construct the frameworks that will offer optimal explanatory power. As we embark on this journey let us draw inspiration from William Blake, "If the doors of perception were cleansed everything would appear to man as it is: Infinite. This I shall do by printing in the infernal method by corrosives, which in Hell are salutary and medicinal, melting apparent surfaces away, and displaying the infinite which was hid" (1794). I will now examine the relative merits of traditional, positivist *vs.* alternative, social constructivist theory construction.

Philosophical assumptions

Traditional theories

Traditional theories great and small contain the imprint of some personal dimension of the authors' lives and their culture. Friedrich Nietzsche is generally credited with the aphorism, "Theory building is autobiography" (paraphrased probably, in part from *The Will to Power*, 1901). Havelock Ellis is credited with a similar sentiment, "Every artist writes his own autobiography" (1890). In the traditional mindset it is widely believed that theories are generalisations about lived experiences. But to what extent can traditional theories satisfy the quest for the formulation of a lawful account of human motivation? Can these idiosyncratic accounts move us toward the construction of a universal formula?

The discovery of knowledge and, by extension, theory building in the "hard sciences", such as physics, chemistry, and biology, rests on the accumulation and deepening of data in a progressive, collaborative way. Investigations proceed by building on the concepts and findings of previous theory and research. A sharp boundary exists between the explanatory systems and empirical phenomena. A physical theory, for example, need only account for physical phenomena without obligation to account for competing theories. Sensitivity to the history of previous discovery is keen. In the "soft sciences", such as anthropology, sociology, and personality psychology, research is carried on in limited domains without much attention paid to competing theories. Consequently, personality psychology is largely a noncumulative affair. In the absence of a unifying theory, a *Weltanschauung*[1] (Freud, 1933a), if you will, competing personality psychology theories abound. The most powerful source for these theories "can be found in the subjective experiential worlds of the personality theorists themselves" (Atwood & Stolorow, 1993, p. 5).

Palombo (1991) makes a useful contribution to this discussion when he constructs a dialectic argument designed to further clarify the distinction between psychoanalytic perspectives in the "hard (natural) sciences" *vs.* the "soft (human) sciences". Palombo reminds us that one of Freud's earliest major undertakings (Freud, 1895a) was an attempt to fashion a psychology that is a natural science. While he failed because he could not adequately conceptualise his understanding of the mental apparatus, especially the concept of repression, in neuronal developments of his day (Sulloway, 1979, pp. 101–131), Freud's quest is taking on renewed interest today as neurobiological research findings open tantalising vistas into the brain's mental functioning. Current psychoanalytic thinking can be divided into two major perspectives; one has it that psychoanalysis is part of the natural sciences, the other that psychoanalysis is part of the hermeneutic discipline. Recognising that the once tight linkage between developmental theory and clinical theory is now considered tenuous, the problem Palombo seeks to address is: what can we reasonably infer about development from data gathered in the clinical setting? With the certitude believed to undergird reconstructions now severely questioned, he proposes to undertake the building of a new psychodynamic point of view to reshape that linkage. With respect to the natural sciences, consonant with the empiricist tradition, a method of investigation emerges which has it that some correspondence must be established between the constructions made in the clinical setting and the historical events that are presumed to be their antecedents. This is called the *correspondence criterion*. With respect to the hermeneutic discipline, empirical data gathering is of a very different order and favours the coalescing of experiential phenomenon into a meaning making stance. Meanings can be apprehended only through understanding. The criterion of coherence, consistence, and completeness has to prevail in the assessment of experience. This vantage is labelled the *coherence criterion* (Palombo, 1991, pp. 151–157). I will elaborate on *coherence criterion* in the following methodological assumptions part and shall return to the perspective of *coherence criterion* in the synthesis of this paper as I attempt to explain my findings.

The psychoanalytic theory building enterprise seems particularly vulnerable to the "substitution of ideology for data" (Sadow, 2000, pp. 176–177). For example, is independence a desirable or even realistic developmental end point? In consideration of this issue, Galatzer-Levy and Cohler (1993, pp. 72–74) question the validity of Mahler's separation–individuation theory, suggesting that it contains an amalgamation of idealised American western emphasis on independence with her own horrific struggle for survival in the Holocaust resulting in an overvaluing of autonomy (Mahler, 1988). In a reconsideration of this issue, Doctors (2000) prefers Lyons-Ruth's phrase attachment–individuation. Similarly, Erikson's emphasis on phase specific crises in the life cycle calls up his own well known adolescent identity struggle (Friedman, 1999; Wallerstein & Goldberger, 1999). And Freud's application of the Oedipus to his own family dynamics illuminated this dimension in his own development, as well as for all mankind. More recently, Kohut's (1984) own narcissistic propensities are revealed and their role clarified in his borrowed formulation of a single line of development of the self with the Oedipus being a phase "rather than some kind of supraordinate experience out of which self structures emerge" (Strozier, 2001, p. 247). Even the attachment theory trailblazer, Mary Ainsworth, appears to have experienced an unstable attachment as a child (Karen, *The Atlantic Monthly, 1990*).

When propounded by heroic figures with compelling rhetorical skills, psychoanalytic developmental theories originating in autobiography can acquire the inexorable qualities of normality and universality. While the Oedipus complex with its variations is considered a cultural universal (Galatzer-Levy & Cohler, 1993, p. 129; Pollock, 1986), its centrality in the "psychoanalytic firmament", as the primary explanatory agent, has been dethroned. Pre- and post-Oedipal dynamics are now considered to have significant explanatory extensions that may supplement, if not supplant Oedipal considerations. Along with the changes in the explanatory domain, there are competing perspectives on adolescent development. The issue of "What is normal?" should be given a wide berth. It is, of course, best to contextualise normality appreciating its enormous relativity (Offer & Sabshin, 1974, 1984). With concern over reductionism, there is a movement away from metapsychological theorising toward empiricism as ways to conceptualise change. As Blos put it, "What we must find is an operational principal, a dynamic concept, which governs the consolidation process of late adolescence and renders its various forms comprehensible" (1962, p. 131). Our quest for a more current explanatory formula now moves on to contemporary contributions.

Alternative theories

Traditional theories are grouped under the modern or positivist philosophical orientation while alternative theories fall under the postmodern philosophical perspective. The reader is encouraged to see Appendix One for a compare and contrast review of these two perspectives, but in the grouping of theories clear category boundaries prove elusive. With the resurgence of neo-positivism through neurobiological research findings, empiricism combines with postmodern thinking to expand explanatory potential. With the "Decade of the Brain" now behind us, we can look at the contribution of real time computerised brain imaging research in the construction of new theory with a remarkable grounding in empirical data with high reliability. Philosophically it is based in what might be called neo-positivism. Still, inferential leaps are taken such as in the formulation of the useful, if controversial, concept of the triune brain (MacLean, 1990), but now with less tendency toward autobiography and the authoritarianism of logical positivism.

The idea that there is a natural lawfulness governing the unfolding of psychological development, such as there is in physical maturation, is not now accepted, as the data supporting this position is tenuous, at best. The belief in a systematic evolution of a generic human psychological organisation stems from an experience distant perspective where theory organises data. The powerful forces represented by Helmholtz and positivism, Darwin and Haeckel, evolution and archaeology, embryology and anatomy, all combined to fuel the intellectual revolution embracing the belief in ontogeny recapitulating phylogeny (Freud 1912–1913, 1930a). This late nineteenth century search for the scientific *Weltanschauung* (Freud, 1933a) governed the pioneering, formative years of psychoanalysis. During the past thirty years, an alternative viewpoint has emerged, primarily from self psychology, grounded in an empathic or experience near data gathering methodology. This perspective allows for a more flexible framework for theory construction (Galatzer-Levy & Cohler, 1990).

Galatzer-Levy and Cohler (1990, 1993) advocate an experience near method of investigating human motives and desires. Hoffman (1998), in describing the difficulty extracting ourselves from our traditional positivist roots has a thorough discussion of this struggle from a postmodern perspective. Jaffe (2000) has proposed the application of a dynamic systems-based theory as a unifying way to think about the psychological reorganisation that occurs in adolescence. Relying on the work of Thelen and Smith (1994, pp. xiv–xvii), the systems approach allows for the "view from below" as opposed to the "view from above". Metaphorically referencing respectively higher and lower orders of magnification, the "view from above" sees development as orderly, linear, progressive or directional, and nonreversible. At the same time, development seen from the perspective of the "view from below" registers an entirely different picture.

From this perspective the developmental process is understood to be,

> ... messy, ... [in which] linearity, uniformity, inevitable sequencing, and even irreversibility break down ... What looks like a cohesive,

> orchestrated process from afar takes on the flavor of a more exploratory, opportunistic, syncretic, and function-driven process in its instantiation . . . At the close-up range, therefore, the rules [for development] seem not to hold. (Thelan & Smith, 1994, pp. xvi–xvii)

In other words, when a new behavioural dimension emerges there are no programmed rules for maturational progress that ultimately govern psychic structure. The illusion of unitary character is created when elements of complex systems cooperate. "The paradox is that the organism moves along as an adapted, integrated whole as the component structures and processes change in fits and starts" (Thelen & Smith, (1994, pp. xvi–xvii) in Jaffe, 2000, p. 31). Rather than an underlying guiding mechanism to account for the general progression, development proceeds by the simultaneous cooperation of multiple subsystems. The assembly process is asynchronous, with early detection of function long before integrated performance, with sudden appearance and with disappearance of behaviours and reversibility.

In my view, Galatzer-Levy, Cohler, and Jaffe, taken together, have formulated a close to real experience, meaning making/systems axis for thinking about development that has considerable utility. The theoretical orientation to development in this paper is regulation theory informed by brain research with the emphasis on system processes and organisational varieties of self-states, now called the neurological or neural self. So informed, the transformational self conceptualisation comes from empathetically gathered data produced from two psychotherapies.

Methodological assumptions

The single case study method optimally describes the methodology used to discover new patterns and themes in the developmental experience of moving from adolescence to young adulthood. The case study method, consisting of an in-depth record of the clinical process, has a long and distinguished history in psychoanalysis. It is the principal research approach used by the major analytic theorists. This method is preferred over other research design methods because "It presupposes that the issues being investigated in personality research can be fully understood only if viewed in the context of the individual's personal world" (Stolorow & Atwood, 1979, pp. 27–28). It is characterised by three general features. First, it is personalistic and phenomenological. Second, it is historical. Unlike academic personality research where to get at objective truths the phenomeno-logical-historical variables are isolated and presumably neutralised, the case study method inserts itself into the temporal real life personal context of the individual being studied. Third, it is clinical and inter-pretive rather than experimental and deductive.

In other words, data is gathered directly from the clinical process in an empathic, intersubjective context with the therapist and client engaged in the task of co-constructing a narrative account of the conditions that brought the client into and out of treatment. The ther-apist acts in a participant–observer role (Sullivan, 1953) and becomes one of the subjectively understood elements in the ecological human system of the client. Because data is derived from the clinical process, not from concepts originating in meta-psychology, it is an example of an experience near, view from below perspective. This perspective allows for a theory to be constructed that is data, rather than theory, driven. Therefore, the phenomenon gathered through empirical means should enable future studies to confirm my hypothesis with high research study replicability.

Kazdin (2011) further clarifies the single case research design. It is the oldest of the research designs with a rich experimental legacy in biology and psychology including Wundt (1862) investigating sensory and memory processes, Ebbinghaus (1885/1913) using himself as the subject in examining the nature of memory, Pavlov (1927) studying learning (respondent conditioning) in animals and formulating the famous dichotomy of independent variables (e.g. conditions of train-ing such as the number of pairings of various stimuli) and dependent variables (e.g., drops of saliva), and of course Freud (1905d) using the case of Little Hans to validate his Oedipal hypothesis. In these designs many observations were made on one or a few cases, rather than the now dominant larger-sample-size research evaluated by statistical tests where many systematic, psychometrically regulated observa-tions are made on many subjects. This larger-sample-size paradigm essentially involves a basic control group design where one group, that received the experimental condition, was compared with another group (the control group) that did not. Random assignment of subjects to these groups is carefully administered. While there needs to be equivalence among subjects they need to be selected in the absence of any systematic bias (Kazdin, 2011, p. 12).

With respect to research in clinical settings focused on personality psychology, for example, in single case designs a distinction is made between controlled and uncontrolled types. In the controlled type, in order for scientifically acceptable inferences to be drawn, the design must be empirically evaluated in order to measure change or growth. The primary investigative tool is carefully controlled assessment procedures or measurements (e.g., of discrete personality features subjected to measurements over time using a dimensional framework) administered in a rigorous fashion analysing the effects of independent and dependent variables. In the uncontrolled type, periodic measurements are replaced by anecdotal process recording that is permitted to unfold, systematically collected, and evaluated, allowing for hermeneutic inferences to be drawn. Beyond this core distinction, additional differences are noted: naturalistic *vs.* contrived observation, natural *vs.* laboratory (or clinic) settings, obtrusive *vs.* unobtrusive assessment, and human observers *vs.* automated recording (Kazdin, 2011, pp. 89–97). In the two psychotherapies, from which my general thesis is framed, the data gathered is from contrived observation in a laboratory/clinic setting employing obtrusive techniques. In other words, the clients are aware that their behaviours are being assessed, with the psychotherapist being, obviously, a human observer in a participant–observer role.

What can be said about the efficacy of clinical procedures in single case research designs? General statements that changes in behaviour should constitute criteria for judging intervention effects have proven unsatisfactory. Two broad and related strategies are used to judge the impact of a clinical intervention: social validation and clinical significance. Social validation refers generally to consideration of social criteria for evaluating the focus of treatment, the procedures that are used, and the effects that these treatments have on performance. The social validation of intervention effects can be accomplished in two ways, which have been referred to as the social comparison and subjective evaluation methods. With the social comparison method, the behaviour of the client before and after treatment is compared with the behaviour of nondeviant ("normal") peers. The question asked by this comparison is whether the client's behaviour after treatment is distinguishable from behaviour of his or her peers who are functioning adequately in the environment. Presumably, if the client's behaviour warrants treatment, that behaviour should initially deviate from "normal" levels of performance. If treatment produces clinically important change, at least with many clinical problems, the client's behaviour should be brought within normal levels. With the subject evaluation method, the client's behaviour is evaluated by persons who are likely to have contact with him or her in everyday life and who evaluate whether distinct improvements in performance can be seen. The question addressed by this method is whether behaviour changes have led to qualitative differences in how the client is viewed by others (Kazdin, 2011, pp. 306–312).

"Clinical significance strategy has been introduced as a way to supplement statistical evaluation in the same way social validation was introduced to supplement visual inspection" (Kazdin, 2011, pp. 312). Three methods are used to implement this group strategy:

1. Falling within a normative range involves comparing pre-treatment with post-treatment measures of subjects against a sample of subjects grouped for normative functioning.
2. Departure from dysfunctional behaviour involves selecting patients for a focal problem and measuring improvement at the end of treatment.
3. No longer meeting diagnostic criteria involves the inference that if the individual no longer meets criteria, then improvement can be assumed to have occurred (Kazdin, 2011, pp. 312–322).

It seems that the clinical significance strategy will become more visible when the American Psychiatric Association incorporates more dimensional diagnostic methods into its *Diagnostic and Statistical Manual of Mental Disorder* manual in *DSM-V* scheduled for publication in 2013.

In the two psychotherapies that I shall present, efficacy of the treatment methods will be evaluated by the social comparison method in the judgment of this psychotherapist.

The discovery of the transformational self is an exercise in inductive reasoning ("inferring possible conclusions from available evidence," Spear, 2010, p. 101), as inferences about two older adolescents are formulated and applied to the larger late adolescent cohort.

Coherence criterion

Coherence criterion is a term consonant with postmodern philosophy and the discipline of hermeneutics. In this philosophical orientation prediction is eschewed as a scientific objective in favour of under-standing, deconstruction, and emancipation as hermeneutic objectives. It refers to an alternate set of criteria by which efficacy in the psychoanalytic psychotherapy process can be assessed (as the creation of a coherent narrative co-constructed by the therapist and client through the application of semiotics and semantics or metaphor and language), by which development can be reconsidered (as a unique interpretation of particular life episodes), and by which psychopathology can be reconfigured (as reflective of the interferences to the integration of self experience into a meaningful narrative) (Palombo, 1991, p. 166). I find myself in agreement with Palombo in recognising the privileging of coherence criterion over correspondence criterion as the superordinate principle in the construction of theories and understanding of the clinical process. Coherence criterion allows for a different set of measures (coherence, consistence, and completeness) to be brought to bear on the analysis of the efficacy of the psychoanalytically informed therapeutic enterprise. These measures are more consistent with contemporary philosophical trends and will be applied in the reflection of the two psychotherapies in the synopsis. The reader is encouraged to see Appendix One for comparing and contrasting the modern with the postmodern philo-sophical paradigms.

The value of a systems approach

The dominant "way of thinking" about the living world has become general systems theory. It is a loosely connected group of theories derived from both the "hard" and "soft" sciences that for the past 125 years has generated increasingly useful hypotheses about the processes and structures across the range of living entities. Formative contributors have been Talcott Parsons (1960) in sociology, Ludwig von Bertalanffy (1967) in biology, Arthur Koestler in philosophy (1967, 1971; Koestler & Smythies, 1979) and, more recently, Ilya Prigogine (Prigogine & Stengers, 1984) in chemistry who has analysed the dimensions of non-linear dynamic systems. Non-linear systems thinking is evolving and is alternately labelled complexity theory or chaos theory. Complexity theory refers to the notion that an examination of the non-linear system and its parts can appear so disordered, that the overall pattern of stability or directionality can become obscure. I prefer the term complexity theory because I believe it captures the inordinately knotty and labyrinthine nature of the processes attending the transformational self.

Of the many concepts associated with complexity theory, I want to highlight but three that seem of unusual significance in order to get us oriented properly:

1.   Components in systemic relationships interact in complex feedback loops. The resulting interaction of system parts, therefore, produces a nondeterministic causality that is multidirectional, multiple, mutual, and retroactive.
2.   The system is hypersensitive to any perturbations, that is, all internal and external stimuli. A small input of energy can produce a disproportional outcome.
3   All living systems, including leaves, coastlines, crystals, social groups, and human minds, are thought of as dissipative structures. In other words, they run down, distribute or export energy from the system. Energy is dissipated randomly so that it becomes less accessible, less capable of organised work, a process called entropy. Entropy is, "the tendency of an unattended system to move toward an unorganized state that is characterized by decreased interactions among its components; this is followed by decrease in usable energy". As the term entropy comes from physics, a disjuncture is noted. It has been recognised that living systems do not move toward a state of total energy distribution; rather, they tend to maintain themselves in a high degree of disequilibrium, "on the edge of chaos" (Anderson, Carter, & Lowe, 1999, pp. 10, 18-21, 289, 290).

The reader is directed to Chapter Nine for a detailed discussion about the nature of non-linear dynamic systems theory or complexity theory and how that theory helps to explain the processes associated with the transformational self.

I now turn to the subject of positioning the transformational self in a developmental context.

Note

1. "A Weltanschauung is an intellectual construction which solves all the problems of our existence uniformly on the basis of one overriding hypothesis, which, accordingly leaves no question unanswered and in which everything that interests us finds its fixed place. . . . Psychoanalysis is incapable of creating a Weltanschauung of its own. It does not need one; it is a part of science and can adhere to the scientific Weltanschauung. Scientific thought is still very young among human beings; there are too many of the great problems which it has not yet been able to solve. A Weltanschauung erected upon science has, apart from its emphasis on the real world, mainly passive traits, such as submission to the truth and rejection of illusions" (of religion) (Freud, 1933a, in Abstracts . . ., 1973, pp. 506–507).

PART II
THE NATURE OF THE
TRANSFORMATIONAL SELF

INTRODUCTION TO PART II

Part II consists of three chapters dedicated to the subjects of formulating the nature of the transformational self and positioning it within a systems framework. In Chapter Three, I present the transformational self from a micro perspective and discuss the self concept and various ways to think about adolescent development in contemporary circumstances. In Chapter Four, I review the transformational self from a meso perspective and deal with the issue of positioning the transformational self within a pluralistic family attachment context that promotes differentiation. In Chapter Five, I approach the transformational self from the macro perspective. This involves comparing and contrasting the dominant self-system frameworks and locating a comfortable conceptual home for the transformational self.

CHAPTER THREE

The transformational self in adolescence

Orientation

Few concepts in psychology can rival the term "self" when it comes to expansive theoretical application and explanatory utility. Subject to definitional broadening on a remarkable scale, we have grown familiar and comfortable with the sociological selves (Harter, 1999, pp. 1–11; Offer, Ostrov, & Howard, 1981), the self as a social construction (Harter, 2012, pp. 11–26), a wide array of psychological and psychoanalytic selves (Galatzer-Levy & Cohler, 1990; Schafer, 1968), and, currently, a neurobiological self (Feinberg, 2009; Levin, 1980). By simply altering the adjective we are ushered into different contexts on dozens of self dimensions and constructs, designed by their authors to convey various and different aspects or domains of the individual and interpersonal mind-brain experience. The confusing multiple usages often contribute more ambiguity than illumination to the task of using shifts in self-states to clarify the nature of movement through the life cycle. The task at hand is to find a self construct that adequately conveys the sense of self-organisation required to explain the intrapsychic shift from adolescent to young adult functioning. As Ovid suggested the task is not easy,

Then the noble hero, looking forth upon the wide water spread before his eyes, pointed with his finger and said: "What place is that? Tell me the name which that island bears. And yet it seems not to be one island." The river god replied: "No, what you see is not one island. There are five islands lying there together; but the distance hides their divisions". (Ovid, 2004)

For the purposes of this paper I have constructed the term "transformational self" to herald the attainment of a cluster of self-state capacities, that positions the individual to assume mature status in society. The conceptualisation of the transformational self is an interdisciplinary construct formulated as regulation theory, which is located conceptually in the emerging neural self theoretical orientation. It embraces an amalgam of contemporary ideas constituting leading edge thinking that point to non-traditional ways to consider transitional phases in development.

In this chapter I will discuss: 1) part of the key literature on the self concept (without being exhaustive or comprehensive) and develop the point that the neural self should be the contemporary overarching self definition; and 2) some of the forces in society and science that have impacted on how we think about adolescence.

Literature review of self constructs

There is general agreement that Freud used the terms soul, psyche, mind, and ego to convey in the original German language aspects of emphasis which have been lost in the Strachey English translation (Bettelheim, 1983). "In 1923, Freud altered his model to posit relatively stable mental structures that were categorised not by their relationship to consciousness, but rather by their distinct functions" (Makari, 2008, pp. 350–351). Subsequently, the ego has enjoyed a rather fixed definition as "a coherent organization of mental processes" (Freud, 1923b, p. 17). The same cannot be said for the self. While Freud used the term self as an adjective or adverb as in self-reproach, self-analysis, self-injury, or self-destruction, he appears not to have used the term self to denote a psychical agency (Freud, 1974, p. 372; Laplanche & Pontalis, 1973, pp. 413–414; Rothgeb, 1973, p. S-154). Strachey seems to have done a disservice to Freud in that where Freud wrote "das Ich" Strachey chose to translate "das Ich" into "the I," "the self," or "the ego" depending upon Strachey's own interests in structural distinctions (Ornston, 1992, p. 71).

Controversy grew as to what was meant by self. Was the self part of the ego? Was the ego part of the self? Should the self be thought of as an intrapsychic representation of the individual or as a source of action and agency in its own right? In Kohut's early writings he "used the concepts of self and self-representation interchangeably" (Palombo, Bendicsen, & Koch, 2009, p. 263). Hartman suggested (1964) a compromise to this confusion by referencing the interactional contexts of ego and self. In this view the ego interacted with the other intrapsychic agencies, the id and superego, while the self interacted with objects. Some believe this distinction created a framework for the theory of object relations with the self emerging as the result of inter-actions with significant objects in the environment and with corre-sponding internal objects (Gabbard, 1994; Kernberg, 1982; Meissner, 1986). In the ensuing years a profusion of psychoanalytic selves evolved. I will attempt to categorise the most significant ones.

The distinction for being the first to use self as agency (i.e., as an overarching intra-psychic structure) seems to belong to Karen Horney (1950) who described the "real self" "not as a fixed entity but a set of intrinsic potentialities, including temperament, talents, capacities and predispositions—that are a part of our genetic makeup and need a favorable environment in which to develop" (p. 17). The real self is "the alive, unique, personal center of ourselves, the actualization of which is the meaning of life and alienation from which may be called a 'psychic death' " (p. 155). It is "the repository of the healthy conscience, which is the reaction of our true self to the proper func-tioning or the malfunctioning of our total personality" (p. 131; and Paris, 1999). Horney's description of the "real self" with its capacities and properties presage later self formulations. In these enunciations of the psychoanalytic selves, I will consider normal variations, not those associated with psychopathologies.

The classical psychoanalytic self

As I survey the literature on the concept of the self, there seem to be four major streams of influence that suggest ways to think about the evolution of self. The first may be said to take into account the drive/defence psychoanalytic positions that believe that self and other differentiation, and the relationship between the two, emerge as a consequence of the discharge of the drives and their subsequent developmental vicissitudes. This position was modified by a shift in the 1940s to the ego psychological stance with its emphasis on ego adaptation. At about the same time an object relations position crystallised, initiated by the work of Abraham (1927) and Klein (1946), where formulations about self and object representations flourished. Now the drives were not seen as seeking discharge, but rather as object-seeking. Formative contributors to this stream are Abraham (1925), Freud (1905d), Hartmann (1939, 1964), Jacobson (1954), Klein (1946), Mahler (Mahler, Pine, & Bergman, 1975), and Winnicott (1960). This stream may be said to have culminated in the remarkable attempts at revision and synthesis by Kernberg (1976, 1982). The drive/defence, ego psychological, and object relations schools are based in the positivist tradition. They are epigenetic in nature, essentially non-empirical speculations and organised by mixtures of the mechanistic (like a machine or computer) and the organismic (taking in psychological nutrients to build psychic structure) metaphoric orientations in sometimes elegant meta-psychological formulations (Palombo, Bendicsen, & Koch, 2009).

The relational self?

A second stream I consider is the interpersonal/relational/intersubjective (hereafter called relational) school. It is located within the post-modern, constructivist philosophy, is non-empirical in its data collection, and is organised primarily by the contextual metaphor. In this metaphoric organisation the person's experiences are subjectively woven together to create an ideological, historical account. The account is a narrative story of the various meanings ascribed to those experiences by the individual. Formative contributors to this highly diverse stream are Sullivan (1950), Chodorow (1978), Benjamin (1988, 1998), Stolorow and Atwood (1992), Mitchell (2000), and Dimen (2003). The origins of this school are traced to Sullivan (1950) who departed, with one exception, from psychoanalytic theory and language in the formation of his theoretical position. He did construct a developmental model, a dimension of relational theory that has been of little concern to later adherents of this school because of the emphasis on the here and now interaction between patient and therapist.

Past factors in development are of questionable value due to the primary emphasis placed on present experience. In addition, developmental theories are believed to reflect biased social and cultural viewpoints and are regarded as "ethnocentrically derived narratives whose validity is difficult to establish" (Palombo, Bendicsen, & Koch, 2009, p. 226). Consequently, in the relational school there is no generalised developmental theory out of which the self can emerge. In this school primary emphasis is placed on the interaction of social relationships to the avoidance of a discussion of the internalisation of those relationships. Development is thought to proceed from interpersonal interactions, not from endogenous drive or maturational forces.

What can be said about the self concept in the relational perspective? In the later relational school the self is fused with the other.

> There is no "self", in a psychologically meaningful sense, in isolation, outside a matrix of relations with others. Neither the self nor the object (other) are meaningful dynamic concepts without presupposing some sense of psychic space in which they interact, in which they do things with or to each other. (Mitchell, 1988, p. 33 and in Berzoff, Flanagan, & Hertz, 2008, p. 216)

Consequently, the relational self (actually the self–other dyad) is fluid, complex, and ever changing, but also opaque and shapeless in the absence of the other in their psychic matrix space.

The attachment self

A third stream is suggested by the positivist contribution of traditional attachment theorists such as Bowlby (1969, 1973, 1980, 1988) and empiricists Ainsworth, Blehar, Waters, and Wall (1978) and Main, Kaplan, and Cassidy, 1985 (see also Morgan, 1996; Solomon, 1990). Attachment theory is primarily a theory of development. Bowlby gathered data from ethologists and animal psychologists. He was a Darwinian evolutionist who grew to believe that attachment behaviours are species specific, instinctive, and activated in the service of survival. Self and other differentiation is organised by evolutionary imperatives initially composed of separate instinctive responses that are independent of each other. The component responses gradually merge through interactions between infant and care-giver. Through this process, the infant acquires an internal working model of the external milieu and the internal milieu of the infant–care-giver relationship. A secure or an insecure attachment is subsequently formed based on the predictability and quality of nurturing that shapes interaction of the self with the care-giver and other relationships. The internal working model was differentiated eventually into four distinct patterns of attachment in the toddler population. In studying "states of mind with respect to attachment", Main and colleagues identified attachment patterns in adults. These patterns revealed a high degree of correlation to attachment styles of their children, leading directly to the remarkable discovery that among human beings there is an intergenerational transmission of attachment patterns. Attachment theory has become a widely respected framework for understanding and shaping responses to attachment disorders.

The attachment literature does not seem to have evolved a framework for thinking about the self concept. Of course, distinctive attachment patterns stamp the self with some measure of stable and durable individuality, but there is little written about the nature of the attachment self (inferred from Cassidy & Shaver *Handbook of Attachment*, 1999). It is Wallin who fills this void (2007, pp. 59–83) with a discussion of four intersecting domains of self-experience in attachment relationships. These domains are located in diverse interdisciplinary constructs and are brought together by Wallin to create a theoretical amalgam I call the attachment self.

The attachment self consists of:

1. The somatic self is the earliest experience of the self and it is registered in the body. Stern (1985) refers to this experience as the core self that emerges from self-invariants, the consistent somatic structure of the physiological body and its boundaries.
2. The emotional self emerges from the feeling of security (Sroufe & Waters, 1977) which now is considered a more basic goal of attachment than Bowlby's (1988) need for proximity and protection. The feeling of security is felt as an emotion and soon differentiates into a form of affect communication embodied in the emotional self. As Schore (1994) puts it: "The core of the self lies in patterns of affect regulation" (p. 33). Emotions are the individual's intuitive appraisals either of his own organismic states

and/or the succession of environmental situations in which he finds himself, the force that drives actions and are the immediate connections to the body.

3.   The representational self is derived from Bowlby who "argued that it was an evolutionary necessity to have a representational world that mapped the real one" (Wallin, 2007, p. 64). The representational self at its earliest manifestation is a memory of past and present experiences useful to make predictions about future experiences. This memory is characterised by Stern (1985) as "representations of interactions that have been generalized" (p. 97).

4.   The reflective self (Fonagy & Target, 2006) and the mindful self (Siegel, 2005) are taken as a single self in that they represent a potentiality for psychological liberation. The reflective self through "mentalizing promotes internal freedom by enabling us to act as 'mental agents' ", while "mindfulness fosters freedom by enabling us to act as 'attentional agents' " (Wallin, 2007, p. 68).

Bridges to the neural self

The narcissistic self or the cohesive self

> Until now we have examined very different views of the self. In drive theory, the self is a cauldron of seething impulses of sexuality and aggression. In ego psychology, the self is that agency that mediates between the drives, reality and morality. In object relations theories, the self is made up of internal representations of relationships with others. (Berzoff, Flanagan, & Hertz, 2008, p. 161)

In self psychology, the self is focused on maintaining an internal subjective sense of cohesion. The self attends with its own specificity to the kinds of life experiences that contribute to the formation of a vibrant sense of the self as a cohesive whole.

I now turn to a discussion of Kohut's narcissistic self with its distinctive emphasis on its cohesive properties. The study of self psychology is often approached through a compare and contrast exercise with ego psychology. The reader is encouraged to see Appendix Two for a compare and contrast chart detailing differences between these two psychologies. I will discuss the morphology of the tripolar self and set aside the bulk of the contextual and theoretical issues. Kohut's framework began in a positivist, hypothesis testing perspective as an ego psychology expert. His later work is organised around both the organismic and contextual metaphors. More specifically "Although his [Kohut's] clinical theory is consistent with a hermeneutic approach, the developmental model we infer from his formulation is a hybrid nonepigenetic organismic model that incorporates a narrative perspective" (Palombo, Bendicsen, & Koch, 2009, p. 262).

Kohut's (1977, p. 171) final definition of "the self is a supraordinate configuration that exists from birth. It is the source 'for our sense of being an independent center of initiative and perception, integrated with our most central ambitions and ideals and with our experience that our body and mind form a unit in space and a continuum in time' " (in Berzoff, Flanagen, & Hertz, 2008, p. 163). Kohut also defined the self in terms of subordinate and supraordinate viewpoints that I will not review here because I have discussed that topic as an aspect of locating the transformational self in a developmental framework in Chapter Five. Kohut's mature self formulation, the tripolar self (1984), originates in three essential needs of man necessary for the sustenance of the self: his need to experience mirroring and acceptance; his need to experience merger with greatness, strength, and calmness; and his need to experience the presence of essential likeness from the moment of birth to the moment of death. Each need requires empathic self-object responses to grow and flourish. Each need is associated with a pole of the self respectively: the pole of ambitions or the grandiose self, the pole of ideals (and the intermediate area of talents and skills) or the idealised parent imago, and the pole of twinship or the alter ego (Kohut, 1984, pp. 192–194). The word pole refers to a pathway of development within the self that has its own energy and needs. Each pole is considered to be a "flexible, ever changing, relational web of aspects or polarities of the self". The energy motivating the self is different than that of the drives associated with structural theory and refers to a "biological growth force" that pushes the person toward the completion of maturational tasks. The needs of each pole are met by care-givers who provide distinct self-object responses (Berzoff, Flanagan, & Hertz, 2008, p. 173).

The term self-object is original to Kohut and may be understood as follows:

An object may be defined as a self-object when it is experienced intrapsychically as providing functions in an interpersonal relationship that add to or maintain the cohesive self. This includes affect attunement, consensual validation, tension regulation and soothing, recognition of one's autonomous potential, and restoration of a temporarily threatened fragmentation of the self through a variety of activities and comments. (Chessick, 1993, p. 357 in Flanagan, 2011, p. 167)

The developmental line of self-growth was left vague by Kohut. He thought there was a general sequence in tripolar development with the needs of the grandiose self dominating until age four, the needs of the ideal self being most intense from four to six, and those of the twinship self needing optimal responses during latency and adolescence. In optimal development the self-objects adjust their responses to the growing needs of the self in a phase specific manner. The self-object functions are gradually taken into the psychology of the individual in an altered manner so that the self is not simply a replica of the self-object, but rather is a unique person with separate desires and motivations. The term "transmuting internalisation" was carefully selected by Kohut to designate that the taking in of self-object functions was transformative in nature, not just an imitation of self-object behaviour. It was not until recently that a developmental line of the narcissistic self, inferred from Kohut's writings, was outlined by Palombo (Palombo, Bendicsen, & Koch, 2009, pp. 262–272). The periods include: the virtual self (birth to two months), the cohesive self (two to thirty months), the Oedipal period (thirty to forty-eight months), latency (four to thirteen years), adolescence (fourteen to seventeen years), late adolescence (eighteen to twenty years), and entry into adulthood (nineteen to twenty-five years). During the cohesive self period, the core self, designated as the nuclear self, emerges and is referenced as the "I" for the rest of life.

Of concern to the transformational self is the last two periods in Kohut's developmental framework. In late adolescence the nuclear self undergoes a reconfiguration organised by four processes: 1) adolescents reassess their past in light of their present experiences resulting in a new perspective in their personal past-present-future continuum; 2) self-object experiences can be utilised in a symbolic, not just a concrete level; 3) gender role and sexuality become focal preoccupations; 4) formal operational thought generates an avenue for titrating experience that can lead directly to mature appraisal of aspirations and goals. The late adolescent nuclear self creates an inner program of these possibilities, the actualisation of which firmly shapes a coherent developmental trajectory (Palombo, Bendicsen, & Koch, 2009, pp. 274–275).

In early adulthood, the nuclear self undergoes consolidation and moves beyond adaptation to the adoption of internal values, acquiring a sense of purpose, and adjusting to more of a sense of mutual interaction with the matrix of self-objects in the world in which joy, pride, and enthusiasm become longings and strivings (Palombo, Bendicsen, & Koch, 2009, pp. 275–276).

At this point I want to turn to Kohut's formulation of the transformations of narcissism which have a direct bearing on the transformational self. "They are: (i) man's creativity; (ii) his ability to be empathic; (iii) his capacity to contemplate his own impermanence; (iv) his sense of humor; and (v) wisdom" (1966, p. 257). Kohut suggested a developmental line for these narcissistic transformations. Creativity is a feature of the creator's relationship to his work.

> In creative work narcissistic energies are employed which have been changed into a form to which I referred earlier as idealizing libido, i.e., the elaboration of that specific point on the developmental road from narcissism toward object love at which object love (in the sense of social psychology) is cathected with narcissistic libido and thus included in the cathexis of the self. (1966, p. 258)

Kohut's formulation on creativity suggests that that which is created, either symbolically or in concrete form, is invested with narcissistic libido and becomes a part of the self. So with respect to the transformational self, the appearance of unique self-referencing metaphor during the transition from late adolescence into young adulthood is regarded as an idealisable attribute, invested with libidinal energy as a potential, and becomes a prized creation. It is especially valued for its unique narcissistic properties which contribute to its vitality and reconfigured cohesive tonus.

With respect to a developmental line of these mature forms of narcissism, Kohut seems to suggest that the capacity for empathy and creativity bloom during this transitional period due to a decrease in egocentricity, an increase in idealisable self-objects, and an embrace of the mature value of work. "Ideals are most strongly cathected in youth, humor is usually at its height during maturity; an acceptance of transience may be achieved during the advanced years ... with the attainment of wisdom ... usually reserved for the later phases of life." (Kohut, 1966, p. 268)

Kohut's cohesive self and self-object concepts have spawned creative variations. A notable example is that of Galatzer-Levy and Cohler's (1993) self and essential other framework. Galatzer-Levy and Cohler's (1993) self is defined as, "the experiential cohesive center of initiative", that interacts with the "essential other" (p. 25). The essential other,

> is our experience of other people, and entities in the environment, that supports the sense of a coherent and vigorous self and its develop-ment. The essential other refers to an experience of the psychological life of the individual, not to mention the external reality of these people. We believe that the support of the self is always part of a total experience of other people and entities. This function is never isolated from the additional meanings these others have" (p. 3)

In my opinion, while different, the differences are not of sufficient magnitude to merit a separate discussion in this context.

The sense of self

Stern's (1985) framework is based on infant developmental research gathered in laboratory settings. His aim was to create a fresh approach to psychoanalytic developmental psychology that more closely fit the empirical data. He contrasted his approach with that of Mahler, Pine, and Bergman (1975). He emphasised that whereas her approach was retrospective (clinical dynamics based on adult reconstructions) and pathomorphic, his was prospective and normative. Mahler's infant was understood in a positivist, developmentally linear, epigenetic, ego psychology context whereas as his was grounded in a post-modern, more developmentally non-linear and transactional, non-epigenetic, relational viewpoint. Mahler's infant has to "break" out of its autistic shell, was motivated by drives, and adultomorphised into longing for autonomy and independence. By contrast, Stern's infant from birth has a capacity for subjectivity within a sense of self oriented toward intersubjective transactions. These are sharply different, regrettably polarised, visions of infant development which Stern attempted to mollify, "The clinical infant breathes subjective life into the laboratory infant . . ." (Stern, 1985, p. 14; Applegate, 1989). Stern departs from developmental convention with his use of domains of relatedness, rather than stages or phases, to indicate that when a different sense of self is mobilised it exerts continuing influence throughout the life cycle.

Stern (1985) appears unique in preferring to differentiate between "the self" and the term "sense of self". Stern defines the senses of the self as follows:

> There is the sense of self that is a single, distinct, integrated body; there is the agent of actions, the experiencer of feelings, the maker of intentions, the architect of plans, the transposer of experience into language, the communicator and sharer of personal knowledge. Most often these senses of self reside out of awareness . . . but they can be brought to and held in consciousness. We instinctively process our experiences in such a way that they appear to belong to some kind of unique subjective organization that we commonly call the sense of self. (pp. 5–6)

Stern's focus on the plurality of selves sets the stage for his theoretical emphasis on the multiple subjective experiences of the interpersonal senses of self. Stern is clear about placing the senses of self at the centre of his inquiry. They are invariant patterns of internal organisation understood as: the sense of agency, the sense of physical cohesion, the sense of continuity, the sense of affectivity, the sense of a subjective self that can achieve intersubjectivity with another, the sense of creating organisation, and the sense of transmitting meaning. Developmental organisations occur in quantum leaps at well recognised periods: between two to three months, between nine and twelve months, and between fifteen to eighteen months. These are epochs of great change in human ontogeny from virtually any measurement perspective.

Senses of self unfold according to an innate developmental progression. Each sense is thought to have distinct properties which, once activated, impact the organism for life. The first sense of self is the sense of emergent self with its domain of emergent relatedness that occurs between birth to two months. During this epoch the sense of emergent self experiences a sense of connectedness, a sense of integration between, for example, touching and knowing that which is touched, and exerts vigorous goal-directedness to assure social interactions. The second sense of self is the sense of core self with its domain of core-relatedness emerging between two to six months. During this epoch it registers upon the infant that she and mother are physically separate, are different agents, have distinct affective experiences, and have separate histories. This is one of other possible organised subjective perspectives. The third sense of self is the sense of a subjective self with its domain of intersubjective relatedness emerging between the seventh and ninth months. During this epoch capacities come on line including "sharing a focus of attention, for attributing intentions and motives to others and apprehending them correctly, and for attributing the existence of states of feeling in others and sensing whether or not they are congruent with one's own state of feeling" (Stern, 1985, p. 27). The fourth sense of self is the sense of verbal self with its domain of verbal relatedness which is seen between fifteen to eighteen months. During this epoch the verbal self has the capacity "to objectify the self, to be self-reflective, to comprehend and produce language" (p. 28). Stern later (1989, 1993) introduced a fifth sense of self, the narrative self with its domain of the narrative sense of self emerging between thirty to forty eight months. During this epoch the urge to understand human activity in terms of psychological story plots emerges involving actors with separate motives and goals, stories set in a historical context in specific locations and containing a beginning, middle, and ending set of processes. This synopsis of Stern's framework must omit details which have been summarised in Palombo, Bendicsen, and Koch, 2009. Stern's empirical grounding in infant research blends well into the research into the neurobiological self. Of course, Stern's speculations about the nature of infant cognition must be placed in the same category as that of Mahler's attempts to understand infant thinking through the lens of adult experience.

The neural self

A fourth stream is suggested by contributions from attachment theory, self psychology, the sense of self, and neurobiology to the formulation of the concept of the *neural self*. Direct contributors to this position are Damasio (1994), Schore (2000, 2002), and Feinberg (2009). This fourth stream is essential to the construction of the transformational self and, because it is detailed in Chapter Eight, I will not discuss it here.

This account ends the review of self constructs that serve as background for the transformational self. I now turn to ways to understand the adolescent from the perspectives of contemporary society and science.

The positivist adolescent (five traditional core concepts)

There are five core concepts related to adolescent development which dominated thinking on the subject for more than seventy-five years of the twentieth century. One of the most enduring ideas about adolescent development from a psychoanalytic perspective is that of recapitulation or repetition. It was first propounded by Freud (1905d) when he referred to the process of object choice as diphasic. The first wave begins between ages two to five followed by the interregnum of latency. With puberty the second wave sets in "which determines the final outcome of sexual life" (Freud, 1905d, p. 200). Jones (1922) further codified this and in so doing accorded recapitulation the status of an unquestioned, lawful ontogenetic process in our occidental society. ". . . the individual recapitulates and expands in the second decennium of life the development he passed through during the first five years of life, just as he recapitulates during these first five years the experiences of thousands of years in his ancestry and during the pre-natal period those of millions of years" (1922, pp. 397–398). Bernfeld (1938), Blos (1962, 1967, 1976), Colarusso (1990), Erikson (1950, p. 261, 1958), Fenichel (1945, pp. 110–113), and A. Freud (1958) all supported the view that in adolescence the first years of development, in particular, the Oedipus complex, gets re-experienced and/or reworked as a necessary step in the journey into adulthood.

The four other core concepts come from the co-inventors of adolescence: Rousseau (1762, 1782) and Hall (1904) (Kaplan, 1984, pp. 51–80). Rousseau is credited with the ideas of adolescence being a repetition or rebirth (although what he had in mind was very different from what Jones advanced) in that adolescence is the platform and point of departure for an advanced stage of humanity and the need to sublimate sexual passions in the service of higher accomplishment. In 1904 Hall published the authoritative, encyclopaedic work on adolescence: *Adolescence: It's Psychology and Its Relations to Physiology, Anthropology, Sociology, Sex, Crime, Religion and Education*. Without acknowledging

Rousseau's earlier work, Hall incorporated Rousseau's positions. Hall is credited with the ideas of adolescence being a normal time of storm and stress, of alternating polarities (i.e., the adolescent could be selfish and altruistic, gregarious and solitary, etc.), and the desirability of postponing or elongating the adolescent phase in order primarily to undo the negative effects of masturbation and, second, to account for the emerging legal requirements to keep children in school through high school. These five concepts: recapitulation, storm and stress, prolongation, alternating states, and sublimating sexuality became the unshakeable foundation for thinking about adolescence and working with adolescents (Hall, 1923; Rousseau, 1782).

Of these five core issues, three have been replaced: the storm and stress hypothesis as a universal adolescent developmental phenomenon has been discredited (Arnett, 1991; Offer & Sabshin, 1974); the recapitulation theory has been supplanted (Palombo, 1988), and the neurotic preoccupation with masturbation with its focus on sublimating sexuality has been surpassed by an educational emphasis on the development of the whole person (see e.g., Samuel, 2008).[1]

The social constructivist adolescent (contemporary concepts)

Prolongation of the adolescent phase and alternating polarities

Of the five aforementioned concepts, two have contemporary relevance in today's adolescent world: prolongation and alternating polarities. First, the prolongation of the adolescent phase, now lasting approximately ten years, remains a central part of how we currently think about adolescence (Urdang, 2008, p. 398).

Second, the concept of alternating polarities is empirically verified in Harter (1999, pp. 59–88) who has extensively studied self-representations as an aspect of normative adolescent developmental change. In so far as alternating polarities refer to behaviours, we can comfortably say that self-representations drive and/or organise those behaviours. In early adolescence positive and negative attributes commonly alternate leading to inaccurate overgeneralisations about the self. By middle adolescence there is keen awareness of the alternating attributes with instability leading to confusion and inaccuracies about the self.

Given the cognitive limitations of the phase and along with heightened awareness of discrepancies an early type of "normative dissonance" (Colarusso, 1990, p. 184) or "normative distortions" (Harter, 1999, p. 87) emerge with intrapsychic conflict, accompanied by anxiety that threatens the integrity of the vulnerable self state, being experienced among the contrary self-representations. (Harter, 1999, p. 70) With the arrival of late adolescence a more resilient self attains greater capacity for adaptation. "Attributes reflecting personal beliefs, values, and standards become more internalized, and the older adolescent would appear to have more opportunity to meet these standards, thereby leading to enhanced self-worth" (p. 85). The self is more balanced in its registering of the alternating attributes, has increased accuracy in self-evaluation and greater acceptance of limitations because of increased cognitive capacities (pp. 85–86).

A different model of the adolescent developmental trajectory

Despite the fact that the storm and stress model was endorsed by the psychoanalytic establishment, most notably by A. Freud (1958), it was obvious that many adolescents seemed to experience adolescence as a reasonably calm period in their lives. In the 1970s the empiricists began to impact the conceptualisation of adolescence most notably with the work of Offer and Sabshin (1974, 1984) and Offer, Ostrov and Howard (1981). Their survey of thousands of adolescents from middle and upper class families and economic circumstances in Western, industrialised countries reversed the notion of adolescence being a normative time of storm stress. They concluded that eighty per cent of adolescents perceive themselves as "normal" in terms of self-esteem, accepting the changing body, looking forward to the future, minimising intergenerational conflict, and orienting themselves in a positive way to studying and working. In other research Offer and Offer (1975) concluded that there were essentially three pathways through the adolescent journey: a pattern of smooth, "continuous" growth, a rapid pace of "surgent" growth, and a roller coaster pattern of "turbulent" growth. This research became widely accepted and reoriented those who work with adolescents away from the powerful bias of adolescence being a normative phase of storm and stress. Arnett (1991) "supports a modified storm and stress view that takes into account individual differences and cultural variations" (p. 317).

Ego psychology gives way to philosophical and methodological pluralism

Also in the 1970s, the hegemony of ego psychology began to wane. This trend was solidified with the publication of *DSM-III* in 1980 and with the *Osheroff vs. Chestnut Lodge*[2] (Klerman, 1990) lawsuit settled in 1982. Both of these events contributed to the end of the dominance of psychoanalysis as the central mental health and illness framework. Best practice standards were ushered in, biological psychiatry was in the ascendancy, as was cognitive behavioural therapy, and the multi-disciplinary team approach reinvigorated. The spectre of managed care with its reliance on evidence based methodologies was beginning to be felt.

In addition, the emergence of Kohut's self psychology (1971, 1977) provided an alternative framework from which to view development, a framework more compatible with postmodern philosophical thinking. In 1988, Palombo was one of the first to articulate the notion that the adolescent phase need not be thought of as essentially a recapitulation or revisiting of earlier phases. Palombo argued instead, from a self psychology perspective, for the unfolding development of a sense of self as agency with increasing self-cohesion culminating in a new, strengthened or enhanced psychic structure at the close of adolescence, the nuclear self.

The nuclear self is understood to be a self-state that is the experience of a subjective sense of dual unity, identity, and satisfying interaction with the self-object world. In the nuclear self, the three self-object needs organised according to an approximate developmental timetable, are responded to as follows:

1. Mirroring resulting in the grandiose self with accompanying feelings of firmness, harmony, vitality, and a sense of worthiness. For the adolescent it is first, the wish for affirmation in the midst of a changing body, preoccupation with appearance and exhibitionistic longings that require self-objects beyond what parents can provide. Second, the adolescent's desire to feel valued and worthwhile is intensified by her uncertain self-confidence and need for ever more authentic responses to bolster self-esteem.
2. Idealisation with accompanying feelings of power, being protected with a feeling of safety and trust, capacity for the modulation of affects, and internal regulation of self-experiences and the

acquisition of values and ideals. For the adolescent it is first managing the disillusionment and de-idealisation subsequent to the re-evaluation of parental omnipotence; second, building the capacity for affect self-regulation and, third, internalising a value system experienced in both symbolic and concrete dimensions.

3.   And finally alter-ego or twinning, with the experience of a common bond to others as human beings, the feeling of being like others, the possession of competencies, and capacities for effectiveness. For the adolescent it is the need to belong to a group of like minded others where differences are minimised and contagion can lead to participation in mass activities.

The adolescent nuclear self acquires a new level of stabilisation with the capacities to remain cohesive, resilient, and flexible. However, because the word "nuclear" conveys the sense of early, primitive, or archaic development and is too closely linked with self psychology, I believe it cannot be used to designate the "transformational self", a multi-faceted (multi-theoretical) self-state with which the adolescent is transformed into the young adult.

New methods with which to understand today's adolescent

Brain research

An era of accelerated brain research was ushered in when President George H. W. Bush on January 1, 1990 issued a Presidential Proclamation confirmed by separate House and Senate Resolutions declaring the 1990s to be the "Decade of the Brain". He committed millions of Federal dollars to the Library of Congress, the National Institute of Mental Health, and the National Institutes of Health to coordinate studies featuring computerised neuroscience brain imaging. The "Decade of the Brain" was preceded by the mapping of the human genome project and was followed by the "Decade of Human Behaviour" project. When the yield from the "Decade of the Brain" effort produced research studies with high replicability, a resurgence of postmodernism and neo-positivism emerged.

Discoveries from this effort include the following:

1.   New neural cell growth continues well into old age. The brain develops and maintains itself through the removal (pruning) and

construction (neurogenesis) of new neurons and circuits. The most energetic phases seem to occur in a pattern resembling waves during childhood and adolescence.

2. The brain continues its most expansive growth up to between eighteen to twenty-five years of age as a result of continual inter-action with the environment. It turns out that the brain is highly responsive to external stimuli and can rapidly change connec-tions between neurons within minutes of stimulation, a process called neuroplasticity.

3. Mental disorders such as schizophrenia, bipolar affective disor-der, and obsessive-compulsive disorder began to be understood as brain disorders and still later as circuit disorders. Unlike Alzheimer's, which is understood as a neurological disorder involving tissue loss or damage, the aforementioned disorders appear to be better understood as one or more disruptions in circuitry.

4. Neuroscience research is contributing to the understanding of the ataxias such as Parkinson's and Huntington's diseases which have been linked to gene mutations within familial histories.

5. The treatment of conditions such as trauma have been signifi-cantly impacted through the understanding of chemical and anatomical brain changes.

6. The study of the brain's limbic system, which supports emotion and motivation, along with its interaction with multiple neuro-transmitters and the subject's genetic make-up are contributing to the understanding of alcohol intoxication and addiction, a process called neuroadaptation.

7. New knowledge emerged about olfaction, cognition, and the nature of dreaming, imagination, memory, mood, reason, judg-ment, consciousness/self-awareness, human identity, and the nature of the neurological self (Dana Foundation, 2011).

The nature of the neurological or neural self is one of the major contri-butions to my thinking in the construction of the transformational self.

Non-linear dynamic systems theory

With the advent of computerised mathematical computation, a col-lection of principles has been derived "governing the behavior of physiochemical systems, such as groups of molecules or patterns of clouds" (Siegel, 1999, p. 215). This exciting vista contributes significantly to understanding the nature of the transformational self. For a discussion of this contribution see Chapter Nine on "The contribution from non-linear dynamic systems theory".

I now turn to a discussion of varieties of transformational selves in an attachment context. Discussions of aspects of attachment theory are contained in Chapters Four, Five, Seven, and Eight. The fact that attachment theory is not able to be confined and presented in a single chapter speaks to the centrality and ubiquity of attachment theory in the elaboration of the conceptualisation of transformational self.

Notes

1. As an example of the contemporary educational philosophy with its focus on the whole person, let us look at the "response to intervention" (RTI) model. While RTI can be individualised to suit specific school needs, four components are necessary in order to fully implement the model: 1) all students are screened at the beginning of the school year; 2) students with unique learning needs are identified and scientifically based interventions are applied; 3) periodic "progress monitoring" takes place throughout the school year to make sure the supplemental learning is working; and 4) if the initial RTI is not working, more rigorous learning is offered including special education services (Samuel, 2008).

2. Dr Rafael Osheroff, a forty-two-year-old white male , married with three children, medical doctor with a specialisation in nephrology, was admitted to Chestnut Lodge hospital in Maryland with a diagnosis of depression and narcissistic personality disorder. Psychoanalysis was the only treatment offered. At the seven month mark in treatment his condition worsened to the point where his parents intervened and transferred him to Silver Hill Foundation hospital in Connecticut. At Silver Hill he was diagnosed with psychotic depression and placed on psychotropic medication, including phenothiazines and triclyclic antidepressants. Improvement was dramatic and within three months the patient was back at work. Dr Osheroff initiated a right to effective treatment law suit which was ruled in Dr Osheroff''s favour in an out of court settlement.

P arts of Chapters Two and Three concern a description of the positivist adolescent, the adolescent of ego psychology.[1] What follows is an elaboration of this perspective for historical purposes. Peter Blos Sr. added the dimension that each of the adolescent phases proceeded along three lines: ". . . in terms of typical drive and ego modifications, an integral conflict to be solved and of developmental tasks to be fulfilled". Later Blos (1976) spelled out four ego tasks as developmental challenges necessary to be addressed for adult character formation:

1. completing the second individuation process
2. overcoming the destabilising effects of past traumatic experiences
3. establishing historical ego continuity (similar to Erikson's ego identity and Kohut's cohesive self) and
4. consolidating a sexual identity. (By sexual identity Blos meant the resolution of bisexual impulses with heterosexual object finding, the decline of masturbation, and the resolution of the negative Oedipus.)

For Blos, the central issue in the late adolescent phase is consolidation, that is, the unification of the ego and the means by which continuity within it can be preserved. Continuity is maintained by a stable arrangement of ego functions, character defences and interests, relatively constant self- and object-representations, and an increasing capacity for anxiety tolerance. A state of balance amongst component parts or equilibrium is reached that maintains an intrinsic constancy. An optimal level of anxiety, that favours development, is preserved which gives "tonus to the personality" (Blos, 1962).

Also Blos (1962), expanding on Jacobson's (1954) comments on the development of the self (as a supra-ordinate psychological organiser at the close of adolescence), wrote that,

> ... the self has a long individual history and does not emerge as a psychic formation at adolescence. What is new at the entrance into adulthood is the quality of the self, its relative stability and the effect it exerts on both reality testing and realistic self-evaluation as the basis for thinking and action. Subjectively, the young adult feels he is a different person after the adolescent turbulence is over. He feels "himself," he senses a unity of inner and outer experiences instead of the fragmented excesses of his adolescence. This all amounts to a subjective self-experience, which Erikson (1956) has described as "ego identity". (Blos, 1962, pp. 191–192)

Erikson (1950, 1958) formulated the well-known "Eight Stages of Man". This positivist, epigenetic, developmental, stage scheme integrated a social component into and beyond the five stage psychosexual libidinal framework. Erikson suggested that at each stage a normative ego crisis, with accompanying disequilibrium and critical tasks to master, emerged involving what he called a dynamic polarity representing two possible outcomes, one negative and one positive. If resolution of the crisis was positive a competency or psychological strength/virtue emerged (a process he labelled ritualisation); if negative, a form of estrangement from self and society resulted (a process he called ritualism). The cumulative effect of successful stage resolutions (with corresponding enhancements to self-esteem and successive identifications) of each crisis contributed to one's overall sense of coherent self and healthy ego identity.

Of interest to us is the fifth stage, adolescence, with the primary task of acquiring a sense of identity or its negative counterpart, identity diffusion or role confusion. Erikson struggled to adequately defined "identity". He referred to it as "something in the individual's core with an essential aspect of a group's inner coherence . . . the young individual must learn to be most-himself where he means most to others . . . who mean most to him". "The term identity expresses such a mutual relation in that it connotes both a persistent sameness within one's self (self-sameness) and a persistent sharing of some king of essential character with others" (Erikson, 1956, p. 174). It is a steady ego continuity state recognised by the self and validated by others. Recognising the term's ambiguity, he approached "identity" from a variety of angles. ". . . it will appear to refer to a conscious *sense of individual identity*; at another to an unconscious striving for a *continuity of personal structure*; at a third, as a criterion for the silent doings of *ego synthesis*; and, finally, as a maintenance of an inner *solidarity* with a group's ideals and identity" (Erikson, 1956, p. 109).

At the adolescent stage, the ego strength/virtue that is acquired is fidelity. "The ritualization of this period is commitment to an ideology coupled with a rite of passage involving identification with a peer group different from parents or teachers. The ritualism is *totalism*, in which adolescents commit themselves to an idea, a group or a cause that defines them rather than achieving an individual sense of identity" (Austrian, 2002, p. 133). These two positions are thought of as either identity consolidation or foreclosure, respectively.

A. Freud (1958) earlier discussed central adolescent issues, in polarising fashion following Hall (1904), which needed to be addressed and resolved. These included modulation of impulses, acceptance *vs.* rebellion; love *vs.* hate of parents; revolt *vs.* dependence; and idealism and generosity *vs.* narcissism (A. Freud, 1958, pp. 275–276). These were taken up again in collaboration with Laufer (1965) in the construction of the "Assessment of Adolescent Disturbances: The Application of Anna Freud's Diagnostic Profile". In determining whether the adolescent can make the step to adulthood . . . the following areas should be examined: "social relationships, frustration tolerance, attitude to anxiety, sublimations, attitude to school or work, attitude to the future, attitude to achievements, ability for self-observation, verbalization and comparison of various sectors (In other words, is the personality in balance or harmony with its parts and is it stable?)" (pp. 73–74).

Schafer's (1979) contribution significantly changed the discussion of character formation. He recommended theory builders should turn away from structural and adaptive ideas as too metapsychological. Rather, one should embrace the notion of "character as action" which is defined as, ". . . the actions that people typically perform in the problematic situations that they typically define for themselves". This resulting "action language" is the behaviour manifested in dangerous situations or those in which incompatible choices must be made to accommodate a conflicted course. "Character change in adolescence refers to the changes in the adolescent's 'expectable ways of unconsciously constructing conflicted situations, of acting in these situations, and of developing experiential reports of these situations and their correlative actions' " (Richmond & Sklansky, 1984, p. 106).

Heinz Hartmann (1958) postulated the idea of an undifferentiated id–ego matrix at birth out of which the ego differentiates from the id. Differentiation and fitting together (synthesis and integration) are coexisting processes in varying states of equilibrium. The autonomous ego functions differentiate within a conflict free sphere, which serve the process of adaptation. While libidinal and aggressive drives constituted the biological "push" to development and maturation, later thinkers have envisioned additional biological and/or adaptational motivators.

Robert White (1959, 1975) maintained that mastery should be viewed as a primary motivational force equivalent in importance to sexuality and aggression. When the organism is not directly involved in activities related to intense need states, it has desires for work, play, exploring/adventure, and learning. "Effectance" and "competence" are seen as "what the neuromuscular system wants to do when it is otherwise unoccupied or is 'gently' (rather than intensely) stimulated by the environment".

In addition to White, others, including Richmond and Sklansky (1984) have argued that autonomy should also be considered a primary motivating force. In their conceptualisation of the autonomous self-organisation, they maintain that "the adolescent psyche's striving for autonomy may be considered an ordering principle of character (and identity) formation" (p. 111). Due to sexual, aggressive, and narcissistic tensions the adolescent virtually insists on striving for autonomy by mastering conflicts in an individual way. The autonomous self-organisation is a composite set of pre-Oedipal, anal, and phallic sexual and aggressive derivatives, grandiose and idealising narcissistic tensions, and a unique value system organised around specific goals and aspirations. "Adolescents who achieve an autonomous self-organization find themselves struggling for self-realization (and the acceptance of adult responsibility) and the satis-factions of sexual intimacy while their goals are rapidly changing" (p. 111). Earlier Sklansky noted that the striving for autonomy has the quality of an intense drive and is considered a regulatory principle (Sklansky & Rabichow, 1980).

Although the phrase autonomous self-organisation is tied to the idea of the transformational self, it is too closely linked to separa-tion–individuation thinking with its emphasis on "independence" and consolidation over transformation. It therefore cannot be used to designate the metamorphosing features represented in the transfor-mational self. Furthermore, while the autonomous self-organisation seems to capture the experience of the late adolescent male, it does not explain the affiliation, caring/maternal, and joining needs of the female. Parenthetically, it is understood that while females also have autonomy strivings, they tend to be contextualised in relational inter-actions involving, for example, decision making and choice selection.

Note

1.   Incidentally, for a restatement of this classical position reinvigorated with intersubjectivity and neurobiological dimensions, see Lucente (2012).

CHAPTER FOUR

Classification of transformational selves

In this chapter I employ an attachment framework in the classification of transformational selves. If the reader is unfamiliar with attachment theory a review of attachment dynamics is provided in Chapter Seven. Furthermore, I expand on Lyons-Ruth (1991) and Doctors' (2000) felicitous phrase "attachment–individuation" to convey the idea that positive intersubjective connectedness to phase specific self-objects is a developmental imperative if the person (i.e., the adolescent) is to attain and maintain a functional, adaptive sense of competence in her place in society. Doctors cites Lyons-Ruth's (1991) use of "attachment–individuation" as "emphasizing the child's 'propensity to establish and preserve emotional ties to preferred caregivers at all costs, while simultaneously attempting to find a place within these relationships for his or her own goals and initiatives' " (Lyons-Ruth, 1991, p. 10 in Doctors, 2000, p. 5). I am in full agreement with Doctors in her application of attachment–individuation to adolescents.

> My intention is to highlight the crucial role of the nature of the adolescent's tie to the parent, for too often clinicians focusing on separation forget that the tie to the parent isn't the same for each adolescent.

When the role of insecure attachment is given its due, then the vulner-ability an insecure child brings to the developmental process—and the desperation, depression, and (sometimes) aggression that grow from that vulnerability—can be recognized and not mistakenly attributed to the pain attendant on so-called disengagement. Intense ambivalence is recast, a la Lyons-Ruth (1991), as a hallmark of insecure attachment complicating normative adolescent developmental expansion (e.g., individuation). (Doctors, 2000, p. 6).

As we move forward, building theory from empirical data, let us not get overly confident in our formulations remembering Popper's (1965) cautionary words,

Science is a house built on piles above a swamp . . . The piles are driven down from above into the swamp, but not down to any natural or "given" base; and if we stop driving the piles deeper, it is not because we have reached firm ground. We simply stop when we are satisfied that the piles are firm enough to carry the structure, at least for the time being.

From a heuristic perspective, it is useful to think of two types of trans-formational selves, the secure and the insecure, related to each other as if on a developmental continuum. First, let us consider the secure transformational self.

The secure transformational self is a self-state with a confident sense of expectancy and hopefulness. This adolescent believes, or rather somehow knows, that dependable self-objects will be found and will be available when needed. This is due to having had a good enough sense of attachment and stable, internalised self- and object-representations, which have conferred object constancy. This adoles-cent does not get anxious about whether the self-objects will appear, but when they will appear.

In the 1970s, Offer and colleagues studied the longitudinal devel-opment of a cohort of fourteen to twenty-two year old middle class males and found three developmental pathways through adolescence described as continuous, surgent, and tumultuous patterns (Offer & Sabshin, 1984, pp. 417–422). The secure transformational self probably falls best into Offer's continuous growth category. These adolescents experience "a smoothness of purpose and self-assurance of their progression towards a meaningful and fulfilling adult life". The fami-lies of these adolescents tended to be intact, stable, and functional.

The second type is the insecure transformational self. This adolescent experienced an insecure transformational object without subsequent sufficient repair, and has not internalised a sense that sustaining self-objects will be there for her. In other words, this adolescent has not acquired a sense of basic trust (Erikson, 1950). Consequently, the resulting character structure/self-state is vulnerable and brittle. The insecure transformational self may be grouped into the tumultuous growth category. These adolescents are the ones customarily described in the literature on the psychopathology of adolescence. Families of these teenagers tend to be unstable, dysfunctional, and from lower middle class circumstances (Offer & Sabshin, 1984, pp. 417–422).

Using Modell's (1997) bifurcation of metaphors[1] (see Chapter Six for details), the capacity for open metaphor may well find a closer fit with the secure transformational self and the foreclosed metaphor may well serve to further explain the dynamics associated with the insecure transformational self. The key here may be understood to be a greater capacity for resilience and adaptation in the secure attachment out of which follows the transformational self.

Expanding on Palombo's (1988) outline, the capacities of the transformational self include:

1. Those which have to do with the actualisation of an inner programme:
    a. The ability to connect with and use self-objects so that the three self-object need states are satisfactorily responded to.
    b. The ability to form a developmentally appropriate attachment–individuation programme, that is, a set of reconfigured interdependencies, which are synchronous with societal expectations (Doctors, 2000).
    c. The ability to think in higher abstract forms.
    d. The ability to use biological potentials in an acquired program for survival and propagation.
2. Those formed in response to the need for adaptation:
    a. A firm sense of ego/psychosocial identity (Erikson, 1959a,b) self sameness over time.
    b. A solid sense of gender identity.
    c. A solid sense of work/vocational identity.
    d. The capacity to tolerate ambiguous self and object representations (Bendicsen, 1992).

A central idea about the transformational self-state is the adolescent's belief that she can metamorphose into a new, augmented, or different person as a young adult. This belief takes on the quality of an intense drive and is an ordering principle of the transformational self. The conviction that one can transform oneself through the conscious and not so conscious absorption of idealisations, selective identifications, and trial self-object experiences associated with mastery, differentiation from the family system, individuation from the developmental trajectory (in the sense of functional, mutual interdependence), and transformational strivings is essential to the shaping of the transformed self-state.

From an attachment framework, Ainsworth, Blehar, Waters and Wall (1978) and Bowlby (1988) intend "secure base" to be that centre "from which the child or adolescent can make sorties into the outside world and to which he can return knowing for sure that he will be welcomed when he gets there, nourished physically and emotionally, comforted if distressed, reassured if frightened" (Bowlby, 1988, p. 11). The care-taker's role in the "secure base" is one of being available, intervening only when necessary.

The "secure base" has a close linkage with child development research findings into mother–infant mutual influence (Beebe & Lachman, 1988). Mutual attunement, as the synchronous mother–infant preverbal interaction is called, is a precursor to empathic responsiveness, a capacity laid down in neuronal structure that influences both emotional self-regulation and behaviour connected to relatedness. For an informed discussion of the interconnectedness amongst affect, attachment, and memory see Amini et al. (1996).

A secure attachment to a "good enough environment/mother" (Winnicott, 1941, 1950) facilitates differentiation and is the container making possible the evolution of other primary self functions. It seems that the secure transformational self should be understood as developmental in nature in the sense of promoting healthy coping skills, fostering secondary process thinking with open metaphor, and, otherwise, facilitating adaptation. On the other hand, the insecure transformational self is more defensive in nature in that resilience[2] is compromised; there is a too frequent retreat into primary process thinking and closed metaphor when problem solving and adaptation are too linear.

Fliess' (1942) phrase of "working metabolism", used to refer to the process by which the projective identification framework is used to formulate empathic interpretations in the analytic situation, gets at the metaphor I wish to use. The adolescent "tastes" potential transformation and through trial experience with trial self-objects comes to adopt a set of modified or reconfigured self-constructs (Galatzer-Levy & Cohler, 1990). The excitement of being playful with metaphoric self-constructs, testing new capacities and competencies and having those consensually validated (Sullivan, 1953, p. 29) by others affirms the belief that potentials do indeed exist, are attainable, and can be actualised. This becomes one of the main engines that drive development, especially at the juncture of late adolescence into young adulthood.

The final point I will make in this chapter deals with the critical importance of maintaining family connections for the late adolescent. Adolescents require a recalibration of their family attachment bonds in order to differentiate in a healthy, functional manner. Rather than emphasise autonomy through separation as a developmental goal, I will stress individuation through attachment. This goal has been presented as the attachment–individuation process (Lyons-Ruth, 1991 in Doctors, 2000). I will discuss this in more detail in Chapter Seven.

Let us now turn to Chapter Five and a discussion of the self construct with reflections on traditional *vs.* alternate ways to think about the adolescent developmental process.

Notes

1.   Open metaphor indicates the capacity for trans-correspondence among past and present metaphors enabling the individual to mix metaphoric meanings. In the opposite, closed metaphor is frozen in the present inhibiting recontextualisation of metaphoric meanings.

2.   Resilience is alternatively defined as the capacity for "successful adaptation despite adversity" (Fraser, Kirby, & Smokowski, 2004, p. 23) or as "the self-righting tendencies within the human organism" (Werner & Smith, 1992).

CHAPTER FIVE

Locating the transformational self within the larger self system

In this chapter I will 1) formulate criteria for a psychic self-system, 2) briefly consider some existing self-system concepts attributed to Coppolillo (1980), Damasio (1994), Kernberg (1976), Mitchell (1988, 1993), Siegel (1999) , Stern (1985), and Sullivan (1953), and finally, 3) position the transformational self in a developmental systems framework. Conceptually, the self cannot exist outside of a developmental context and so the self needs to find itself a home. Using complexity theory, the author proposes a heuristic device: it is necessary to describe the context as a psychic self-system.

As we approach this varied material it is wise to keep in mind the perspective of Charles Jaffe (2000),

> The study of adolescents strikes me as a bustling marketplace of issues. Picture the open markets in Florence during the Renaissance or London's Portobello Road of today. In the marketplace of adolescent psychology, everyone gathered seems to have one thing in common: that somehow, roughly in the second decade of life, people transform from a state in which they mostly behave and think like children to a state in which they mostly do not. Merchants from diverse cultures converge with a variety of wares in the market place. They loudly trumpet their products and proclaim their power and efficiency to

understand development, to describe its problems, to supply a fix. Biologists abound. They proclaim the power of their hormones to jump-start development and to shape body and brain. Psychoanalysts, having placed many of their kiosks close together, intend to drown out the cries of competitors with claims of superior power to explain and effect change. In this niche of the market especially, merchants tend to want their wares to dominate and others' to occupy a subsidiary role at most. Academics fill every spare inch. They act as monitors of truth in advertising, as referees reminding others not to occupy more space than they deserve, and as perspective enforcers who remind merchants that their touted products are merely necessities of modern culture, with questionable enduring value or universal marketability. (pp. 40–41)

First, let us consider the nature of the psychic self-system. Thelen and Smith (1994) state "that self-organization in natural systems can only occur when these systems are both complex and open to flux with the environment" (p. 55). Complex, open systems refer to systems that are characterised by an enormous amount of behavioural variability, with dynamics that arrange in non-linear, heterogeneous, and "noisy" interaction in varying degrees with all environmental forces. These systems are in modes of potential cooperation with matter and energy that attract neighbouring elements which, in turn, generate local points of instability causing continuous shifts in the overall level of thermo-dynamic equilibrium. Consequently, new stabilities are always emerging. While the early work on complex systems began with chemical and physical systems, attention has turned to the properties of complex biological systems. We can easily imagine that in a psychic self-system, cognitive, affective, and behavioural elements form local asymmetries which can become amplified. In this amplification, one mode may arise to constitute a new organisational parameter. So the psychic self-system is constantly creating while being created (pp. 55–56). Let us now review examples of self-systems. Details can be found in the after notes immediately following this chapter.

This journey begins with an interpersonal perspective (Sullivan), proceeds to integrative attempts to blend drive theory and object relations (Kernberg, Coppolillo, and Mitchell), through the intersubjective viewpoint (Stern), and brings us to the neurobiological position (Siegel).

Sullivan (1953) proposed a self-system concept, that occupied a central part of his interpersonal perspective. Sullivan distinguished needs for security from needs for satisfaction. The self-system gradually emerges to maintain a steady state of reduced anxiety and so is primarily an anti-anxiety, security agency. Anxiety operates as a destructive tendency and always acts to compromise integration. Anxiety is managed through a type of human dynamism, such as the self-system, which is defined as an enduring pattern of energy transformation exerting a regulating force. The origin of the self-system is grounded in three aspects of education for survival through interpersonal cooperation. From experience with these three parts of mother–child interaction, or socialisation, the child differentiates into an initial three-dimensional personification of *me* consisting of *good-me* (those activities of the child that tend to generate approval and are organised together under a generally positive valence), *bad-me* (those activities that generate anxiety and are organised together under a negative valence), and *not-me* (those activities that promote intense anxiety, generate points of amnesia for the experience immediately preceding it and become dissociated states that do not get organised into any form the child, or later adult, can recognise as himself) (Mitchell & Black, 1995, p. 69). The next step in the child's assumption of some degree of control over his own experience is to shape his own activities that will maximise the appearance of *good-me* (non-anxious states), minimise the appearance of *bad-me* (anxious states), and exclude altogether the terrorising state of *not-me*. At this point the self-system organises, with the specific purpose to minimise anxiety (Sullivan, 1953, pp. 102–103, 108–109, 161–165). Sullivan's formulations have not caught on and are considered historical starting points for the relational perspective (Palombo, Bendicsen, & Koch, 2009, pp. 227–240).

Kernberg (1976) referred to a self-system only as a stage four aspect of his five stage developmental model.

> Stage four extends throughout the oedipal period and is characterized by the solidification of libidinally and aggressively invested self-images into a "definite self system" and good and bad object images into a "total object representation". Also id, ego and superego become differentiated as defined psychological structure. Finally, integration takes place in stage four of self and object representations evolving into ideal self and object representations. (Summers, 1994, pp. 195–196)

Kernberg's use of self-system is a minor, almost incidental, aspect of a larger theoretical effort to combine the ego and object relations perspectives and, consequently, is too limited in its scope to be of value to us (Palombo, Bendicsen, & Koch, 2009, pp. 181–196).

Coppolillo (1980) constructed a model of adolescence involving an emphasis on the ego functions of integration, organisation, and regulation. Integration is defined synergistically "as the fusion of two or more functions of lesser complexity to produce a number of functions of greater complexity. The repertoire of behavior or the number of functions available to the individual after integration has taken place is greater than the sum of the individual functions prior to integration". Organisation is defined as "the manner in which ego functions are deployed or grouped at any given period to meet the requisites of the individual and of the environment or to relieve the strain between environmental constraints and individual wishes". Regulation is defined as "the process of first perceiving the need for a change in the deployment of ego functions (or the need to maintain them in an unchanged state) and then the process of undertaking these changes or stabilizing maneuvers" (Coppolillo, 1980, pp. 397–398). In Coppolillo's model the ego organisation is the supra ordinate structure conceptualised as a triangular configuration involving perception of external reality, perception of instinctual drives, and perception of self in varying states of developmental balance. The early self evolves into a self-system that is regarded as a regulatory function. Regulatory functions become internalised in two ways.

> One portion of it represents the subjective sensor. The other portion groups together traits, values, beliefs, and experiences to serve as the composite mental representation of the self as the person interacts with the external world or seeks to regulate his own drives and their derivatives. Thus the subjective "I" of the self-system observes and evaluates the particular objectified qualities, traits and equipment that are marshaled to achieve a task and that represent at that time and in those circumstances the composite "me." The composite me is a constantly changing mélange of qualities and traits that present themselves to the subject. (Coppolillo, 1980, pp. 409–410)

Coppolillo's model can be thought of as a bridging device in conceptualising the transformational self. Coppolillo's attempt to fashion an ego organisation/self-system with regulatory properties moves us toward a neurobiological self-construct with emphasis on capacities that have to do with the actualisation of an inner programme. However, Coppolillo's mixing of ego- and self-metaphors lends itself to conceptual confusion (Palombo in Palombo, Bendicsen, & Koch, 2009, p. xxxvii).

Mitchell (1988, 1993) has perhaps the clearest, most recent, outline of the struggle to integrate the traditional drive/defence model with the relational model. In the drive model, the self is grounded in positivism and is understood to be layered, singular, continuous, and represented by the spatial metaphor. In the relational model, the self is grounded in social constructivism and is understood to be interactive, multiple, discontinuous, and represented by the temporal metaphor. Mitchell decided to move away from the classical model and constructed an integrated, relational perspective omitting the concept of the drives. I am unsatisfied with Mitchell's model in that it does not offer sufficient explanatory power to describe the characteristics of the transformational self. Recognising inherent incompatible assumptions and theoretical inconsistencies in blending the drive with the relational framework, the transformational self remains a theoretical hybrid with an innate quality of drivenness embedded in a "relational matrix". Mitchell defines the relational matrix as an organising principle and a frame for integrating data, the content of which includes the self, the object, and interactional patterns (Mitchell, 1988, p. 41 in St Clair, 2004).

Stern (1985) formulated the intersubjective hypothesis in which a developmental progression of the sense of self is the primary organising principle. The five senses of self emerge on a predictable timetable each accompanied by a respective domain of social relatedness. The framework is non-epigenetic in that each sense of self does not come into ascendancy, impact the organism, and then recede into the background. Rather, each sense of self with its domain of relatedness contributes to the developing self-experience during its formative sensitive period and continues to contribute throughout the life cycle. The senses of self are inferred from five developmental epochs each based on infant observations of mental and physical capacities that mature in quantum leaps or in systematic bursts of potential. The basic clinical issues such as autonomy and object constancy are seen as issues for the lifespan and not as issues of developmental phases. The unfolding senses of self are: the sense of an emergent self (birth to two to three months), the sense of a core self (two to three months to seven to nine months), the sense of a subjective self (seven to nine months to fifteen months), the sense of a verbal self (fifteen months to thirty months), and a sense of narrative self (thirty months to forty-eight months). Stern considers his approach normative and prospective rather than pathomorphic and retrospective. Stern's framework, based on empirical data collection, has an intuitive feel about it as closer to real experience than the traditional epigenetic models. It, therefore, allows us to use it with some measure of confidence as a foundation for the later transformational self.

Siegel (1999) states that,

> The mind as a whole, although it exists across time and is composed of many relatively distinct but interdependent modules, functions as a system itself. As a complex system, it is made up of subcomponent specialized self-states, as well as itself being a subcomponent of a larger interpersonal system. (p. 230)

> The proposal here is that *basic states of mind are clustered into specialized selves, which are enduring states of mind that have a repeating pattern of activity across time.* (p. 231)

These specialised selves or self-states have their own ways of processing information and achieving goals with each person having multiple such independent and yet distinct processes. These self-states maintain a sense of continuity over time and so create the experience of the mind. Siegel cites the work of Alan Sroufe (1990) and Susan Harter (1999) who maintain that each of us is composed of many selves which interact with other multiple states of selves that cluster together in the service of a specialised activity processing information in order to achieve a particular goal and creating cohesion in the moment and continuity across time. Of considerable relevance to the formation of the transformational self, Harter (2012, p. 61) has studied the phasic nature of adolescent self-states and has created an empirically derived developmental progression leaving the average late adolescent with a more stable self that has enhanced features of resilience and adaptability. For the late adolescent, the critical issue now is ". . . how the mind integrates a sense of coherence—of effective functioning—across self states through time" (Siegel, 1999, p. 231).

While Kohut did not create a specific developmental line for the self, one has been inferred and reconstructed from Kohut's writings by

Palombo (Palombo, Bendicsen, & Koch, 2009, pp. 257–281). As Kohut's thinking evolved he distinguished between the self and self representation. Kohut defined the self as the overarching psychic structure, a structure that incorporates the ego, id, superego, and ego ideal, functions with agency, and contains the natural history of the individual's relationships with self-objects. Kohut divided the self structure into sub-ordinate and supra-ordinate dimensions (1977, p. 97, 1991). The sub-ordinate view of the self included a developmental line that paralleled Mahler, Pine, and Bergman's (1975) separation–individuation trajectory of object cathexis and thus was a record or time line of attachment status. The supra-ordinate view of the self described the psychological evolution of the person. The sub-ordinate view was more grounded in empirical data, while the supra-ordinate perspective was a level of abstraction removed from empirical data and described the psychological development of the person.

Kohut's concept of the self-structure is the primary psychic agency that is incorporated into the transformational self's self-system which is operational from birth and spans the entire human developmental life cycle. Its primary properties are its organisational, integrative, and regulatory roles of affective, cognitive, and attachment aspects of the individual's life over time. As development unfolds certain bursts of achievement are empirically observable. As Stern (1985, p. 8) put it, "new integrations arrive in quantum leaps".

I want to advance the following formulation. I will substitute Greenspan's functional emotional developmental model (Greenspan, 1979, 1989; Greenspan & Lourie, 1981; Greenspan & Porges, 1984; Greenspan & Shanker, 2004, pp. 53–54) and its self framework for that of Mahler, Pine, and Bergman's because Greenspan's model challenges the prevailing deterministic framework and advances the hypothesis that "the critical learning steps leading to symbolic thinking are embedded in our cultural learning processes and not in the structure of our genes" (Greenspan & Shanker, 2004, p. 5). While genetic structure may form constraints on the evolving morphology of the self, environmental experiences grounded in interpersonal exchanges may function like a switching device turning on or off certain regulator genes which in turn influence gene expression and behaviour (p. 5). Greenspan holds that global physiological affective states differentiate into complex emotions. These emotions serve as the primary architect of the mind in terms of being the functional element in social referencing, symbol formation, and meaning making and human interaction. Greenspan is clear in privileging affects over cognition. Cognition flows from emotional life; ". . . emotions are the architect of intelligence" (Greenspan & Shanker, 2004, p. 283). Through a process of dual coding of experience the infant learns to register experience through both its physical and affective properties. For example, a baby touches an ice cube and feels coldness. As experience builds, more and more of the physical world becomes "known", and more and more of the associated emotional patterns of pleasure/unpleasure take shape. Growing motor and emotional signalling capacities enable the child to separate perceptions from action facilitating the formation of more symbols. In normal development these patterns move from pre-symbolic to symbolic status, and a discriminating psychological level of experience, now called consciousness or self-awareness, emerges. Eventually, the refrigerator, January in Chicago, and even some people will symbolise different types of coldness.

Greenspan's developmental hypothesis is set in an evolutionary context. It incorporates current infant observational data, is informed by the study of autistic children, and is grounded in neurobiological research findings. The author recognises that Kohut's psychological self is somewhat different from Greenspan's empirical self, but the fundamentals of each self perspective allow for a dynamic integration without doing violence to either perspective. Greenspan's self or sense of self is defined as the agent of reflection locating the self in the larger interpersonal context of other selves and serving as an internal compass or frame of reference for thinking and making judgments about one's own behaviour and thoughts and comparing them to perspectives of others (Greenspan & Shanker, 2004, p. 52). Both Kohut and Greenspan's selves have in common the self as the primary psychic structure, the self as the sense of agency, and the self as the organiser of behaviour and judgment. Consistent with Kohut's division, Kohut's supra-ordinate self will be the overarching framework and Kohut's sub-ordinate dimension will contain that of Greenspan's functional emotional developmental model in place of Mahler's. In some cases, consistent with Greenspan, the author believes it necessary to incorporate concepts from other perspectives, such as Mahler's self and object constancy and Erikson's ego identity.

Based on findings from infant development and neuroscience research, there seems to be consensus on nine biological epochs from birth to young adulthood. The first five follow Greenspan and Shanker's (2004, pp. 51–92) outline. (For a review of Greenspan's framework see Palombo, Bendicsen, & Koch, 2009, pp. 113–126; Kohut's developmental framework is found in Palombo, Bendicsen, & Koch, 2009, pp. 265–227). Numbers six to ten are well-established parameters. The tenth is the transformational self. Chronologically, from birth through young adulthood, they include:

Periods follow Kohut and *Stages* follow Greenspan

I.   The virtual self period (birth to two months)
     Stage 1, Birth to two months: the earliest self: regulation and interest in the world
II. The cohesive self period (two to thirty months)
     Stage 2, two to five months: the related self: engaging and relating
     Stage 3, four to ten months: the wilful self: intentionality
     Stage 4, nine to eighteen months: the preverbal self: problem solving, mood regulation, and a sense of self
     Stage 5, eighteen to thirty months: the symbolic self: creating symbols and using words and ideas
III. The Oedipal period (thirty to forty-eight months)
     Stage 6, thirty to forty months: the emotional self: emotional thinking, logic, and a sense of "reality"; self and object constancy is attained along with the capacity to tolerate separation
IV. Latency period (four to thirteen years)
     Stage 7, four to seven years: Multiple cause and triangular thinking; the Oedipal self—the capacity to accept that two can have a relationship that does not include "me" and the school self—the capacity to "go off to school"
     Stage 8, ten to twelve years to puberty: grey area, emotionally differentiated thinking; the pubescent self—the biological passage into adolescence
V.   Adolescence period (fourteen to seventeen years)
     Stage 9, ten to twelve to early adult years: a growing sense of self and an internal standard the teenage self—the development of an ego identity
VI. Late adolescence period (eighteen to twenty to twenty-five years): the transformational self—cortical maturation and the biological gateway into adulthood

Stage 10, Early adolescence through late adolescence: an expanded sense of self

Stage 11, Reflecting on a personal future

Stage 12, Stabilising a separate sense of the self

Stage 13, Intimacy and commitment

Stage 14, Creating a family

Stage 15, Changing perspectives on time, space, the cycle of life, and the larger world: the challenges of middle age

Stage 16, Wisdom of the ages.

These are massive biological affective/cognitive changes around which psychology emerges to make coherent meanings for the shifting self-states. These ten epochs, encompassing the development of the transformational self, can be understood as periodic focal systems within the larger (supra-ordinate) self-system. Each focal system (the system receiving attention, the system being studied) has its maturationally appropriate time of imprinting on the self-system, an imprinting that continues to exert influence throughout the self-system's life cycle. These focal systems constitute domains of biopsychosocial synergy as bursts of growth compel new integrations and present opportunities to actualise the individual's potentials. The times between biological epochs are opportunities for consolidation of self-system processes. Schematically, this system (encompassing supra-ordinate, focal, and sub-ordinate system components) can be represented as an inverted cone with developmental geographies occupying successive focal system areas of differentiated activity and expanded adaptive accommodation.

I propose that a transformed self at the close of the adolescent phase is the focal system (state of mind) of a larger self-system (multiple states of mind or "inner community") with maintenance of self-cohesion, personal integrity, and self-esteem as essential features. The idea of inner community comes from Badenoch (2008, pp. 36, 102) who used it to refer to the position that, at any point in time, we exist in a state of coexistence with our multiple states of mind. These states of mind are thought of as neural nets that have been created and reinforced by repeated experience and essentially constitute self-representations that may be concordant and/or discordant with each other. They may exist in history and/or present reality. They tend to be dualistic in nature so that a memory of an angry father is paired internally with a frightened child, or a cold mother with a lost, shamed child. Also, we can imagine a warm, caring mother linked with a calm, peaceful child (Badenoch, 2008, p. 36). What is paired, then, is fundamentally an object representation with a self-representation. As we think about states of mind, each of us is both a teacher/student, parent/child, performer/spectator, and so on.

In summary, the transformed self of the late adolescent/early adult is a phase specific dimension of the neural self[1] and is a multifaceted, interactive series of organisational, integrative, and regulatory processes stabilising in the developmentally appropriate self-state with dynamic properties the author designates as the transformational self.

The dynamic properties associated with the transformational self include:

1. the actualisation of the individual's aspirations in alignment with talents and competencies organised by the ego-ideal (or the idealised parental imago)
2. the emergence of a reconfigured/modified self-state buttressed with new, embodied metaphorical self-references organised within an enlarged belief system
3. an enhanced meaning making capacity with synergistic potential for guiding behaviour
4. the shaping of a set of consistent coping processes and living skills for the handling of anxiety and associated affects that are resilient and adaptive and for the enhancement and protection of the self-system and
5. the regulation of the operation of the transformational self within the self-system, understood through the use of non-linear dynamic system processes.
6. the impact of the respective neural selves within the developmental line, a force for the entire life cycle.

Let us now turn to the critical subject of metaphor and how it shapes the formation of the transformational self.

Note

1. In Chapter Three in the literature review section I discuss the evolution of the self concept. I make the point that, while each theorist's definition

of self makes for different meanings of the term, there is enough overlap and similarity to warrant using the neural self concept as the overarching definition. In Chapter Eight, I discuss Feinberg's concept of the neural self (or neurobiological self) in detail. I use the neural self as the overarching self construct. Feinberg (2009) defines "the self essentially by its coherence: *The self is a unity of consciousness in perception and action that persists in time*" (p. xi).

AFTER NOTES TO CHAPTER FIVE

I n Chapter Five I elaborate on self models and touch on that of Sullivan. I discuss Sullivan's self system here for its historical interest. Its current usefulness as a self model is limited because of its absence of a neurobiological perspective.

In Sullivan's developmental model the *self system* is central to each person's personality. The *self system* involves the following considerations: 1) personality traits coalesce around the person's self esteem; 2) anxiety results primarily from social interactions; and 3) the unconscious depends upon the individual social context.

1. The infant learns to access more or less of mother's *tenderness* as a function of what the "mothering one" regards as good behaviour, that is, compliance with the respective social ritual is prehended as a *reward* by the infant and added to its feeling category of satisfaction in the context of appropriate functioning in specific zones of interaction. (Zones of interaction are the respective relational component Sullivan uses to replace each of the traditional psychosexual stages.)
2. The infant learns, via the primary method of adjusting behaviour, of *grades of anxiety*, gradually accommodating to those activities that are attended by less anxiety.

3.   The infant learns *uncanny emotion* in the discrimination of (espe-
      cially dangerous) situations, which is remembered resulting in
      avoidant behaviour due to the anticipation of a repetition of the
      sudden severe anxiety situation.

Good-me is the beginning personification which organizes experience
in which satisfactions have been enhanced by rewarding increments
of tenderness, which come to the infant because the mothering one is
pleased with the way things are going; therefore, and to that extent,
she is free, and moves toward expressing tender appreciation of the
infant. Good-me, as it ultimately develops, is the ordinary topic of
discussion about "I". (Sullivan, 1953, pp. 161–162)

Bad-me, on the other hand, is the beginning personification which
organizes experience in which increasing degrees of anxiety are associated with behavior involving the mothering one in its more or less
clearly prehended interpersonal setting. That is to say, bad-me is
based on this increasing gradient of anxiety and that, in turn, is dependent, at this stage of life, on the observation, if misinterpretation, of the
infant's behavior by someone who can induce anxiety. The frequent
coincidence of certain behavior on the part of the infant with increasing tenderness and increasingly evident forbidding on the part of the
mother is the source of the type of experience which is organized as a
rudimentary personification to which we may apply the term bad me.
(Sullivan, 1953, p. 162)

Not-me is part of a different field, which we know about through
certain, and very special circumstances. Not me is encountered most
conspicuously by all of us occasionally in dreaming, but it is very
emphatically encountered by people who are having a severe schizo-
phrenic episode, in aspects to them, which are most spectacularly real.
This is a gradually evolving personification of an always relatively
primitive character, which is tangled up with the growing acceptance
of "my body". It is parataxic (untrue; distorted thinking and feeling
about another, which gets corrected through consensual validation
with others). It is about poorly grasped aspects of living regarded as
"dreadful" and differentiated into incidents attended by awe, horror,
loathing and dread. (Sullivan, 1953, pp. 162–163)

Central to the self-system is the concept of dynamism. Sullivan
believed that the ultimate reality in the universe is energy, that all
material objects are manifestations of energy and that all activity
represents the dynamic or kinetic aspect of energy. A doctrine of force,

which has as its underpinning energy, is naturally a conception of a dynamism of the universe. If the whole organism is considered a dynamism, then the individual cell is a subdynamism. With respect to the morphology or organisation of the living dynamism, the cell is the ultimate entity or smallest useful abstraction that can be employed in the study of functional activity of the living organism. This is the dynamism itself, the relatively enduring pattern of energy transformations, that recurrently characterise the organism in its duration as a living organism (Sullivan, 1953, pp. 102–103).

With respect to human dynamisms, there are two kinds (of particular interest to psychiatry). Primary dynamisms are those that refer to the sundry recurring tensions, that disturb the euphoria of the living creature and manifest themselves as integrating, disjunctive, and isolating tendencies. On the other hand, those tensions with "primary reference to the energy transformations characteristic of particular zones of interaction" constitute secondary dynamisms as in, for example, the *oral dynamism* (Sullivan, 1953, pp. 108–109).

The "self-system", the anti-anxiety system, is a secondary dynamism. While it does not have any particular zone of interaction, any particular physiological apparatus behind it, it literally uses all the zones of interaction and all physiological apparatus that are integrative and meaningful from the interpersonal standpoint. The components of the self-system will exist and manifest functional activity in relation;

1. to every general need that a person has, and
2. to every zonal need that the excess supply of energy that the various zones of interaction give rise to, and
3. throughout interpersonal relations in every area where there is any chance that anxiety may be encountered (Sullivan, 1953, pp. 164–165).

For a fuller account of Sullivan's ideas the reader is directed to Chapter 12, "Harry Stack Sullivan (1892–1949)" in Palombo, Bendicsen, and Koch, 2009.

PART III
CONTRIBUTIONS TO THE UNDERSTANDING OF THE TRANSFORMATIONAL SELF

INTRODUCTION TO PART III

P art III consists of five chapters discussing the contributions to the transformational self from very different disciplines, or domains of knowledge. In Chapter Six, I present contemporary thinking about metaphor as a core component of the transformational self. In Chapter Seven, I approach attachment theory as the framework allowing us to place the transformational self in a state of ongoing interpersonal connectedness. In Chapter Eight, I discuss discoveries from neuroscience research findings and hypotheses about those findings as generating meaningful linkages to the biological roots of the transformational self. In Chapter Nine, I reflect on how non-linear dynamic systems theory explains functional aspects of the transformational self. In Chapter Ten, I elaborate on the conceptual significance of prefrontal cortical maturation along with its enhanced neural connectivity and the opportunity it provides for thinking in a different way about closure to the adolescent phase. In addition, I discuss formal operational thought in adolescence and the cognitive development of types of post formal operational thought as ways to extend modes of thinking in adulthood.

CHAPTER SIX

The contribution from the linguistic theory of metaphor

The arrival of the transformational self is preceded by the use of different metaphorical self-references. As the transformational self begins to organise, stabilise, and eventually characterise the late adolescent/young adult, different ways to refer to the self emerge in the form of new, selective, trial identifications. These identifications manifest as behaviours, verbalisations, and/or as differentiated affective states, but most significantly as self-representations. At this juncture we need to spend some time reviewing the rapidly changing conceptual landscape of metaphor theory.

The traditional definition of metaphor is "a figure of speech in which a word or phrase literally denoting one kind of object or idea is used in place of another to suggest a likeness or analogy between them (as in the ship plows the seas or in a volley of oaths)" (*Webster's Third New International Dictionary*, 1993, p. 1420). Metaphor derives from the Greek verb *metaphora* meaning to transport or transfer (meta=beyond, over+pherein=to bring, to bear). Sharpe's (1940) observation that the use of metaphor is a regressive revival of affective language, first experienced by the infant and conditioned by language, is consistent with traditional usage. These experiences mirror control and discharge of affect that later, at all developmental levels, reflect the literal meaning of its origins. Sharp maintained that all metaphors evolve from the feelings and sensations associated with mastery of bodily orifices. Words derive from onomatopoeia and roots. Onomatopoeia is the naming of a thing or action by a vocal imitation of the sound associated with it like the teapot's hiss and the cuckoo's cuckoo. Roots is the organised, crystallised sounds that emerge, by necessity, from earliest civilization naming the relation-ships between man and man, man and his environment, his self-preservation, and procreative powers. Onomatopoetic words imply sense perception, not thoughts. Ideational language evolves from roots. Both derivations find their origins in affective experiences, which have become concretised and forgotten. Examples such as, "I see your point of view, but I don't take it in" and "I can't get the whole day squeezed in, it's too much" are metaphors originally referring to specific suckling experiences. Sharpe's observations are enjoying renewed attention in the context of an expanded metaphorical, theo-retical framework.

In psychoanalysis, metaphor has historically been regarded as an aspect of symbolisation in primary process activity, such as dreaming and symbol formation. Prior to verbal language, it is not unreasonable to assume that the capacity for symbolisation in the form of protometaphors appears early in development (Modell, 2000, p. 143).

Earlier, Levin (1980) proposed that metaphor used in interpretive work had synesthesic properties. "Metaphors cross (sensory) modali-ties; they relate one sensation to another and the various hierarchical levels of (developmental) experience to each other" (p. 12). The use of metaphor contributes to the analyst's affective (communication) and seems to create the general affective arousal level that is required for synthetic activity to occur. Levin seems to be asserting that the useful-ness of a metaphoric interpretation is related to the degree by which the unity of the senses are (re)connected or strengthened by the cross modal exchange of sensory information. In metaphorical research work involving a view of mind-brain transference that predates both Lakoff and Modell, Levin postulated the existence of a mechanism that involves the formation of novel neural networks in relation to subjects the patient and analyst understand are of special interest to the patient. When these subjects and corresponding neural networks are activated by metaphorical interpretations embedded in language the patient can use, they produce a state of general psychical arousal (optimally, the surprise response) that stimulates interest, synthesis, and insight (Levin, personal communication with the author). Later we will work this idea into the formation of the transformational self. See Stern (1985) for a vivid, developmentally based discussion of metaphor and the transposition of amodal information (pp. 138–161).

In the new definition, logical similarity of words and phrases changes to include associations between irrational, different, and *visceral* (my emphasis) concepts and thoughts. Somatic experiences, such as affects, can be transformed into metaphor enabling otherwise inchoate experiences to be understood. As Modell puts it, "There is a privileged connection between affects and metaphor" (Modell, 1997, p. 219).

Modell maintains that "Affects, metaphor, and memory form a synergistic, unified system". Reviewing the work of Edelman (1992), Modell stresses that memory is both retranscriptive and categorical and that,

> what is stored in the brain is not something that has a precise corre-
> spondence with the original experience, but is a potentiality awaiting
> activation. The perceptual and motor apparatus serve memory by
> means of a scanning process in which there is an attempt to match
> current experience with old memory categories. What is stored in
> memory is not a replica of the event, but the *potential* to generalize or
> refind the category or class of which the event is a member. What is
> significant for the psychoanalyst is that activation of these potential
> categories is evoked through cognitive metaphors, which form bridges
> between the past and present; metaphor allows us to find the familiar
> in the unfamiliar. (p. 220)

Affective memories are also potential categories and subject to retrieval in the same way.

Modell has proposed that modern metaphor be divided into fore-closed and open types. In the foreclosed metaphor the correspondence between one domain and a dissimilar domain is unvarying and unambiguous. In traumatic events the metaphoric memory connection between past and present is frozen involving a telescoping of time so that the affective experience of past and present are identical. Categories of affects are remembered and repeated, not recontextualised, constituting a resistance to treatment. Examples of such "metaphors can be found in transference repetition, traumatic memories and in certain inhibitions" (p. 220).

In contrast, the open or fluid metaphor, facilitates the recontextualisation of affects and the generation of new meaning. Ambiguous correspondence between past and present metaphors facilitate imagination. The capacity for open metaphor contributes to the individual's resilience to trauma (p. 221).

The next dimension of metaphor theory I shall discuss as we move into contemporary metaphor theory is that of Ricoeur (1977) and his contention that metaphor works, not at the level of individual words, but at the level of sentences. For Ricoeur, hermeneutics is more than the interpretation of symbols. It is a theory of symbols within texts and a theory of texts, or textuality. The task of hermeneutics is to discover meaning, and the goal of hermeneutics is understanding. This is accomplished through an understanding of knowledge mediated through an expansive definition of language (Simms, 2003, p. 31–43). Consider "Achilles is a lion". Metaphor works not by substituting one "deviant" word for another "proper" word, but rather by the interaction between the focus, a lion, and the frame, Achilles. This interaction entails three tensions: between the focus and the frame, between the literal and the metaphoric meanings, and within the word "is", which in metaphor also contains the meaning "is not". This last tension is the most important because it is the pathway to metaphorical truth and the way of seeing something as something. In other words, seeing something in a new light increases human knowledge and I will extend this to mean knowledge about the self. This is only possible as a result of a hermeneutic process on the part of the reader of the metaphor. Metaphor is that part of language that invites interpretation, and thus invites us to do hermeneutics. Ricoeur contrasts dead Aristotelian metaphors with living metaphors. The living metaphor "is the creation of new metaphor which not only keeps language alive, but which vivifies human thought through its compulsion to exercise the imagination in an interpretative manner" (Simms, p. 77). For example, let us consider the proposition "Faith will enable us to derive hope from our despair". This utterance is hardly likely to rouse us to action. Now consider the same words expressed by Martin Luther King Jr. (King, 1963): "With this faith we will be able to hew out of the mountain of despair a stone of hope". Metaphor enables abstract language to be made concrete, and, consequently, it becomes the language of action (Simms, pp. 79–99).

Before I move into new metaphor theory, I want to reference the work of Langer (in Browning, 2006) who argued for integrating the empirical and interpretive sciences via the capacity to feel as the centre of her theory of mind. Thinking about our internal state in terms of feelings is the framework used to conceptualise all conscious knowing, both of the objective (via sense perception) and subjective (via hermeneutic activity) worlds. Next,

> To imagine is to feel spontaneously. Imagination can function *invol-untarily*, as it does in dream consciousness, or *voluntarily*, as it does when we speak. To speak is to render the world and ourselves into a "new key" through our imagination. *It is the capacity to voluntarily control our imagination that is the basis of our symbolic activity and that produces our pursuit of meaning.* Langer argues that our symbolic activity developed not for survival purposes, but for the purpose of self-expression. (Browning, 2006, p. 1135)

Langer's emphasis on imagination for the purpose of self-expression reinforces the motivation for the transformational self.

New metaphor theory distinguishes itself from the traditional metaphorical thought of Aristotle and over two thousand years of *a priori* philosophical views. Historically, there have been four under-pinnings to metaphorical thought:

1. Metaphor is a matter of words.
2. Metaphor is based on similarity.
3. All concepts are literal and none can be metaphorical.
4. Rational thought is in no way shaped by our brains and bodies, that is, it is disembodied.

Lakoff and Johnson (1980/2003) maintain that all four propositions are false.

1. The locus of metaphor is in concepts (thoughts) not words (language).
2. Metaphor is, in general, not based on similarity, but rather it is typically based on cross-domain correlations in our experience, that give rise to the perceived similarities between the two domains within the metaphor. For example, the persistent use of a metaphor may create perceived similarities, as when a love relationship, conceived as a partnership, goes awry when respon-sibilities and benefits are not shared equally.

3.   Even our deepest and most abiding concepts—time, events, causation, morality, and mind itself—are understood and reasoned about via multiple metaphors.
4.   The system of conceptual metaphors is shaped to a significant extent by the common nature of our bodies and the shared ways we all function in the everyday world.

The modern definition of metaphor is, "the mapping of one conceptual domain onto a dissimilar conceptual domain." . . . "So that in the use of a metaphor there is a juxtaposition between different domains resulting in a transfer of meaning from one to another" (Lakoff, 1987, in Modell, 1997, p. 220). Continuing, Lakoff and Johnson argue that conceptual metaphor is not just linguistic expression (a matter of words), but is a natural, embodied phenomenon, part of human thought and human language. Moreover, the metaphors we have and what they mean depend on the nature of our bodies, our interactions in the physical environment, and our social and cultural practices. Every question about the nature of conceptual metaphor is an empirical question, that is, it is a matter of cognition and, unlike *a priori* philosophy, it can be empirically measured.

Major advances in metaphor theory came in 1997 with fundamental insights by J. Grady (1997), C. Johnson (1999), and S. Narayanan (1997).

> Grady showed that complex metaphors arise from primary metaphors that are directly grounded in the everyday experience that links our sensory-motor experience to the domain of our subjective judgments. For example, we have the primary conceptual metaphor Affection Is Warmth because our earliest experience with affection corresponds to the physical experience of the warmth of being held closely. (Lakoff & Johnson, 1980/2003, pp. 254–255)

Johnson demonstrated

> that children learn primary metaphors on the basis of the *conflation* of conceptual domains in everyday life. He studied how the Knowing Is Seeing metaphor develops, demonstrating that children first use "see" literally, that is, only about vision. Then there is a stage when seeing and knowing is conflated, when children say things like "See Daddy come in" or "See what I spilled"; seeing occurs together with knowing. Only later do clear metaphorical uses of "see" like "See what I mean"

occur. These uses are about knowledge, not literal seeing. (Lakoff & Johnson, 1980/2003, p. 255)

Consider this remarkable statement, "Metaphor is a neural phenomenon" (Lakoff & Johnson, 1980/2003, p. 256). Narayanan "Using computational techniques for neural modelling, . . . developed a theory in which conceptual metaphors are computed neurally via neural maps–neural circuitry linking the sensory-motor system with higher cortical areas. . . . In the visual system of the brain, neurons *project*, that is, extend, from the retina to the primary visual cortex (PVC, author's change from V1), with neurons that are adjacent or nearby in the retina projecting to neurons that are adjacent or nearby in PVC. The neurons active in PVC are said to form a map in PVC of the retinal image. The metaphor here is topographic, with the retina as territory and PVC as the map" (1997, p. 255).

Similarly, the motor cortex is understood to contain a map of the body in which specific, visceral neuronal clusters project throughout the body enabling a correspondence between body parts and their respective actions. With repeated usage learning about those parts and actions takes place. Now the topographical map metaphor literally takes on a whole new meaning with neural circuitry linkages corresponding to body sites. "Affection is warmth" evolves into "He is a warm person" arises from the child's experience of being held affectionately by a loving parent. This conflation of warmth, affection and relationships can be detected by computerised neuroimaging in which two separate parts of the brain are activated: those devoted to emotions and those devoted to temperatures because they are neuronally linked. (Lakoff & Johnson, 1980/2003, pp. 255–256)

In addition to new metaphor being a neural phenomenon, it is also embodied.

> Simulation semantics is based on a simple observation of Feldman's: if you cannot imagine someone picking up a glass, you can't understand the meaning of "Someone picked up a glass." Feldman argues that, for meanings of physical concepts meaning is mental simulation—that is, the activation of neurons needed to imagine perceiving or performing an action. Thus all mental simulation is embodied, since it uses the same neural substrate used for action, perception, emotion, etc. (Lakoff, 2009)

How, in understanding the use of metaphor from a neurobiological perspective, can we gain an expanded perspective on the transformational self? At this point let us revisit Levin (1980) and his proposition that ". . . metaphorical language may even serve as a functional bridge between various psychical agencies that might not be otherwise connected at the time, and in a manner that would allow transfer and creative synthesis of information" (p. 14). Sensory modalities may serve as mnemonic organisers and seem functionally dispersed in the brain's topography. Levin conceives of a multidimensional grid consisting of four developmental layers of patient experience arranged hierarchically beginning with sensorimotor schema (representing the encoding of autonomic affective experience organised into idiosyncratic rhythmic patterns). The second level moves through evocative recall of memories of experiences associated with accidental properties of fragments of data prior to the characteristics of classes of categorisation. The third level is called presentational symbolism, following Langer (1967), (coinciding with Piaget's concrete operational level of thought) in which past and present time qualities are associated with objects now considered in terms of their properties. The fourth level is called discursive symbolism, an advanced form of abstract thought. This schematic demonstrates the potential, unifying effects of a bridging function provided by metaphor, which can produce a "state of general, psychical arousal that allows for synthetic activity" (p. 15). "Vertical" bridging function involves making connections between past and present experiences, affect and cognition, sensations and memories, or between conflicting tendencies or drives (p. 1). Levin is in agreement with the concept (referring to Shannon & Weaver's (1949) communication theory) that with the use of metaphor in interpretation, the value of the message rises to a maximum. Building on this schematic with respect to the formation of the transformational self, it may be possible to think of the appearance of self-metaphor in late adolescence as a catalytic agent that allows for "transfer and creative synthesis of information", advancing the potential actualisation of the reconfigured self.

As regards the transformational self, current metaphor theory makes it possible to link the development of affect attunement states with largely unconscious, primary metaphors, enabling us to deepen the organic nature of the relationship between metaphor, the attachment milieu, and the transformational self of the late adolescent phase.

The transformational self is an actual integration of the embodiment of the new metaphorical self (or selves) with a sustaining belief in internal, guided direction for self-actualisation, the functional ego ideal. In other words, the late adolescent who has had a childhood fascination with trains and bridges and who enjoys high school mathematics, now realistically envisions herself becoming a structural engineer.[1]

Let us now shift to the subject of narrative and metaphor. Cozolino (2002) points out that "The combination of goal-oriented and linear storyline, with verbal and nonverbal expressions of emotions, activates and utilizes contributions from both right and left hemispheres, as well as, cortical and subcortical processing" (p. 169). The left hemisphere interpreter may be the present day descendant of the first evolving language system. Only with the specialisation of the left hemisphere in navigating the verbal language of the social world can the full potential of the neural self be actualised through metaphor.

More specifically, "We believe that early caretaking builds and shapes the cortex and its relationships with the limbic system, which supports emotional regulation, imagination, and coping skills. To this we must now add the development of the parietal lobes in the construction of inner space". From childhood on, the capacity to imagine oneself in other worlds involved in adventures and fantasising about future exploits is a foundation for imagination. It has been suggested that during meditation the frontal lobes become less active while the parietal lobes become more active capturing perhaps the shift from outer to inner attention. "The evolution and expansion of the parietal lobes were likely essential to the emergence of this kind of imaginal self". Interestingly, the inferior regions of the right parietal lobe become activated when we witness others being still, suggesting how we may feel centred when looking at an inanimate object such as a statue of a tranquil Buddha, as well as internalising calm parents as a model for self-reflection (Cozolino, 2010, p. 146).

Cozolino continues,

> Johnson (1987) asserts that the experience of our bodies provides the internal basis for meaning and reasoning with our sense of numbers, quantity, and space growing out of bodily experience. The brain's ability to take our physical experience and use it metaphorically is the basis of imagination. For example, jumping down a slide may serve as a sensory-motor metaphor for falling in love. The child's experience of emerging from under the covers into the light of day provides a

metaphor for the religious enlightenment later in life. The balance provided by the vestibular system may be the model for psychological and emotional stability, and ultimately for leading a more balanced life (Frick, 1982). Physical metaphors provide a contextual grounding in time and space that helps us to grasp our experience and may serve as an infrastructure of higher cognitive processes. (Cozolino. 2010, pp. 146–147)

Through embodied phenomenon the context is established for the linkage of metaphor to attachment.

With a mind that is embodied, we feel grounded, our actions directed from within. We have useful, psychologically enriching access to our somatic sensations and our emotions. The felt sense here is that the ways in which we think as well as feel 'arise from, are shaped by, and are given meaning through living human bodies. (Lakoff & Johnson, 1999, in Wallin, 2007, p. 79)

Let us now turn to Chapter Seven and a discussion of how the transformational self is embedded in attachment dynamics.

Note

1. Up until this point, the use of metaphor has been discussed as an aspect of development. From a treatment perspective, however, it is not uncommon to speak of a patient generating one or more "organising metaphors" as a carrier of themes and meanings in various phases of psychotherapy (Almond, 1990; Benveniste, 1998; Brems, 2002). In remarks made in a mental health workshop in Chicago, on May 15, 2004, seventy-year-old Joanne Greenberg/H. Green (1964) described her reactive psychosis at age sixteen as a "... rupture of the metaphor. It (the metaphor) means nothing. When meaning returns, then healing begins". In her horrifying fantasies and dreams, to which she could not attach logical meaning, she saw blood coming out of faucets and snowfalls of maggots, instead of snowflakes. She characterised the return of metaphoric coherence as her triumph over psychosis.

CHAPTER SEVEN

The contribution from attachment theory

With respect to attachment theory, contemporary neurobiology takes the position that, "repeated experiences become encoded in implicit memory as expectations and then as mental models or schemas of attachment, which serve to help the child feel an internal sense of what John Bowlby called a 'secure base' in the world" (Siegel, 1999, p. 67). As reviewed in Chapter Five, "the impact of attachment relationships registers in the interrelated, indeed overlapping domains of the body, the emotions, and the representational world shaping the stance of the self toward experience in each". Each domain constitutes a dimension of the self so that we can speak of a "somatic self", an "emotional self", and a "representational self". These three domains of the self are considered inherent in the human attachment experience while the "reflective self" and the "mindful self" are considered potentialities available to those with secure attachments leading to "pathways of psychological liberation". Secure attachments refer to those "with the internalized secure base that makes resilience and exploration possible" (Wallin, 2007, pp. 61–68).

The patterning or organisation of attachment is associated with characteristic processes of emotional regulation, social relatedness, access to autobiographical memory, and the development of self-reflection and narrative. Main, Kaplan, and Cassidy (1985), extending the work of Mary Ainsworth, have outlined five principles of attachment:

1. The earliest attachments are usually formed by the age of seven months.
2. Nearly all infants become attached.
3. Attachments are formed to only a few persons.
4. These "selective attachments" appear to be derived from social interactions with the attachment figures.
5. They lead to specific organisational changes in an infant's behaviour and brain function (Siegel, 1999, p. 68).

Also, Siegel extends Main's principles to include:

6. Attachments are characterised within the broad categories of either "secure" or "insecure".
7. The attachment system serves multiple functions:
    (a) For the infant, activation of the attachment system involves the seeking of proximity which protects the infant from a variety of dangers.
    (b) The attachment system has a direct effect on the development of the domains of mental functioning that serve as our conceptual anchor points: memory, narrative, emotions, representations, and states of mind.
    (c) Insecure attachment may serve as a significant risk factor in the development of psychopathology.
    (d) Secure attachment appears to confer a form of emotional resiliency.
8. Minds communicate with each other in a form of "co-regulation" called "affect attunement."
9. The infant's developing mind uses the mind states of the attachment figure to help organise its own states.
10. "Mental state resonance" refers to the alternating misalignment and alignment of attunement signals, often non-verbal.
11. Intimate relationships involve alternating moments of engaged alignment and distanced autonomy.
12. Attuned communication involves the resonance of energy and information.

13. The nature of an infant's attachment to the primary care-giver will become internalised as a working model of attachment.

14. And I want to include a dimension of attachment that holds for the mother–infant relationship as well as for all other relationships through the life cycle, "That which we cannot verbalize, we tend to enact with others, to evoke in others, and/or to embody" (Wallin, 2007, p. 121).

Mary Ainsworth, a student of John Bowlby, systematised the study of attachment by devising the infant strange situation (Ainsworth, Blehar, Waters, & Wall, 1978). This research instrument studied the behavioural reactions when a one-year-old is separated from its primary care-giver for twenty minutes within a strange environment and at times with a stranger. At the time of reunion, the infant's response to the mother's return is encoded for the way he seeks proximity to the mother, the ease with which he can be soothed, and the rapidity of his return to play. The basic idea is that if there exists an internal working model of a secure attachment, the infant should be able to use the primary care-giver to soothe himself quickly and return to his childhood tasks of exploring and playing. Four behavioural responses have been identified: secure, avoidant, resistant or ambivalent, and disorganised/disoriented. Primary care-giver attachment patterns have been identified that correspond to the infant behavioural responses. This research has been replicated hundreds of times with very high reliability (p. 73).

Main and Goldwyn (1994) devised the adult attachment interview (AAI), which studies the adult state of mind that has become engrained and organised at a particular point in time. Using a structured interview method, the respondent's narrative responses are carefully analysed for coherence with respect to attachment. Elements of mental functioning such as autobiographical memory and social communication are fundamental integrating processes with which the mind creates coherence across mental states.

How stable are our mental models when we find ourselves with a very different experience of the self and the self with others within different relationships?

These social-context-dependent changes reflect the capacity of the mind to adapt to new situations. However, attachment research and clinical experience suggest the existence of some tenacious process that maintains similar characteristics of the individual over time. Some of these traits can be seen as elements of implicit memory, mental models of the self and others, behavioral response patterns, and emotional reactions. As an individual reflects on the self across time, these characteristic traits can be seen within the autobiographical narrative process within the AAI. Main's term "state of mind with respect to attachment" refers to an engrained, temporally stable, self-organizing mental state. This is not a transient, randomly activated state, rather, from repeated experiences with caregivers, it has become a characteristic self defining state—or "trait"—of that individual. (Main & Goldwyn, 1994, p. 83)

The AAI has been matched with the strange situation at five-year intervals with the interviewees. After two decades of comparison studies, there has been a remarkably "robust association with the specific classification of infant–parent attachment". In other words, the strange situation classification is a very good predictor for later adult patterns of attachment. Main and Goldwin have developed adult attachment patterns, which correspond well to earlier infant attachment patterns (Siegel, 1999, p. 74):

Infant Strange Situation behaviour		Adult state of mind with respect to attachment
Secure	→	Secure/Autonomous
Insecure/Avoidant or Dismissive	→	Insecure/Dismissing
Insecure/Resistant or Ambivalent	→	Insecure/Preoccupied
Insecure/Disorganised/Disoriented	→	Insecure/Unresolved/Disorganised

What are the characteristics associated with secure and insecure attachments in adults? Main and colleagues have identified five primary characteristics in parents judged to have secure attachment. They generally,

1. valued attachment relationships
2. believed that their attachment relationships had a major influence on their personality
3. were objective and balanced in describing their relationships
4. showed a readiness of recall and ease in discussing attachment, that seemed to suggest they had reflected on their experience, and

5.   took a realistic rather than a idealistic view of their parents (Main, Kaplan, and Cassidy, 1985 in Davies, 2004, pp. 25–27).

While many of the secure adults described good early experiences and relationships with parents, some described difficult histories that included trauma and loss. What distinguished the adults who were judged secure was not their actual experiences, but rather how well they had remembered, understood, and integrated their early experiences. The quality of their discourse tended to be fluent, coherent, and organised, and they easily included positive and negative feelings about their experiences. Talking about their experiences did not cause them to become overly anxious or cause them to resort to obvious defence mechanisms. This finding is consistent with findings from traumatised people in that the more they could recall and understand what happened, the less likely they were to develop post-traumatic stress disorder symptoms (Davies, 2004, pp. 25–26).

With respect to insecure attachments, the internal working models of these adults were characterised by the following factors. They generally

1.   felt less positive about attachment relationships
2.   tended to deny the influence of attachment experiences on their personality
3.   did not seem objective in their descriptions, and
4.   had great difficulty recalling some or all aspects of attachment relationships attributed to a complication of memory process Bowlby labelled as "defensive exclusion of information" (Bowlby, 1980 in Davies, 2004, p. 27).

Beyond these general characteristics, the insecure parents fell into three main patterns matching those described by Ainsworth. The dismissive adult described attachment relationships as being of little concern, value, or interest, did not have vivid memories of attachment experiences, and described current relationships with parents as cut-off. Infants of these parents tended to be unconcerned about the returning parent and were classified as dismissive (Main, Kaplan, & Cassidy, 1985, p. 91, in Davies, 2004, p. 26).

The preoccupied adult described attachment relationships as being overly concerned with dependency on their own parents and actively struggled to please them. They tended to hold themselves responsible for the difficulties in their attachment relationships and to idealise their parents. They revealed anxiety about their current relationships and tended to worry about how others perceived them. The infants of these parents were anxious about the availability of their care-givers and were most often described as ambivalent (Main, Kaplan, & Cassidy, 1985, p. 91 in Davies, 2004, pp. 26–27).

The unresolved adult described histories of unresolved trauma including physical and sexual abuse, death of a parent, with ongoing symptoms of disordered mourning. They continued to be fearful about loss and held irrational views such as tending to blame themselves for the loss and having caused the abuse. Their accounts of attachment were disorganised and lacked coherence. The infants of these parents were most often classified as disorganised/disoriented (Main & Morgan, 1996; Main & Solomon, 1990; both in Davies, 2004, p. 27).

Insecure attachments, while not equivalent to *DSM-IV-TR* mental disorders and specific types of psychopathology, do create a risk of psychological and social dysfunction. Brain growth can be adversely affected by prolonged and severe insecure attachments. In toxic attachments,

> The release of stress hormones leads to excessive death of neurons in the crucial pathways involving the neocortex and limbic system—the areas responsible for emotional regulation. (Siegel, 1999, p. 85)

Dysregulation of this central integrating process will undermine successful self-organisation. In short, secure attachment conveys resilience while insecure attachments conveys risk (p. 87).

At this point a cautionary comment from Wallin (2007) regarding the fluid nature of attachment classification types should be highlighted. With respect to the usefulness of considering patients and their "prevailing state of mind toward attachment, the fact is that their complexity as whole people can never be adequately captured by a single descriptor—secure, dismissing, preoccupied, or unresolved" (pp. 96–97). Rather, the relative prominence of two dimensions: avoidance (of closeness and dependency) and anxiety (about abandonment), where anxiety corresponds to Ainsworth's ambivalence and Main's preoccupation, could serve as an alternative framework. Moreover, over time, patient's reveal multiple states of mind with respect to attachment that are context dependent and are suggestive of a layering effect. To minimise obfuscation, good critical thinkers will quickly reaffirm that clinicians and theorists alike must carefully define terms and conditions of observation.

The analogy between parenting and psychotherapy has been frequently reaffirmed.

> Therapy is not just the rewriting of a client's story; it is the teaching of a method, a process of integration, an assessment and recalibration of perception, and a set of principles for future organization. In this way, therapy is both a form of reparenting and the learning of a strategy for reediting the self. (Cozolino, 2002, p. 170)

> The affectively attuned responses of the parent or therapist that help the child or patient to feel felt may depend upon what Schore (2003) calls right-brain-to-right-brain communication. (p. 50)

Schore's idea is "that our receptivity and responsiveness to the affective signals of others are a product of the right brain's capacity (largely through the orbitofrontal cortex) to process emotion that is expressed non-verbally—that is, through facial expression, tone of voice, posture, gesture, and so on. A patient of mine put it this way, 'I say something and then you get this look on your face, so I *know* that you know what I feel' " (Wallin, 2007, pp. 106–107).

With respect to the treatment of individuals suffering from insecure attachments, an attachment relationship is prescribed. A state of reparability/treatability is suggested (at least up to a point) using "intervention via a secure attachment with contingent, collaborative communication that involves sensitivity to signals, reflection on the importance of mental states, and the nonverbal attunement of states of mind" (Siegel, 1999, p. 86). Psychotropic (especially the SSRIs) intervention may be useful to augment treatment.

Fonagy's (2001; Fonagy, Gergely, Jurist, & Target, 2002) work on integrating object relations with attachment theory needs to be highlighted at this point, in so far as his work and that of his collaborators serves as a sturdy conceptual bridge spanning attachment theory, psychoanalytic object relations, and neurobiology. Fonagy's contribution may be said to begin with a shift in the emphasis in attachment theory "from a *behavioral perspective* to an understanding of *the role that internal representations* play in social relations" (Palombo, Bendicsen, & Koch, 2009, p. 338). For traditional attachment theorists, infants internalised care-giver's responses through adequate maternal sensitivity that occurred via exposure to the mother's behaviour and personality. For psychoanalytic theorists, it is assumed that "the 'good enough mother's' responsiveness involved much more, including *her own psychic organization and the manner in which the child internalized those experiences*" (Palombo, Bendicsen, & Koch, 2009, p. 338). In other words, this additional level of internalisation meant that the infant acquired the care-giver's psychodynamics and the capacity for self-reflection. Self-reflection or mentalisation, was the specific outcome of the care-giver's mirroring responsiveness that left the child feeling understood and affirmed resulting in a secure attachment. In the obverse, the insecure attachment was defined as having occurred when the infant identified with the care-giver's defensive behaviour in which infant–care-giver naturally occurring, episodic attunement and miss-attunement mismatches continued and did not adequately resolve. So in contrast to the internal working models of traditional "attachment theory, children form internal representations through their reflection upon the mothers' mirroring of their internal state" (ibid., p. 339). In his updating of attachment theory, Fonagy reformulates the internal working model to include mentalisation (ibid., pp. 338–340).

There is a second concept devised by Fonagy and his collaborations which extends mentalisation and is vital to furthering the explanation of the development of the attachment, psychoanalytic, and neurobiologically informed self. A critical aspect to this self needed to be explained. How is it possible for the infant to interpret and otherwise ascribe psychological meaning to the experiences to which they are exposed? To solve this problem Fonagy (2003) hypothesised the existence of the interpersonal interpretive mechanism (IIM). The IIM is a brain function that requires environmental stimulation, specifically the mother's sensitive responsiveness, in order to be activated. This overarching neural structure is thought to be localised in the medial prefrontal cortex. The IIM is a genetic potential which, in the context of a secure attachment, mobilises in the developing self allowing for the flourishing of interpretive capacity and mentalisation. The emphasis in contemporary self theory construction seems to be placed on evolutionary regulatory processes. I am reminded of the regulatory emphasis Schore (2002) placed on secure attachment as an affect state regulatory process. So it seems with Fonagy's IIM in that it provides *"the opportunity to generate a higher order regulatory mechanism: the mechanism for the appraisal and reorganization of mental contents"* (Fonagy & Target, 2002, p. 325, my italics; Palombo, Bendicsen, & Koch, 2009, p. 342). When the IIM is compromised through trauma, environmental toxins, or developmental insufficiency, the result is disordered attachment, dissociation, and/or borderline psychopathology as children struggle to find solace in terrifying unpredictability (Palombo, Bendicsen, & Koch, 2009, pp. 340–342).

Let us now turn from the expanding knowledge domain of attachment theory to the subject of the contribution of neurobiological underpinnings to the morphology of the transformational self.

CHAPTER EIGHT

The contribution from neurobiology

The neurobiological self or the neural self

et us now turn to perhaps the most recent interpretation of the self, the neural self. Work is proceeding apace to integrate neurobiological research data into a contemporary, psychoanalytic developmental psychology (Kaplan-Solms & Solms, 2002). Lemche (1998) proposed a maturational progression of the self beginning from proprioceptive and enteroceptive[1] neurobiological substrate that underlies the intrapsychic functioning which contributes to body image self experience. Panksepp (1998) suggested that the origin of the self is located deep within the early brainstem progressing through motor activity coupled with a wide array of regulatory functions. Both self-formulations begin at the cellular level. Both do not elaborate sufficiently on the mature self. They are, consequently, too speculative, too experience distant, to consider in the context of the transformational self. Details of Lemche's and Panksepp's hypotheses can be found in the after notes. More useful formulations come from Damasio, Schore, and Feinberg. Damasio (1994) maintained that the neural self is a repeatedly reconstructed biological state that depends upon the continuous reactivation of images about our identity and our body. Schore (2002), underscored neurobiological findings that the non-verbal right hemisphere is the locus of the non-dynamic unconscious[2] and the emotional self, the site where early attachment is localised and embedded in implicit memory and where the self-object construct plays a vital role in understanding the development of the self. Feinberg (2009) defines "the self essentially by its coherence: *The self is a unity of consciousness in perception and action that persists in time*" (p. xi). I will consider the neurological hypotheses of Damasio, Schore, and Feinberg, in order of progressive relatedness toward a more empirical understanding of the transformational self.

Damasio's (1994) position with respect to the self-structure is that it is almost ephemeral. The neural self is a repeatedly reconstructed biological state that endows our experience with subjectivity (pp. 226–227). "The neural basis for the self . . . resides with the continuous reactivation of at least two sets of representations", each a specialised neural assembly. One set concerns representations of key events in an individual's autobiography, on the basis of which a notion of identity can be reconstructed repeatedly, by partial activation in topographically organised sensory maps. Contained herein are a large number of facts that define our person, unique facts about our past, a collection of recent events along with their temporary continuity, and a number of events, which we plan to make happen or expect to happen. This set is referred to as dispositional representations and held in long-term explicit memory. The second set concerns the primordial representations of the individual's body, not only what the body has been like, but what it has been like lately. This encompasses background body states and emotional states. Early body signals, in both evolution and development, helped form a "basic concept" of self. ". . . this basic concept provided the ground reference for whatever else happened to the organism including the current body states that were incorporated continuously in the concept of the self and promptly become past states" (pp. 238–240). While Damasio is not specific on the type of memory associated with primordial representations, it seems that these representations are held in implicit or procedural memory.

Brain integration accounts for the capacity to reason.

> Both "high-level" and "low-level" brain centers, from the prefrontal cortices to the hypothalamus and the brain stem, cooperate in the

making of reason. . . . The lower levels in the neural edifice of reason are the same ones that regulate the processing of emotions and feelings, along with the body functions necessary for an organism's survival. In turn, these lower levels maintain direct and mutual relationships with virtually every bodily organ, thus placing the body directly within the chain of operations that generate the highest reaches of reasoning, decision making and, by extension, social behavior and creativity. Emotion, feeling and biological regulation all play a role in human reason. The lowly orders of our organism are in the loop of high reason. (Damasio, 1994, p. xiii)

At each moment the state of self is constructed from the ground up. It is an evanescent reference state, so continuously and consistently *re*constructed that the owner never knows it is being *re*made unless something goes wrong with the remaking. (ibid., p. 240)

Present continuously becomes past, and by the time we take stock of it we are in another present, consumed with planning for the future on the stepping-stones of the past. The present is never here. We are hopelessly late for consciousness.

Damasio considers the following point to be perhaps the most critical. How is it possible for an object image and an image of "a state of the self, both of which exist as momentary activations of topographically organized representations, to generate the subjectivity which characterizes our experiences?" ". . .it depends on the brain's creation of a description, and on the imagetic display of that description" (pp. 240–241). The brain reacts to those images and signals arising in those images, which are relayed to several subcortical nuclei such as the amygdala and the thalamus and multiple cortical regions. In turn, those changes alter the body image and thus perturb the current instantiation of the concept of the self.

Damasio posits the following question: how does the brain or its components "know" that responses are being generated to the presence of an entity? The self described above cannot know that the organism is responding. However, a process called the "metaself" might know. The "metaself" might be thought of as a third set of neural structures interconnecting images of the object and images of the self. In other words, a kind of third party neuron ensemble called a convergence zone might build a dispositional representation of the self in the process of changing as the organism responds to an object.

This process does not require language, but the process may be converted into language. In this way attention, awareness, and subjectivity, core components in consciousness, may come about leading to narrative capacities (pp. 243–244).

So to summarise Damasio's position on the neural self: The neural self is continuously being recreated, organised by two specialised sets of neural assemblies understood to be interacting representations, dispositional and corporeal (my term). Dispositional representations concern key past events committed to memory, as well as those anticipated, in an individual's autobiography and reconstructed repeatedly to shape one's identity. These representations are retained in long term explicit memory and also comprise the "memory of the possible future" (p. 239). Corporeal representations involve the archaic and current body and its experience of early as well as recent physical and emotional states. These two sets of representations form an internal coherence with a sense of temporal continuity. But these representations cannot explain how the organism "knows" it is responding to these perturbations. To account for how the neural self acquires self-awareness and subjectivity, a specialised third neural assembly, a "meta-self," is postulated; it is a convergence zone of processes metabolising self representations responding to an object. Damasio's "meta-self" accounts for consciousness, self-awareness in relation to the object world, to form the basis for an interpersonal neurobiology that sustains a constant, yet ever changing, neural self-state (pp. 236–244).

Schore (2000, 2002) has advanced perhaps the most coherent explication to date of the emerging neurological self. Schore (2002) is an ardent proponent of the idea that attachment transactions mediate the social construction of the human brain. He has formulated the hypothesis "that attachment theory is fundamentally a regulation theory; that is, the primary function of attachment is that of regulating the child's affect states" (Palombo, Bendicsen, & Koch, 2009, p. 325). Synthesising data from many researchers, Schore has constructed a model of the early self that positions self psychology and attachment theory as the psychological and relational/intersubjective frameworks, respectively, with which to integrate findings from neuroscience research. Shore maintains that the developing self-system is located in the maturing right hemisphere. The right hemisphere is the dominant hemisphere during the first three years of life. It has extensive connections with the emotion processing limbic system. The limbic system derives subjective information in terms of emotional feelings that guide behaviour and functions to allow the brain to adapt to a rapidly changing environment and organise new learning. While the right hemisphere is important for broader aspects of communication, the left hemisphere mediates most linguistic behaviours. The right hemisphere is the instrument for perception of the emotional state of other selves through facial recognition and expression, that is, for empathy. It communicates non-verbally with objects through the mutual exchange of affects. In addition, the right hemisphere is centrally involved in the analysis of direct information received by the subject from his own body which is more closely connected with direct sensation than with verbally logical codes. This is accomplished by extensive reciprocal connections with the autonomic nervous system. This information exchange provides the locus of the corporeal image of self through the gradual differentiation of mutual co-regulation of state and affective experience between the mothering object and the self. Neurobiological findings indicate that the right hemisphere is specialised for generating self-awareness and self-recognition and for the processing of self-related material. The right hemisphere's orbitofrontal cortex acts as the senior executive of the emotional brain. It is responsible for the integration of past, present, and future experiences and for the ability to mentally travel through time. This unique capacity to self-reflect comes on line at about eighteen months, the time of orbitofrontal maturation (Schore, 2002, pp. 443–448).

From the standpoint of the right hemisphere and neurological pathology, Feinberg (2009, pp. 8, 117) believes that in patients suffering from asomatognosia, a disturbance of the self in which the patient denies ownership of a part of the body itself, the delusional process is possibly located in the right hemisphere, particularly the right frontal lobe. An abundance of metaphors are used to reference the paralysed limbs: "a piece of dead meat", "nothing but a bag of bones", etc. Drawing on the distinction the linguist Sapir (in Weinstein & Kahn, 1959) makes between experiential and referential language, the patient so afflicted makes use of referential language. ". . . referential language is socially conventional language that refers to things as they generally appear to everyone without the personal connotations of individual experience and emotion. Experiential language, in contrast, is based upon one's own personal and emotional experience. Experiential symbols are therefore more often idiosyncratic and may be only meaningful to their user" (Feinberg, 2009, p. 118). Because the neurological patient takes the metaphorical expressions literally, "the right frontal lobe must play some role in enabling the mature brain to put aside or keep implicit (as in implicit memory in the non-dynamic unconscious, author's note) the symbolic expression of normal experience" (p. 119).

Can we combine elements of Damasio's and Schores' frameworks so as to form a working concept of the neural self? Feinberg (2009) suggested that the neural self can be thought of as a set of functions operating within a nested or compositional hierarchy. A non-nested or top-down, control hierarchy has a pyramidal shape with an army being an example. The neural self cannot be so described because in a non-nested hierarchy the higher parts exercise a centralised pattern of constraint upon the lower parts; the "general" makes the large decisions. The nested hierarchy better explains the neural self in that the lower elements are contained or nested within the higher parts to create increasingly complex wholes called holons. Depending upon the nature of the analysis (the element singled out for attention) each component part may be called a holon. The constraint is embodied within the organism and each of the holons so that the collective action creates emergent properties at higher levels which exercises constraint at lower levels. All living organisms are organised as nested hierarchies.

With respect to the anatomical architecture of the neural self, Feinberg posits:

> The medial-lateral trend deals with the organism's internal needs of homeostasis and the internal milieu (medial systems) versus the organism's relationship to the external environment (lateral systems). The caudal-rostral trend takes into account the evolution of the nervous system and the ever-increasing neural complexity that is possessed by more evolved neural systems that makes possible more advanced and abstract behavioral patterns and thought. (pp. 148–149)

The medial-lateral and the caudal-rostral trends have evolved together and function as one system. The medial-lateral refers to growth in a concentric progression, an organisation that is radially arranged such as growth rings in a tree trunk. The caudal-rostral trend (bottom-top, brainstem to prefrontal cortex) refers to growth in a longitudinal progression in an approximate correspondence with MacLean's (1990) concept of the evolutionary triune brain which includes reptilian, paleomammalian, and neomammalian brains nested within each other.

Feinberg has proposed a schematic neural self structure which consists of "three hierarchically arranged and interrelated systems: the *interoself system*, the *exterosensorimotor system*, and the *integrative self system* that is interposed between the other two" (p. 148). The *interoself system* is specialised for the processing and awareness of aspects of the self that pertain to homeostatic internal processes including self-preservation, motivational, and emotional processing. The *exterosensorimotor system's* contribution to the self is to create the quality of projicience, a term which designates the mental projection of sensations into the external environment that are characteristic of the distance receptors such as vision and audition. More specifically, projicience is "the mental externalization of stimuli away from the body that makes self-object discrimination possible, a quality of the mind that is critical for the creation of consciousness" (p. 150). Sherrington (1947), the originator of the term, believed that distance receptors are the key to brain development and to consciousness. Projicience refers to those sensations initiated through distance receptors, as opposed to those initiated through proprioceptice or interoceptive fields, which are immediately projected into the world outside the material me (Sherrington, 1947, in Feinberg, 2009, p. 151). The *integrative self system* serves to assimilate the *interoself system* with the *exterosensorimotor self system* and mediate the organism's internal needs with the external environment (p. 152). Essential to this highly complex task is the processing of self-awareness and the discrimination of self-referential material over and above its emotional content. Feinberg cites the work of Buck (1999) who has generated a hierarchiacal model of emotional functions.

Emotion I is a general state of arousal that serves homeostatic, autonomic, and self-preservative (fight or flight) responses. Emotion II serves emotional expression and expressive displays that serve important signaling functions. Emotion III, the highest emotional level on this hierarchy, entails conscious awareness of emotional states including the subjective experience of feelings and affects. It may be that if a stimulus is related solely to emotion, it has only to be processed within the *interoself system*. However, in order for a stimulus or emotion to have specific reference to the self, it needs to be processed within the integrative zones where emotion is related to cognition and objective self-awareness. (p. 155)

All models of the neural self regard consciousness as the core issue to explain. Feinberg begins to address this issue by focusing on the role memory plays in the creation of the neural self. Citing Tulving's (1985) groundbreaking work on memory, Feinberg iterates that memory also is hierarchically organised in levels of memory systems that correspond to three levels of consciousness, or self-awareness. *Anoetic* (non-knowing) consciousness is considered the lowest level and is supported by procedural memory. Procedural memory "requires only the ability to acquire, retain, and retrieve cognitive, perceptual, and motor skills" (p. 155). Procedural memory allows actions to be performed without being able to verbally explain or remember when or how the knowledge was acquired. Animals at the reptilian level of neural organisation are capable of the simplest forms of *anoetic* consciousness. The next hierarchical level is called *noetic* consciousness. At this level animals possess semantic memory that principally includes factual knowledge of the environment and associated meanings without the memory of specifically experienced events. At the level of *noetic* consciousness, organisms can be aware of and act upon, or cognitively operate on, objects and events in the absence of such. Such symbolic knowledge of the world is possessed by many non-human species, particularly mammals and birds. This capacity is suggestive of these organisms having neural structures at a minimum of up to and including paralimbic cortices. *Autonoetic* (self-knowing) consciousness, a singular human trait, sits at the highest level of Tulving's memory hierarchy. The type of memory used at this level is called episodic memory and is considered the most advanced. On the evolutionary scale episodic memory is late-developing, is early deteriorating with respect to past-oriented memory, is more vulnerable to neurological dysfunction, and is probably unique to humans. "It makes mental time travel possible allowing one to re-experience, through *autonoetic* awareness one's own previous experience . . ." (p. 158). The ability to mentally time travel, to remember and re-experience one's past life episodes, "allows for the emergence of self, self awareness, identity, autobiographical identity and a sense of subjective time" (p. 158). With the ability to imagine a past coupled with self-awareness in the present, a new capacity is formed, to conjecture a potential subjective future, a capacity Tulving called *chronesthesia*. Episodic memory and *autonoetic* consciousness included within the *integrative self system* offer a compelling explanation for the neural self.

Can we combine the positions of Damasio, Schore, and Feinberg into one overarching neural self formulation? Damasio's concept of dispositional representations, corporeal representations and "meta-self" fit comfortably with Feinberg's *exterosensorimotor system*, the *interoself system*, and the *integrative self system* respectively. Schore's right hemisphere orbitofrontal cortex, with the acquisition of the contribution of the maturing the left hemisphere orbitofrontal cortex, combine to correspond to Feinberg's *integrative self system*.

I believe Damasio and Schore would agree with Feinberg's definition of the neural self as being defined essentially by its coherence: "The self is a unity of consciousness in perception and action that persists in time" (Feinberg, 2009, p. xi).

States of mind

Siegel (1999) advanced his "interpersonal neurobiology" hypothesis involving "states of mind" that offers the optimal theoretical fit with the transformational self. *"A 'state of mind' can be defined as the total pattern of activations in the brain at a particular moment in time"* (p. 208). States of mind are organisers that allow the brain to achieve cohesion in functioning in the moment and creates a pattern of brain activation that can become more likely in the future (p. 210). Basic states of mind endure in repeated patterns of activity over time and so can be thought of as being clustered into specialised selves. A state of mind therefore involves a clustering of functionally synergistic cohesive processes that can become a remembered brain activity configuration or neural net profile. "Repeated activation of particular states—for example, a shame state or a state of despair—[author's addition, or an ego ideal representation of a transformative self state] can become much more likely to be activated in the future. In this manner, states (of mind [my addition]) can become traits of the individual that influence both internal and inter-personal processes" (p. 210). Emotion is one of the main adhesives that clusters the activity of specific systems of processing that determines the cohesiveness of states of mind.

A state of mind can be proposed to be a pattern of activation of recruited systems within the brain responsible for (1) perceptual bias, (2) emotional tone and regulation, (3) memory processes, (4) mental models, and (5) behavioral response patterns. (Siegel, 1999, p. 211)

Thinking of the mind as a centralised information processor, mental activity stems from basic processing modules. A module can be defined as a set of neural circuits carrying a certain type of information and utilising a similar form of mental signal or code. For example, a module for processing visual input involves a signal sent from the eyes to the visual cortex. It may then include circuits, which detect certain shapes, contrasts, or angles retrieved from various forms of implicit or explicit memory. These circuits may then cluster sensory representations into perceptual patterns eventually forming a visual mode. In coordination with other modes, a perceptual system is created. If this is further linked to motor circuits, state of mind coordinates activity in the moment, and it creates a pattern of brain activation that can become more likely in the future.

How are states of mind organised? For our purpose, the transformation self, the psychological part of the biological neural self, can become mobilised when an embodied metaphoric self-reference appears, is attached to an emotional charge, gets coordinated as a clustering process of dynamics, and a state of mind is mobilised. The degree to which this clustering is useful, repeated, and effective determines the state's cohesiveness. "The brain is a pattern-seeking organ; in the absence of pattern, it will even try to create one. Down to the very processes of individual neurons, it responds profoundly to repetition, creates expectation" (Fuller, 2007). Dysfunction can be explained by certain self-states coming into conflict with each other or functioning in an anti-synergystic (entropic), asymmetrical manner.

Prefrontal cortical maturation

Kent (1981) studied adaptation and the design of the human brain in an interdisciplinary context and has concluded that the prefrontal cortex "is among the last portions of the nervous system to fully develop, some pathways becoming functional only at about twenty years of age" (p. 209). Using an artificial intelligence model, Kent has formulated a neurobiological explanation to account for judgment, insight, and selective attention in anticipating consequences of likely actions and decision making. When new perceptual data is encountered, Kent postulated a "feed forward" system in which the novel percept is matched with neural networks of existing memories of perceptual data sets. The brain anticipates the appropriate response in part by correlating the new perception with categories of objects for the initial trial matching experience. Levin and Kent (2003) have co-authored a revision of this model in which Levin's "self-in-the-world" concept is used to explain ". . . the well known research finding that mental imagery of movement is fully equivalent to actual movement in its effects on learning" (p. 161).

Through a National Institute of Mental Health grant Giedd and colleagues (1999) in 1991 began to study the changing brains of teenagers. They found that the most significant changes took place in the prefrontal cortex and the cerebellum, the regions involved in control of emotions and higher order cognitive function. They found a time lag between the explosive growth of the limbic system during puberty and the prefrontal cortex which continues to mature for another ten years. Synaptic pruning removes those neurons that are not used and privileges those synapses that are exercised. By age twenty-five the most dramatic growth seems to have taken place with cortical growth continuing, but at a much slower pace (Henig, *New York Times*, 2010).

Kaplan-Solms and Solms (2002) correlate the maturation of the brain with the emergence of the ego's executive functions. Using data derived from computerised functional neuroimaging, they determined that

> Once the prefrontal (cortical) region has been structuralized (which occurs around the fifth and sixth years of life, but continues until late adolescence), it exerts a powerful *regulatory* effect over all cerebral activities. For example, it not only exerts a controlling and binding influence over motor discharge; it also regulates perceptual discharge and thereby binds projection (which prevents hallucinations). This global effect of prefrontal structuralization is described as the "secondary process". (my emphasis)

This secondary process is consistent with the traditional Freudian concept of the reality principle (Kaplan-Solms & Solms, 2002, p. 281). With the maturation of the of the prefrontal cortex, the brain's full executive potential is activated, allowing for "mature" goal directed behaviour involving enhanced functioning of motivation, attention, and sequencing of actions (Sadock & Sadock, 2007, p. 90). The ego functions of reality testing, judgment, regulation of impulses, modulation of affect, object relations, self-esteem maintenance, and mastery fully "come on line," as it were, making possible the mature personality. Biologically timed functional anatomical changes systematically channel psychological cognitive potentialities. With cortical maturation and its enhanced neural connectivity, the personality can stabilise and fully integrate, forming a coherent self-state.

More recent studies (Gogtay, et al., 2004) confirm that the prefrontal cortex is the last part of the brain to mature. Brain imaging reveals a reduction in grey matter density that temporally correlates with increased synaptic pruning during adolescence and young adulthood. This study also confirmed that phylogenetically older brain areas mature earlier than newer ones.

From an ontogenetic perspective, imagine the typical *S* curve of biological growth (Kurzweil, 2005, pp. 43–44) represented by a graph where the horizontal (x) axis signifies time and the vertical (y) axis represents biological growth of cortical maturation. The bottom tail of the *S* gradually ascends to about five to six years of age and then experiences a steep, almost vertical, increase to about eighteen to twenty-five years of age where the top tail tapers off to a gradual ascent for the remainder of the life cycle.

While I have focused on the maturation of the prefrontal cortex suggesting that that particular anatomical change is the *sine qua non* of adolescent neurobiological development, Spear (2010) reminds us that

> The brain is a series of networks, each interconnecting functionally related regions. Activity in one brain region influences activity elsewhere in the network. Indeed, it has been argued that studies of brain development may not be well served by trying to determine when a particular brain region comes "on line", but instead should focus on assessing maturation in terms of developmental changes in the region's pattern of functional connections with other brain regions (e.g., Johnson, 2001)". (p. 73)

For our purposes, the developmental transitional period between late adolescence and young adulthood is the earliest life cycle epoch in which the ego's synthetic properties reach its fullest expression permitting the crystallisation of the transformational self. In other words, enhanced self- and object-representations, contextualised in metaphor and action language, exert a potentiating effect on the ego ideal, which pulls the transformed self into the future.

Parenthetically, the question of whether the transformational self is a developmental endpoint or an ongoing process needs to be raised. It seems to me that it is both in so far as it follows the epigenetic principle. Campbell defines epigenesis as, "Those genetically determined processes that give direction and stability to the organism in its development of species-specific end states" (1996, p. 249). For the late adolescent a normative crisis of development emerges in that further transformation of the self is made possible for each individual by a neurobiological event (cortical maturation) and its respective adaptation sequences.

The neurobiology of adolescence

Spear (2000) makes the point that adolescents must negotiate the sometimes difficult developmental transition from adolescence to young adulthood while acquiring the skills necessary for independence. Risk-taking and novelty-seeking are among the age-related behaviours mammalian species seem to have evolved to aid in this process. Reduced positive incentives from stimuli may lead adolescents to pursue new appetitive reinforces through drug use and other risky behaviours. These behaviours may well stem more from neural alterations in the prefrontal cortex and limbic regions than increases in hormones associated with pubescence. The maturing brain may provide a partial biological basis for these behavioural strategies, although they are not deterministic. The changes in the prefrontal cortex and limbic regions may influence an apparent shift in the balance between the mesocortical and mesolimbic dopamine systems. Dopamine is a key neurotransmitter in motor activity and the main ingredient of reward reinforcement, the so called "pleasure centre". Alterations in this balance in these stressor-sensitive regions, which are critical for attributing incentive salience to drugs and other stimuli, likely contribute to the unique characteristics associated with adolescence (p. 417).

The unique and well known characteristics of adolescence include a disproportionate amount of reckless behaviour, sensation-seeking, and risk-taking. While these behaviours may be hazardous, they may also have some benefits including exploring adult behaviour and privileges, enhancing self-esteem, gaining greater acceptance by peers, and becoming more socially competent. Drug and alcohol use may involve "developmentally appropriate experimentation" for those who can moderate usage. For others, of course, long-lasting negative consequences can occur. While risk-taking may have evolutionary antecedents such as securing physical resources, attracting mates, and denying mating opportunities to competitors, today's adolescent is more regulated by the need to manage stress. The adolescent's vulnerability to stress can involve disruptions in cognition, eating, and sleeping, as well as the increased need for greater levels of novelty- and sensation-seeking. The need for increased environmental stimulation is a powerful predictor for drug and alcohol use.

The brain of the adolescent, in contrast to that of the adult, has greater response sensitivity to a variety of drugs. In addition to different metabolic absorption and excretion rates, the adolescent brain differs considerably in a number of neural systems prominent in the action of psychopharmaceutical drugs, as well as drugs of abuse. The ontogenetic metabolic variations have been studied and with respect to early exposure to drugs of abuse, especially alcohol, the potential for long term adverse consequences is powerful.

"Given the large number of transitions faced by adolescents, they have been viewed to be '. . . in a chronic state of threatened homeostasis' with 'their adaptive responses to this period being crucial' " (Spear, 2000, p. 428). In so far as adolescence is considered a stressful life cycle stage, stress, even if it is only perceived, threatens the adolescents' fragile homeostasis. Changes in brain function may contribute to this instability in that these brain shifts are not yet fully integrated. In addition, exposure to stressors activates the hypothalamo-pituitary-adrenal (HPA) axis, resulting in a cascading sequence of hormone release from the hypothalamus and pituitary, with increases in plasma adrenocorticotropic hormone (ACTH) inducing the adrenals to release cortisol into the blood stream (Spear, 2000, p. 431). Outcome data from some studies suggest a pattern. In adolescents differences in HPA responsivity has been suggested to be related to problem behaviour. In general, individuals with externalising disorders exhibit lower cortisol levels possibly reflecting hypoarousal, and individuals with internalising disorders display elevated cortisol levels suggesting hyperarousal.

With respect to the "raging hormone" folk theory explanation of adolescent behaviour, there is only weak associational data suggesting that adrenarche, the increase in output of adrenal hormones that begins to occur prior to other signs of impending adolescence, and gonadarche, the pubertal increase in gonadal hormones, significantly influence adolescent behaviour (Spear, 2000, pp. 434–438).

Of greater significance in explaining adolescent behaviour is the massive neural sculpting that takes place in late adolescence. The overproduction and pruning of synapses in the human neocortex is thought to be "an example of developmental plasticity whereby the brain is ontogenetically sculpted on the basis of experience to effectively accommodate environmental needs" (Spear, 2000, p. 439). While the massive pruning of synapses has not been causally linked to behavioural changes, there is a focal activation in the brain in, for example, the degree to which both hemispheres can process information independently.

More recently, Spear (2010) has formulated a set of hypotheses which highlight five general features of adolescent brain development.

1. *"Many adolescent-typical brain changes are regressive, with the elimination of a substantial number of synapses during adolescence"*. Synaptic pruning resulting in brain sculpting may reflect developmentally delayed elimination of non-functional synapses or a relatively delayed opportunity for the brain to be reshaped by environmental influences.

2. *"Speed of information flow in brain is increased during adolescence via myelination of selected pathways"*. Myelination appears to regulate the transmission of information in part through its interaction with unmyelinated interconnections. Its developmental course moves from the brainstem to frontal regions. This process also seems sensitive to environmental circumstances.

3. *"During adolescence, both progressive (increases in white matter) and regressive (decreases in gray matter) changes are seen in the brain, resulting in a shift in balance between white and gray matter"*. Brain maturation is uneven. The term white matter derives from the appearance of unstained brain tissue which looks white due to the presence of substantial amounts of myelin, the fatty-like insulation material. Grey matter owes it appearance to lesser amounts

of myelin. The shift in ratio from grey to more white matter is used as a general index of brain development because myelination is a relatively late occurring process in the formation of neural populations (pp. 72–73).

4.   *"The timing of brain development is regionally dependent, with posterior regions (e.g., primary sensory and motor regions of the cortex and subcortical regions) generally developing before more anterior regions (e.g., the prefrontal cortex and other frontal regions)"* The posterior to anterior maturational shift seems to function parallel to and in consequence of the myelination process.

5.   *"The adolescent brain becomes more efficient, streamlined, and cost-effective"*. As a brain region matures research demonstrates the lowering demand for blood flow to that region indicative of a decline in its energy needs (pp. 81–90).

In summary, Spear emphasises that the adolescent brain is a brain in transition. It differs anatomically and neurochemically from the adult brain. Adolescent behaviour is in part biologically determined, but remains highly vulnerable to environmental stressors and cultural influences.

Let us now turn to Chapter Nine and consider how the functional aspects of the transformational self can be explained by applying the postmodern philosophical–scientific framework of non-linear dynamic systems theory.

Notes

1.   Rene Spitz (1945b, 1965) proposed that the human nervous system be divided into two parts: the sensory or diacritic (Gk: dia = through + krinein = to separate) system is centred in the cortex; the emotive or coenesthetic (Gk: koenos = common + eistesis = sensibility) system is centred in the area of the brain now known as the limbic system. Among the functions of the diacritic system are conscious thinking, intentional and volitional acts using the long striated skeletal muscles of the limbs, and sensory perception. Perception is considered localised and circumscribed.

Among the psychic functions of the coenesthetic system are emotions, affects, and certain attributes of dreams. Its somatic manifestations are visceral and postural. "Its perceptive function is better qualified by the adjective 'sensitive' than 'sensory', since its manifestations are perceived as vague, extended, diffuse sensations such as gastro-intestinal, sexual, precordial, or dizziness sensations, etc." (1945b, p. 149). The coenesthetic system has two modes of functioning: the proprioceptive mode refers to internal sensations emanating from the gastro-intestinal tract; the entero-ceptive mode refers to stimuli related to the short, smooth trunk muscles governing posture and balance. Because coenesthetic sensations lack differentiation they are referred to as "reception of stimuli". As the infant grows its sensorium becomes differentiated; internal and external stimuli are distinguished, a condition Spits preferred to label "perception of stimuli".

In other words, particularly during the first six months of life, co-enesthetic reception shifts gradually toward diacritic perception (Spitz, 1965, p. 134).

2.   Explicit memory is roughly coincident with our usual under-standing of the term "memory". As such, it can be consciously retrieved and reflected upon, it is verbalizable and symbolic, and its content is information and images. Implicit memory, by con-trast, is nonverbal, nonsymbolic, and unconscious in the sense that it is not available for conscious reflection. Its content involves emotional responses, patterns of behavior, and skills. Implicit memory entails "knowing how" rather than "knowing that. (Wallin, 2007, p. 118)

To add to this distinction, Levy (2011) states:

Explicit cognition encompasses thought processes that are symbolic in nature (such as words). As a result this form of thought can be consciously recalled. In contrast, implicit cognition involves thought processes that are asymbolic (such as knowing how to ride a bicycle or how to hop on one foot, which can't be described well with words). Implicit cognition therefore occurs outside of conscious awareness because it is not encoded symbol-ically (Fosshage, 2004). In contrast, to the dynamic unconscious, where unconscious material is actively kept out of awareness, one cannot directly become aware of implicit thought because of its essential nature. This form of cognition is thought to operate in parallel to the dynamic unconscious. Although implicit and explicit thought are distinct, they may be integrated to some extent. (p. 50)

AFTER NOTES TO CHAPTER EIGHT

In Chapter Eight I discuss the self, and in particular the adolescent self, from a neurobiological perspective. I excluded details of Lemche's and Panksepp's self constructs because they seem to experience distant and do not hypothesise sufficiently on the nature of the mature self. I present details of their constructs here for general interest.

Lemche (1998) proposes a new approach to constructing a developmental line of body image that goes beyond observable infant data and adult reconstructions. This approach is based on the data analysis of maturational progression of the neurobiological substrate that underlie the intrapsychic functioning that contributes to body self-experience. The earliest aspect of the beginning of a developmental line of body image begins with a centredness on autonomic regulatory processes through establishment of body image boundaries to cognitive differentiation of the inner space of the body image. Lemche's herculean effort compares data across eight parameters to chart a five stage ontogenetic model of body image constitution. Lemche along with Freud (1900a) and Schilder (1935) give proprioception (muscular self-perception) a decisive place in the ontogenesis of the body related sense of self. Later researchers from Glover (1924, 1930) through Anna

Freud (1953), Kestenberg (1971, 1977), Lichtenberg (1975, 1978), and many others have given the development of body image a central place in psychoanalytic thinking about early development. Other theorists take enteroception (the perception of visceral tension) as their specific starting point in defining the beginning of body image development. These include Federn (1926), Greenacre (1953, 1955, 1958), Mahler (1968) and Spitz (1945a). The distinction lies in the belief that, in the proprioception school, body image research begins with the experience of touch, whereas in the enteroception tradition, body image research starts with the experience of tension shifting from inside to outside the body where it undergoes a more differentiated boundary (Lemche, 1998, pp. 221–222).

Lemche considers the following eight parameters to be of significance as he builds his developmental line of body image.

Psychobiological preconditions
1. neuromotor development
2. maturation of the central nervous system
3. differentiation of neonatal states
4. memory capacities of early childhood

Developmental psychological findings
1. the developmental stages of the infant's ability to recognise himself in a mirror
2. body-related systems of mother–child interaction
3. earliest affect development
4. knowledge about the development of imaginative and representational capacities.

These parameters combine to lead to a five phase postnatal ontogenetic scheme of body image constitution and the sense of self. Each phase is referred to as a distinct plateau in which new levels of neurobiological maturation are integrated with psychological and cognitive potentials. The close correlation with Stern's (1985) framework and traditional benchmarks of development are recognised.

1. Extension *vs.* flexion phase—(birth to 2.5 months). In this phase the uncoordinated and undirected kicking and waving of the infant is characterised as extension. At this time the brain is experiencing an unparalleled growth spurt, that is tied indispensably

to incoming sensory experiences. The experience dependent brain is vulnerable and would atrophy under adverse circumstances. The more salient and positive the stimuli, the more differentiated the neuronal networks become, especially those related to the primary sensory fields. Through optimal mutual attunement one or more primary attachment relationships facilitate homeostatic equilibration making it possible for internal state regulation and affect modulation.

2. Cohesion *vs.* fragmentation phase—(2.5 to six months). This name of this phase is derived from the infant's emerging sense of self experiencing increasing directedness as he senses his body holding together as a motor-affective unity. The development of intentionality is tied to the exchange of positive and negative affect with the primary attachment figures. Facial recognition improves as does the capacity for anticipation as memory function increases. The nucleus of the self in consolidated by the seven to nine month time frame as polarity between cohesion and fragmentation is overcome.

3. Comparation *vs.* affination phase—(six to nine months). The title for this phase comes from the comparison of the infant's body with another's. The reciprocal touching between mother and infant creates an awareness of the other and a mutual tendency toward approach. As the neocortex matures and takes over regulation of those functions formerly under subcortical control, memory, affectivity, and crossmodal sensory integration capacities gradually become available. With increased voluntary locomotion various affective patterns of expression gain great significance including fear, anger, sadness and disgust. Approach and withdrawn activities are now played in the form of chasing games accompanied with heightened bursts of affect. Ambivalence over separation is noticeable and the need to maintain physical proximity becomes possible through the transformative potential of intersubjectivity.

4. Expansion *vs.* contraction phase—(nine to thirty-six months). In this phase expanded motor function and the experience of skin–body boundary expansion introduce an ambivalent disposition with respect to distance from the primary care-giver. Emotional states such as elation and sadness are experienced as affective components of the game of disappearing and returning.

5.   Introspection *vs.* pretence phase—(thirty-six months and beyond). The three-year-old is now growing capable of introspection and its opposite, pretence play, in which inner themes are acted out outwardly, of verbal self-referencing, of spatial orientation of its body, of demonstrating empathy (a cognitive ability referred to as "theory of mind"), of the expansion of two word to several word sentences, of gender difference and awareness, and of triangular, relational, and symbolic communication.

The contribution of Lemche furthers the empirical neurological foundation for the framework of the unfolding self-structure though the development of body image. Let us now turn to the work of Panksepp.

Panksepp (1998) is a leading proponent of the existence of a coherent neural representation of the self within the early brain. In his hypothesis, this neural representation elaborates a basic motor representation of the organism as an active agent in the world and may be essential for an animal to have affective feelings. To facilitate talking about such a complex brain function, Panksepp refers to its primordial neural substrates, deep in the brainstem, as the SELF (simple egotype life form). The SELF is multiply represented in the brain during development and it provides the centre of gravity for the emergence of affective consciousness in brain evolution. Although adult human experience also relies on higher brain representations of emotional systems, those higher functions could not subsist without the integrity of the lower functions (p. 224). The archaic SELF is responsible for control of motor tone and simple orienting responses; its intrinsic rhythms can be transiently modulated by a wide array of regulatory inputs and it is highly interactive with all the basic emotional circuits. "Feelings may emerge when *endogenous sensory* and *emotional systems* within the brain that receive direct inputs from the outside world as well as the neurodynamics of the SELF begin to reverberate with each other's changing neuronal firing system" (p. 309).

CHAPTER NINE

The contribution from non-linear dynamic systems theory

Non-linear dynamic systems theory

The expanded use of non-linear dynamic systems theory, alternately referred to as chaos, complexity, or dynamical theory, or as complex adaptive systems, synergetic, dissipative, or self-organising systems, is being increasingly applied to the study of human behaviour, motivation, and development (Galatzer-Levy, 1995, 2004; Galatzer-Levy & Cohler, 1993, p. 290; Jaffe, 2000; Lasser & Bathory, 1999; Masterpasqua & Perna, 1999; Siegel, 1999; Thelen & Smith, 1994).[1] "We are all nonlinear dynamical systems" (Siegel, 1999, p. 235). A single human brain as well as brains interacting with each other can be understood through complexity theory. Both can be understood as examples of open, complex systems, living systems capable of responding and adapting to the environment. The human brain possesses processes that organise its own functioning, a property called "self-organisation". Siegel (1999) cites Boldrini, Placidi, and Maazziti (1998), "the spontaneity, unpredictability, and self-organizing properties of non-linear dynamic systems are well suited to explain the notoriously spontaneous, unpredictable, and creative nature of human beings" (p. 217). Complexity theory now is being used to explain normal human developmental processes, attachment patterns, psychopathology (Siegel, 1999, pp. 208–238), childhood trauma (Lasser & Bathory, 1999), and the postmodern self.

> This postmodern self is never solidified once and for all; it is always in a state of becoming and thus potentially sensitive to perturbations in context. This is a perspective on the human psyche in search of new physical metaphors, metaphors that include dynamically evolving systems continuously engaged with their contexts. We can no longer rely on models based on insulated, linear, and closed systems to explain a self in context and in continuous construction. We see the sciences of chaos and complexity as offering these new models and metaphors. They offer a basis from the physical and natural sciences from which to understand a postmodern self in "continuous construction and reconstruction". (Masterpasqua & Perna, 1999, pp. 6–7)

Additionally, Palombo (2006) employs non-linear dynamic systems theory to integrate data from neurobiological, social, and psychodynamic perspectives in work with children with non-verbal learning disabilities. Using Gleick's (1987) methodology, Palombo asserts, that non-linear equations present an alternative to the view that events are related to each other in a simple linear cause–effect relationship. In a three dimensional field, causality chaos, not randomness, is the term used to refer to a highly structured, non-linear sequence of happenings that produces a set of fluctuating events that retain a more or less constant orderly pattern. I will discuss this vital concept in more detail in the subject of reciprocal causality. Gleick maintains that this pattern is distinctive and reproduces itself at the macro, as well as the micro, level leading to the familiar images that are called "fractals". These patterns are the product of an operator that guides the process, called an "attractor" which shapes the sequence and gives it an orderly appearance.

The term "fractal" was coined by Benoit Mandelbrot (1977) from the Latin adjective *fractus*. The corresponding Latin verb means "to break", to create irregular fragments. Non-linear fractals, microscopic in size, could only be seen with the aid of computers. Fractals make up a large part of the biological world. Clouds, arteries, veins, nerves, parotid gland ducts, the bronchial tree, regional distribution of pulmonary blood flow, and surfaces of proteins all show some kind of fractal organisation. Fractal geometry is non-Euclidian and involves capturing dynamics in complex planes resulting in non-repeating, beautiful, one of a kind, non-conventional, geometric designs (Donahue, 1997).

> Attractors in general are "geometric forms that describe the long term behavior of . . . non-linear systems . . ., that is systems where the output is not proportional to the input". Generally "an attractor is what the behavior of a system settles down to, or is [conceived of being] attracted to . . . such as a pendulum's movement over time toward a fixed point of rest". (Levin, 2003, pp. 199–200)

To further clarify the self-organising aspects of complex systems, "It is important to stress again that self-organization in natural systems can only occur when these systems are both complex and open to flux with the environment" (Thelen & Smith, 1994, p. 55). Behavioural variability is an essential characteristic of making "order out of chaos" (p. 56). Out of the variation, the system selects or is attracted to one preferred configuration out of many possible states. The state outcome depends on the energy flux, the constraints on the system, and the interaction among the actual elements that compose the system. So the once separate elements now communicate and interact "because of the inherent non-linearity in nearly all of our physical and biological universe". As the system elements interact, they combine in a collective action until they appear to dominate and regulate the behaviour of the system. The resulting dominant modes are referred to as "*order parameters* which are capable of *slaving* all other modes of the system" (Haken, 1977, in Thelen & Smith, 1994, p. 55). The resulting mode(s) enable the system to be described in terms of one or a few order parameters, a collective action that regulates the system. When one order parameter dominates the system it is called an attractor state (Thelen & Smith, 1994, pp. 55–56).

At this point I want to review some of the aforementioned concepts in the context of the distinction between prediction *vs.* understanding in scientific undertakings. The quest for the holy grail, as it were, in the positivist, modern philosophical tradition centres around the empirical study of past and current objects and phenomenon in order to predict future events. Galatzer-Levy (1995) makes clear that,

> The notion that prediction is a uniquely appropriate measure of scientific status is faulty. It ignores the historical background of the prestige

> inherent in the capacity of astrologers and astronomers to predict (Schafer, 1993). It also ignores acceptable scientific disciplines, such as plate tectonics in geophysics and meteorology, the study of which do not lead to satisfactory prediction. Conversely, prediction and understanding are not necessarily linked. Many statistically excellent, but meaningless correlations are found in economic data. The most predictive science, quantum electrodynamics, is said by its inventor to provide no understanding of the matters it so satisfactorily predicts (Feynman, 1985). (Galatzer-Levy, 1995, p. 1085)

It seems that the goal of prediction does not necessarily compliment or facilitate movement toward the goal of understanding, the different quest of the post-modern philosophical movement.

Galatzer-Levy (1995) suggests using non-linear[2] dynamic systems theory, or chaos theory, a new branch of mathematics, to address the questions of prediction and data collection in psychoanalysis, if it is to move towards the status of a systematic (scientific) discipline. Chaos theory has revealed that a small input into a system can result in a disproportional outcome.

> This phenomenon came to be known as the "butterfly effect" because it can be shown in studies of long-term weather forecasting that a butterfly flapping (or not flapping its wings) in Sumatra, could result in a 5 degree change in the temperature in Atlanta 8 days later. (p. 1096)

The question of prediction takes on a different dimension. While details of a complex system with its wildly fluctuating internal dynamic shifts are not predictable over a long period of time, system tendencies and reasonably stable overall patterns, called attractors, seem to take on a deterministic quality. Sometimes hyper-energised system oscillations result in more complex forms of attractors called strange attractors, but which, nevertheless, have motion tendencies that can still be represented in patterns. So to repeat, "In the new vision of prediction the investigator predicts patterns of change and stability of systems, not their moment-to-moment status" (p. 1100).

A second kind of order has emerged through the examination of chaotic systems. In addition to a different type of prediction, a clearer understanding of the microscopic elements of the system, called fractals, is emerging. These structures are visible through the power magnification of even modern home computers which reveal that each fractal is connected to other fractals in what is called a Mandelbrot set. This set continues indefinitely repeating self-similar images of remarkable aesthetic beauty and remarkable mathematical features. This provides a new clarity via the extraordinary mathematical power of statistics and probabilities into the core of what we think of as natural phenomenon (Galatzer-Levy, 1995, pp. 1100–1101).

Let us now examine Seigel's (1999) use of complexity theory to explain brain processes. Complexity theory has emerged to become the dominant way to think about interconnected dynamic system processes containing a bewildering degree of complexity (Thelen & Smith, 1994). I shall follow the use of Siegel's (1999) term of complexity theory to denote this process.

The brain is now considered an example of an open system capable of experiencing environmental perturbations (disturbances, vibrations, or influences) in such a manner that affects the brain by altering the strength of its synaptic connections (Siegel, 1999, p. 216). Perturbations can be reinforced by genetic endowment, as in innate preferences, or in learning, as in remembering a face. Strengthened synaptic connections are those that have been reinforced and are contained in variable neural networks in either implicit or explicit memory and so are remembered. Reinforced patterns of interaction within the environmental system, alternately thought of as states of activation, are called attractor states. Attractor states are stabile forms of repeated interaction that give the system shape, stability, and, therefore, some measure of predictability.

Three principles derived from complexity theory deepen our understanding of many aspects of the brain's functioning from emotions to human relationships. First, complex systems possess an inherent orderliness called a self-organisation. The unfolding nature of this self-organisation, as in the human lifespan trajectory, proceeds from a pattern of simplicity toward complexity. The self-organisation pattern at any point or period in time may be considered an "attractor state" in that it is a repeated pattern of activation such that the component parts of the system function as a cohesive unity. The probability of activation of the attractor state depends on the subject's history and present context or environmental conditions. Siegel (1999) proposes that "emotional responses constitute a primary value system that engrains patterns of neuronal firing and shapes the emergent activation of the system" (p. 218). In other words, if the pattern of neuronal firing is experienced often enough and with sufficient emotional intensity, then the repeated instantiation (manifested by a concrete example) of a particular profile of activations may become a deeply engrained attractor state. This attractor may be thought of as a state of mind. For example, if a high school junior gets sufficient satisfaction (emotional intensity) from achieving good grades in mathematics, chemistry, and physics over time (instantiation of a neuronal firing pattern through repeated activation), then the self-representation (considered the attractor), "I am a competent science student" becomes engrained as a state of mind. Repeated exposure to experiences of "I am a competent science student" can promote adaptability and flexibility. Conversely, repeated academic underachievement and classroom disappointments can undermine self-confidence and may promote in the student a state of mind that is characterised by vulnerability, inflexibility, and resistance to change.

Second, complex systems are non-linear in that a small input can generate a disproportionately large outcome. As Siegel puts it ". . . small changes in the micro-components of the system can lead to large changes in the macro-behavior of the organism" (Siegel, 1999, p. 220). Consider for example, the case of an individual with obsessive compulsive disorder, a minor non-reality based fear stimulus can trigger a cascade of varied system responses from panic behaviour with a racing heart rate, accompanied by obsessive thoughts of catastrophe followed by compulsive rituals designed to contain the anxiety. On the more beneficial side of complexity theory, ". . . is the finding that small changes in a person's perspective, beliefs, or associations of particular forms of information processing can suddenly lead to large changes in state of mind and behaviors" (p. 221). An example would be that of an abused teenaged girl who retreated into anxious silence in order to feel safe, years later has a fantasy one day in the school cafeteria that she can bellow like an assertive female rhinoceros, finds her voice, and dares to speak up in class.

Third, complex systems have emergent patterns with recursive characteristics. To elaborate, "emergent" refers to the dynamic of each of us being "filled with a flow of states that evolve over time" and "recursive" designates "that the effects of the elements of a given state return to further influence the emergence of the state of mind". These properties operating in tandem give the sense of freedom as well as cohesion within the system over time as we flow from state to state

(Siegel, 1999, p. 221). Like Heraclitus who said, "You could not step twice in the same river; for other waters are ever flowing onto you" (Bartlett's Familiar Quotations, 1980, p. 70), we are never the same, existing in a state of perpetual change, creating and being created. As our states of mind flow in a dynamic of progressive differentiation, the self-organisation emerges ever anew while re-experiencing those features that convey the continuity of self-identity.

At this juncture, let us remember the question posed in the Introduction with respect to the effects on the entire family when adult children return home (pp. 3–6). We can now examine these effects from both state of mind and complexity theory perspectives. Let us consider Siegel's (1999) example of

> . . . how an adult can experience a shift in her state of mind when she returns home for the holidays. If a family is viewed as a supersystem, a cluster of the smaller systems of its individual members, then we can begin to make sense of this common phenomenon. As we've seen, a state of mind includes the assembly of various processes via reentry loops, each of which may emanate from the activity of relatively distinct circuits in the brain. A state of mind involves the recruitment of these various subsystems into activity together—in other words, the coupling of disparate processes into a simultaneous set of reentrant, coassembled activating components. The adult child has her own developmental history in which her genetics and repeated encounters with the environment have reinforced her state of mind—specific patterns of clustered neural activations that are sensitive to initial, specific environmental conditions. Her parents also have their own developmental histories (part of which include having her as their child), which have created specific states and patterns of response. They may have been quite happy during the years since their daughter has moved away, but somehow on these holiday visits things for them, and for her, fall back into old patterns.

> The context shift of the grown child's returning home—possibly sleeping in the same room, eating meals with her parents, having siblings present, and experiencing other old and familiar conditions—reestablishes a fertile setting in which each family member's mind can respond. The new contextual frame evokes old attractor states. Literally, what this means is that each of their brains is responding to this new setting with an alteration in its individual constraints to make old patterns of states of mind more likely to occur. The recruitment or coassembly of components of the individuals within the family allows

us to see how the larger framework of a supersystem contains its own developmental history, with attractor states and coupling processes of its own. Recruitment is often automatic, without conscious awareness or intention. The family now functions as a whole system, reinstating its old attractor states. For the adult child , the experience may be one of being drawn back into old sensations and patterns of behavior without her initial awareness or sense of control. (Siegel, 1999, pp. 233–234)

Masterpasqua and Perna (1999) consider the brain a complex adaptive system. Complex adaptive systems exist everywhere including insect colonies, political systems, economies, immune systems, and the mind/brain/body system. These systems are adaptive and dynamically roam between stability and chaos. They dump (dissipate) entropy[3] into the environment, a constructive role, while assimilating negentropy (essentially synergy), from the environment. The ensuing interchanges can result in novel reorganisations. These systems do not devolve into randomness and disorder. Rather they organise and reorganise into more complex and integrated structures. Characteristics of complex adaptive systems include: 1) There is no master control centre. Rather, regulation depends on the connectedness and interplay of billions of agents in a relational context. 2) There is no hierarchical arrangement of system elements. Instead, the elements are heterarchically connected to be optimally responsive to the system's context. 3) The future is anticipated through internal models that emerge as a result of system-environment transactions. Feedback plus the system's history guide predictive capabilities. 4) In a state of perpetual novelty, equilibrium is never attained. At the edge of chaos, complex adaptive systems are constantly reorganising (pp. 31–33).

Lasser and Bathory (1999) emphasise that reciprocal causality is an essential, perhaps the core, component of chaos theory. They consider reciprocal causality fundamental in applying chaos theory to dealing with clinical examples such as childhood trauma. They maintain that "Chaos theory has two important mathematical characteristics: (a) it is concerned with dynamics, or how things change over time; and (b) it is concerned with nonlinearity, or with the mutual interaction of cause and effect variables" (p. 148). In contrast to linear mathematics where initial size differences in systems can be expected to produce proportional outcomes, non-linear mathematics in the 1960s began to understand the significance of disproportional outcomes. This is due to one overriding consideration, that "Nonlinearity produces the *sine qua non* of chaos theory: sensitivity to initial conditions. Small differences in where systems begin can produce large differences in where they end" (p. 148).

Lasser and Bathory base this consideration on three assumptions. First, in reciprocal causality, determinism acquires a different perspective. Two events may interact in simple or complex ways, but in either case freedom is restricted. However, with additional events interacting with each other the effects become distributed in unpredictable ways. The effects are, however, not random. They are still determined, but in ways that may be completely unpredictable resulting in the possibility of increased freedom. Another consideration in chaos theory that influences reciprocal causality is iteration, the capacity of an event, or variable, to influence itself. Iteration contributes to multi-directionality making complex behaviour and its psychology more comprehensible. Some consider iteration a fundamental developmental mechanism. Originally a concept derived from mathematics, "An iteration is a process that takes its output as its new input, produces new output, which it takes as input, and so on, ad infinitum" (van Geert, 1994, pp. 14–15). Mandelbrot's chemical fractals and human sexual reproduction are common examples of iteration.

The second assumption differentiating linear from non-linear mathematics or reciprocal causality concerns discrete and non-discrete variables. Discrete variables are non-continuous, individually distinct, isolated (relatively speaking because even isolated events are contextualised) events "such as behaviors, reinforcements or clearly operational goals" (Lasser & Bathory, pp. 152–153). Non-discrete variables consist generally of more complex behaviours, thought patterns, and especially, meaning making. The essential subjectivity of meaning making and the creativity of such, especially in brutalising circumstances, gives additional exploratory capacity to understanding the continuous construction and reconstruction of the self.

The third assumption differentiating linear from non-linear mathematics or reciprocal causality involves the handling of contiguous and non-contiguous time. Events occurring in close temporal proximity to each other are highly suggestive of having a causal relationship in a linear perspective. However, events occurring in a distant temporal relationship to each other, such as revenge taken, for an affront that occurred decades earlier, may be more adequately explained in a reciprocal causal framework (pp. 153–154). Lasser and Bathory demonstrate the usefulness of these three assumptions in exploring the domestic violence impact on a six-year-old boy receiving treatment from a neurobiologically informed therapist thinking about psychopathology in a developmental model context.

The complexity of the human mind, human psychology, human development, and the evolution of the psychoanalytic process are being subjected to increasing scrutiny through the application of complexity theory. Of concern to us, in general, is the blending of human biological and psychological processes and the evolution of motivational tendencies and, in particular, the unfolding of the psychotherapies of two adolescent girls. The study of the trajectories of these psychotherapies will help us clarify the development of the transformational self. The application of coherence criterion and the social comparison method will help us in understanding these processes through the subjective meaning the individual makes of changes, as well as the behavioural changes themselves.

I invite you now to turn to Chapter Ten and consider a fresh approach, derived from neurobiological research findings, to determining when adolescence ends along with exploring different forms of cognition available to the young adult.

Notes

1.   Masterpasqua and Pena (1999) cite the work of Ganz (1993) and Mahoney (1991) who has divided the history of ideas into three periods. The first way of knowing is taken from Hesiod's poem *Theogeny* which contains a description of Chaos and Gaia. Gantz maintains that Chaos is a neuter noun meaning "yawning" or "gap". Chaos was originally a gap between heaven and earth. Eventually Chaos differentiates as a kind of foundation and is followed by "Gaia, the earth, broad bosomed and a secure seat for the gods to come" (Ganz, 1993, in Masterpasqua & Pena, 1999, pp. 1–2). Hesoid's story was based on mysticism in which supernatural forces beyond the ken of mortals hold sway. At about 600 BC the first period of knowing emerged dominated by organised religion and rational philosophy, exemplified by the Socratic method. A second period of knowing followed the Dark Ages. Beginning in the 1300s until the twentieth century the Enlightenment, the Renaissance, and empiricism merge to allow mankind to measure reality and form the notion that there is a clocklike reality "out there" that is predictable and can be discerned

through our senses. The mechanistic perspective, the industrial revolution, and the scientific method became the gateway to discovery and domination of nature. The third period began with the discovery of quantum mechanics and the revelation that particles could never be measured with certainty. Either the velocity or the location of atomic particles could be known, never both. In psychology, the subject and object, the knower and the known, are now understood to live in an interactional realm of uncertainty and unpredictability, a realm governed by the dynamical laws of chaos or complexity theory (Mahoney, 1991, in Masterpasqua & Pena, 1999, pp. 3–5).

2. "In mathematics the word *linear* means that the equation involves adding together derivatives that are multiplied by constants. None of the terms of a linear differential equation involve multiplying variables or their derivatives by one another. Mathematicians do not mean by linear that the solution is a line, is simple, proceeds step by step, or is easy to conceptualise. Nor do they mean by "nonlinear" anything mysterious, mystical, or related to "new age" thinking".

"Only confusion results when analysts and others borrow technical terms from other disciplines and use them in ways suggested by their common rather than their technical usage. The term *nonlinear* has a particularly unfortunate history in this regard, having been taken up as part of psychobabble to refer to nonpropositional thinking. Chaos theory is in the process of suffering a similar fate. Confusion of technical terms and common usage leads to attributions to the mathematical theory that are not supported by their actual content" (Galatzer-Levy, 1995, p. 1090)

3. Entropy is the tendency of an unattended system to run down. It is the quantity of energy not capable of conversion into work (Anderson, Carter, & Lowe, 1999, pp. 289, 292).

CHAPTER TEN

The contribution from cognition

The beginning and the ending of the adolescent phase

"Adolescence may be said to begin with pubescence. In no other phase is the direct correlation of the physiological with the psychological as obvious as it is in adolescence" (Kestenberg, 1967 in Sklansky, 1991, p. 63). Maturationally timed, hormonal productions from the hypothalamus, the pituitary, and the gonads sequentially intersect in concert to produce the cascading physical changes and gender differentiation associated with pubescence. It is often said that it is easier to mark the beginning of a particular developmental phase than its closure. This has certainly been true for adolescence.

Spear (2010) takes issue with the traditional position of Kestenberg and Sklansky, "*Adolescence* and *puberty* are not synonymous terms" (p. 5). She maintains that adolescence covers the entire developmental transitional position from childhood to adulthood while puberty is restricted to the physiological changes of sexual maturation. Spear is correct in asserting that characterising the course of adolescence is difficult due to the well known variables of environmental conditions (e.g., peer influences, conflict with parents, rites of passage, etc.), nutritional states (diet, family eating patterns, etc), sex (e.g., "hooking up", early romantic encounters, etc.), and socio-cultural values (e.g.,

polygamous *vs.* monogamous societies, the nature of paternal investment, abuse, stereotypes of masculinity and feminity, etc). However,
recognising the broadening definitions of adolescence, for the purpose
of this monograph, I take the position that adolescence will be defined
as that developmental period between puberty and prefrontal cortical
maturation. I will refer to this period as adolescence proper.

Cultural determinants indicating closure to the adolescent phase,
especially those viewed through a psychoanalytic lens, have been
imprecise. Theorists have struggled to describe the psychological
achievements with the associated phase specific developmental tasks.
Two examples of the emphasis on tasks are those of Blos and
Colarusso. Blos (1962) writes,

> With respect to the close of adolescence . . . First, the psychic appara-
> tus which synthesizes the various phase-specific adolescent processes,
> renders them stable, irreversible, and gives them an adaptive poten-
> tial; Second, the source of the specific residues from earlier develop-
> mental periods which have survived adolescent transformations and
> which continue to exist in derivative form, contributing their share to
> character formation; and finally, the source of the energy which
> pushed certain solutions into the foreground and leaves others in
> abeyance, thus lending the consolidation process a quality of deci-
> siveness and individuality. These qualities, which often bring about
> sacrifice and pain cannot wholly derive from the maturational push; I
> suspect that other forces combine their efforts within this process
> (1962, pp. 131–132).

Colarusso (1992), building on the work of Blos (1962, 1976), Settlage
(1973), and Wolf (1980) states that the developmental tasks of adolescence include: 1) accepting the physically and sexually mature body; 2)
separating physically and psychologically from parents; 3) accepting
sexual maturation and establishing an active sexual life; and 4) preparing to work (pp. 92–96). The developmental tasks of young adulthood
include: 1) developing a young adult sense of self and other: the third
individuation; 2) developing the capacity for intimacy: becoming a
spouse; 3) becoming a biological and psychological parent; and 4)
separating psychologically from parents while facilitating their midlife
development (pp. 134–142).

With respect to the subject of phase specific developmental tasks, I
want to be quick to add that I am not relegating Blos, Colarusso, et al.,
to anachronistic status. Far from it. The highly nuanced thinking of

these specialists in adolescent and adult development, form a homogeneous developmental continuum of considerable utility, grounded in positivism and ego psychology. It may be said that they form a first order level of complexity framework. However, with rapid advances in other disciplines, a second order level of complexity is required, one that offers a new explanatory matrix consonant with postmodern philosophy.

As I consider the developmental shift from late adolescence into young adulthood, it is necessary to move beyond a discussion of tasks to a consideration of the processes involved in the formation of the transformational self. Tasks associated with a particular phase convey a sense that once they are addressed successfully, the individual experiences some sense of closure and is ready to move to the next phase. The development trajectory associated with the transformational self is different. Five main threads weave together to form the transformational self. The threads consist of contributions from metaphor theory (Chapter Six), attachment theory (Chapters Four, Five, Seven, and Eight), neurobiology factors (Chapter Eight), non-linear dynamic systems theory (Chapter Nine), and cognition (Chapter Ten). Specifics on these factors can be found in the cited chapters. The process can be understood through a systems approach and through an intra-psychic perspective in which the manifestation of one or more self-referencing metaphors reveal the adolescent's new self-representations that drive the process of change.

So with the familiar, dramatic biological pubescent changes signalling the beginning of adolescence proper, we can now use prefrontal cortical maturation and its enlarged neural connectivity to herald the biological closure to adolescence proper. It is now possible to think of different biological maturational markers as bookends to the adolescent life cycle phase.

Piaget's model of cognition

Piaget considered himself a genetic epistemologist, one concerned with the questions, "How does knowledge grow?" and "What is the process by which knowledge judged to be inadequate and insufficient is replaced by knowledge assessed to be more efficacious and adaptive?" (paraphrased from Greenspan, 1979, pp. 59–60). For a compelling discussion attempting to synthesise Piaget's cognitive framework with psychoanalytic developmental psychology see Greenspan (1979). Since the publication of Piaget's model (Piaget, 1962; Piaget & Inhelder, 1995), it has, like Erikson's psychosexual model, undergone many attempts by researchers to modify it, but it still remains the gold standard by which all other cognitive models are compared. "Kegan (1982) credits Jean Piaget as being the central figure in the development of developmental–constructivist thought, in his studies of how children make sense of the world, and begin to reason" (Urdang, 2008, p. 19). Innate knowledge of how people and things work does not come with children as they are born. Figuring out how the world and the people in it function evolves with maturity and experience as the individual engages the process of mental construction. More specifically, "Piaget . . . identified three factors that contribute to mental development: 1. Maturation (the genetically controlled growth of the brain and nervous system—the hardware necessary for cognitive processing), 2. experience in the world of nature and objects, and 3. interaction with others—particularly interactions that challenge the individual's existing understanding of things" (Lemme, 2006, p. 80; see also Greenspan, 1979, p. 61). Recognising that the mind just does not passively accept and manipulate new information, Piaget described three intellectual tendencies to clarify this process.

> The first is the tendency to organize information into meaningful units called schemas. The second is to adapt to new information by either assimilating it (adding to it) to existing schemas or accommodating it (changing existing schemas or creating new ones). The third tendency is to maintain a sense of harmony or balance, similar to the biological concept of homeostasis, which Piaget referred to as equilibration. (Lemme, 2006, p. 80)

Lemme continues.

> Information inconsistent with our existing worldview disrupts this equilibrium, placing us in an unpleasant cognitive state (conflict, dissonance, inconsistency) and requiring us to adapt in some way. Disequilibration is, in fact, the major impetus for cognitive development: as our current level of thinking becomes increasingly inadequate to deal with the information and experiences we are confronting, we become motivated to develop a more effective (and advanced) level of cognitive ability. Human beings are viewed, then, as active constructors of knowledge and understanding—of their reality. (Lemme, 2006, p. 80)

With respect to the transformational self, this sequence describes the process by which self-referencing metaphors enter the individual's existing cognitive schema state, disturbing the current harmony and creating affective and cognitive dissonance. Anxiety signals an emerging condition of cognitive disruption referred to as disequilibration, which is the impetus for accommodation and/or assimilation to integrate the self-referencing metaphor(s) into a new state of mind. This new edition of the neural self awaits the next perturbation and joins the ever changing community of enlarging selves. This enhanced self may, through long term potentiation, becomes a stable coherence of potentialities in the ongoing process of attachment–individuation.

Formal operational thought

Piaget's epigenetic, organismic model consists of four sequential stages beginning with the Sensorimotor Phase (birth to two years of age), followed by the preoperational phase (two to seven years of age), then the operational phase (seven to eleven) culminating in formal operations (from eleven to the end of adolescence).

> In the organismic model, cognitive development is understood to proceed through a series of sequential, universal stages, tied to age and dictated by a genetic timetable, with each stage representing a qualitative change in cognitive ability. The source of development is primarily internal, within the organism (the individual), who is viewed as actively involved in constructing knowledge and adapting to the environment. (Lemme, 2006, p. 125)

Other models of cognitive development include the mechanistic, the contextual and the psychometric, but here we shall concern ourselves only with the organismic model and an elaboration of the last phase and beyond.

Piaget believed that all adolescents with normal endowment can obtain the capacity for formal operational reasoning. However, formal operational thought is neither attained at the same time by adolescents nor is it attained for all adolescents. Some remain egocentric in their way of thinking rather than become sociocentric. This stage is so named because thinking now operates in a formal, highly logical, systematic, and symbolic manner. "The concept *formal* implies that what matters is form and logic rather than content" (Muuss, 1996,

p. 158). Formal operations is characterised by the ability to think abstractly, to reason deductively (from the general to the particular), and to define concepts in the process of critical thinking. The adolescent can form a hypothetical analysis and then seek out empirical data to confirm or refute the hypothesis, a process known as hypothetico-deductive thinking (Ginsburg & Opper, 1988, p. 201). Also, two cognitive structures emerge, combinatorial systems and propositional logic. These structures enable complex scientific experiments to be performed leading to combining propositions. The concept of probabilities can be grasped, and the adolescent attempts to use all possible relations and hypotheses in order to explain data and events. Language usage reaches its highest level of complexity following formal syntactic rules and grammatical correctness.

The distinction between necessity and possibility is understood early in development, but reaches an advanced level when the adolescent can appreciate the possibility that sometimes one outcome will occur conditional to something else (Muuss, 1996, p. 186). In this context, formal operational thought enables the adolescent to realise the possibilities inherent in the potential of the transformational self.

The capacity for abstract thinking enables the adolescent to cultivate deep interest in philosophy, aesthetics, religion, ethics, logic, and politics. Because the adolescent can reflect on ideological issues, the adolescent can view the perceived world as only one among many possible worlds, thus opening up the impulse to transform the world and/or transform the self. This urge is accompanied by an emotional investment in the change that can manifest in narcissistic grandiosity, omnipotence, and megalomania in a phase normative manner (Austrian, 2002, pp. 134–135; Greenspan, 1979, p. 95).

Post formal operational thought

Some cognitive researchers take issue with Piaget's position that formal operations constitutes the apex of human reasoning (Inhelder & Piaget, 1958, p. 332). They postulated a fifth stage of cognitive development, the post-formal stage, that may be attained in adulthood. If formal thought is mankind's crowning cognitive achievement, logic suggests that new and different thought patterns that follow must necessarily conform to patterns of decline and regression (Labouvie-Vief, 1984, p. 158). Four models will be highlighted, each from different organisational perspectives, which comprise a set of alternative, more hopeful approaches.

Richards and Commons (1984) propose the structural analytic thought model that attempts to understand relationships among systems. Richards and Commons extend cognitive stage theory by formulating four levels of post formal thought: 1) the systematic order; 2) the metasystematic order; 3) the paradigmatic order; and 4) the cross-paradigmatic order. Each level is an advance over the structure and function of the previous level. Only a very few highly educated people have been recognised as moving through these levels. Richards and Commons deconstruct Piaget's logical progression of ever more complex thought assumed to take place as the child's thinking advances. They emphasise that the individual's imaginative cognitive independence can account for some of the creativity and innovation found in culture (Commons & Richards, 2007).

Basseches (1984) offers a dialectical thought model that synthesises perspectives. Basseches believes that dialectical thought seeks conflict and contradiction or paradox in systems, rather than attempting to remove the inconsistency, as a positive source for understanding change. This type of thinker understands how every effort to organise knowledge omits something that will threaten the system with contradiction and create change (Stevens-Long, 1990, p. 131 in Urdang, 2008, p. 399).

Labouvie-Vief (1984) formulates an autonomy model from an inductively derived perspective in which "Structures of formal thought are merely a precursor form of those thought structures that permit the expression of the characteristics often associated with maturity: moral integrity, constructive generativity, social responsibility, and individual agency and autonomy" (p. 160). She suggests that Piaget's over reliance on logic as the main characteristic of mature thought closed off other possibilities for considering different characteristics. Piaget's overall aim seems to have been to describe the formal laws of logic for a particular form of self-regulation that allows for the goal of sustaining equilibration-maintaining mechanisms for the cognition system as a whole. In other words, Piaget's thought system was formulated with a sense of certitude in which maturity, or developmental competence, was equated with attaining and maintaining formal thought through logic. The autonomy model accommodates a shift from the logic of formal systems to the logic of self-regulating systems. Truth is now propagated by individuals. "Questions of truth thus acquire dimensions that are unabashedly pragmatic, social, cultural, moral, and personal" (p. 177).

Sinnott (1984) suggests a relativistic stage model from a social reasoning perspective that permits the adult thinker to operate in a world of relative choices in an interpersonal subjectivity. "Interpersonal relations seem to change constantly in their reality as a function of their being known or perceived in different ways by different individuals in the relationship . . . It requires cognitive operations that take necessary subjectivity, and the unavoidable unity of subject and object, into account in structuring knowledge" (Sinnott, 1984, pp. 298–299).

A common theme "running through most of these descriptions of post formal thought models is an increasing relativism, the realization that real-life problems do not have absolute answers, that contradictions and uncertainties are realities of life, and that knowledge and reality are only true temporarily"(Stevens-Long, 1990, in Lemme, 2006, p. 147). In other words, post formal thought models are attempts grounded in postmodern philosophy to interpersonally contextualise adult cognitive development. Piaget's model is undergoing deconstruction in which its core assumptions, stage sequencing, its universality, and its remove from cultural variables are all being questioned (Lemme, 2006, pp. 147–148)[1]. Postmodern philosophers and human developmental theorists are most comfortable with post-formal thinking as are all who have acquired the capacity to tolerate ambiguity (Bendicsen, 1992).

A non-linear dynamic systems theory perspective on cognition

Thelen and Smith (1994) maintain that "Viewed from afar, cognitive development fits Piaget's description . . . At a global level the intellectual differences between children of different ages are very much as Piaget described them" (p. 21). However, on an individual scale when Piaget's framework is placed under a microscope, the scientific consensus is that the monolithic, invariantly ordered, sequential march of changes in the logicomathematical structures that underlie cognition is wrong. In a highly stable, controlled laboratory learning environment the model holds. But, in real world learning environments, what are seen are "instabilities, context dependencies, and fluidity in cognition". (p. 22) In other words, "Cognitive development does not move forward in lockstep. Cognitive development does not look like a marching band; it looks more like a teeming mob. Piaget's theory fails to fit the view from below" (p. 22).

The global or macro view from above supported three central claims to Piaget's theory: "(1) an impoverished beginning state, (2) global discontinuities in cognition across stages, and (3) monolithic cognitive growth". However, from the perspective of the view from below, that of the individual, the theory fails to support these assumptions. The Piagetian infant was understood to be a bundle of reflexive responses to external stimuli. The micro view from below paints a very different picture. Contemporary developmental research demonstrates that the human infant is not impoverished, but rather "is highly 'competent' and possesses highly structured perceptual and conceptual skills" (Thelen & Smith, 1994, pp. 22–23). The Piagetian infant was also conceptualised as experiencing cognitive discontinuities across stages. The opposite is true. Continuities are recorded in infants that "show elements of abstract numerical thought (e.g. Wynn, 1992), a complex naïve physics (Spelke, 1990), and 'theories' of causality (Bullock, Gelman, & Baillargeon, 1982)" (Thelen & Smith, 1994, pp. 22–23). In both babies and adults a common core of continuity exists. And last, it has been demonstrated that individual cognitive growth moves forward as wide discrepancies are noted in various competencies across domains. One such a domain to consider is the transitive inference task in which a third relation is inferred from two others. "For example, we might infer 'the blue rod is longer than the yellow rod' from 'the blue rod is longer than the green rod' and 'the green rod is longer than the yellow rod' " (Thelen & Smith, 1994, pp. 22–23). Piaget empirically supported this claim that preschool children could not accomplish this task, but subsequent research demonstrates that when the children's immature memories are taken into account and the research design adjusted accordingly, they can make transitive inferences.

Thelen and Smith (1994) review contemporary theories in explaining the continuities and discontinuities in development, the irregularities in children's performances in related tasks, and the mix of competence and incompetence. While it is beyond the scope of this monograph to summarise this outstanding discussion, the hypothesis they formulate is in agreement with,

> Cairn's [sic] (1988) analogy between evolution and development: evolution is to biology what development is to psychology—the

process behind the structure. . . . we propose a developmental process that is like evolutionary process. Evolutionary process is mindless and opportunistic. There is no design, no blueprints, no 'pregiven' specifications for the species that can emerge. There is no end-state—only context-specific adaptations. Yet from the opportunistic and context-specific, we get marvelous species of many kinds, each reflecting its unique evolutionary history and each finely honed to its place in the whole. Might not the developmental process over time work like this? Might not the origins of knowledge in an individual emerge in opportunistic and context-specific psychological processes that reflect the unique developmental history of the individual and fit together to make a living and thinking whole? (p. 34)

In summary, Thelen and Smith, rejecting traditional definitions of cognitive development, offer a definition consistent with non-linear dynamic systems theory: cognitive "development is the outcome of the self-organizing processes of continually active living systems" (p. 44).

A neurobiological perspective on cognition

What can we add to our understanding of cognition from neurobiological research findings? Spear (2010) has summarised this highly complex array of research data and has concluded that ". . . there is little evidence of either a single set of cognitive skills that would be characteristic of the formal operations stage, or any indication of a step-like shift in cognitive function from stage to stage" (p. 102). In other words,

rather than talking about a stage of cognitive activity characteristic of adolescence, . . . it is more accurate to depict these advanced reasoning capabilities as skills that are employed by older children more often than by younger ones, by some adolescents more often than by others, and by individuals when they are in certain situations (especially, familiar situations) more often than when they are in other situations. (Steinberg, 2005, p. 73)

So it seems simplistic to equate adolescent cognition with formal operational thought. Furthermore, it seems equally simplistic to maintain that a causal relationship exists between adolescent cognition and the maturation of the prefrontal cortex.

Thus, rather than viewing adolescent brain maturation merely as the last remnants of a series of brain regions sequentially maturing and coming "on line", a more contemporary view of brain development is that it reflects a dynamic process of network organization, with different regions competing, influencing, and cooperating with each other over time during development, and in the process acquiring new (and often more efficient and able) roles in the modulation of cognitive abilities. (Spear, 2010, pp. 119–120)

Having said that, the data suggests that adolescent cognition is more mature than that which preceded it.

1. Information processing abilities are enhanced due to the combination of advances in processing speed, working memory, and problem solving, reasoning, and planning skills. Each dimension contributes to increased information processing even though each dimension follows its distinct maturational time course (Spear, 2010, p. 102).
2. While it is also simplistic to say that during adolescence executive function ability increases, research does support improvement in specific functional domains including selective attention, goal setting, rule discovery, planning, decision making, response inhibition, and, as mentioned earlier, working memory. Again, each functional domain follows its distinct maturational time course (Spear, 2010, pp. 105–106).
3. Some decline in aspects of cognitive performance is an expected part of development, but especially so during exposure to stressful circumstances. In some early adolescents, exposure to stressful stimuli has caused transient developmental decline in certain cognitive tasks such as "matching faces with emotional expressions to words describing those emotions" (Spear, 2010, pp. 107–108). Performance in tasks such as exploratory proclivities can also be compromised under stress.

At this early stage in adolescent cognitive research, limitations are apparent. Research is exploding and the diverse findings often do not reflect consensus. Furthermore, findings emerge from both animal and human research, due to ethical constraints on research with human subjects. Given these limitations, it is possible to infer that the increase in adolescent cognitive capacities seems due to maturational changes in brain activity "in the activation of frontal-parietal regions and associated networks interconnecting these regions with other cortical as well as subcortical regions". It may be "more appropriate to view adolescent neural development as a transition from diffuse task-related activation to more focal activation, as the progressive emergence of neural networks recruiting more distant regions, or simply as age related activation of different brain regions" (Spear, 2010, pp. 128–129).

To summarise, the process of brain maturation in the late adolescent, which links the prefrontal cortex with other network assemblies and regions, both distal and proximal, results in increased functional neural connectivity. This explanation may account for the changes in adolescent cognition seen in the second decade of life and beyond.

Another significant contribution from the neurobiology of cognition relates to the concept of hot cognitions. In stimulating circumstances where the excitement of associating with peers in unstructured, emotionally charged situations exist, rational decision-making can easily be compromised increasing the likelihood that adolescents will engage in risky behaviours. Sensation/thrill/fun-seeking adolescents, especially those under the influence of alcohol and/or drugs, are particularly vulnerable. The emotional brain (bottom-up processing involving greater activation of amygdala and ventral prefrontal cortex regions) can override the rational brain (top-down processing involving greater regulation of dorsal prefrontal cortex regions) resulting in impulsive behaviours with logical decision making taking a back seat. On the other hand, cold cognitions involve less stimulation in low emotional contexts such as those ordinarily seen in school, at home or in the laboratory (Spear, 2010, pp. 139–140, 154, 158, 187–188). There well may be a dimension of hot cognition in the formation of the transformational self in that the emergence of one or more self-referencing metaphors may lead to modulated risk-taking in the sense of testing new identities and self capacities.

The organismic metaphor gives way to the biotope metaphor

Piaget's original framework is traditionally associated with the organismic metaphor. The organismic metaphor is one of the root metaphors which Pepper (1942) described as an original idea in search of comprehension through a basic analogy or root metaphor. The root metaphor serves as an aid in description and classification of phenomenon of the universe that enhances overall understanding. "Developmental theorists who favor this metaphor conceive of the human mind as an organism that becomes progressively more differentiated from less developed (i.e., immature) to more developed (i.e., mature) states" (Palombo, Bendicsen, & Koch, 2009, pp. xxxvi–xl). Piaget continuously fought against the idea of his model containing the formulation of an innate plan that unfolds over time, consequently being reduced to a form of predeterminism. "His transition model (Piaget, 1975; Moessinger, 1978) is highly reminiscent of what we currently see as a dynamic systems model; a simple iterative mechanism operating in an environment that is both internal and external, thereby transforming the environment and itself" (van Geert, 1993, p. 265). Consequently, Piaget's transitional model fits poorly into the organismic metaphor category. If we must keep this metaphor it might best be labelled a degraded organismic metaphor model.

A better solution is to design a new metaphor. Van Greet (1993) proposes the biotope metaphor (bios—Greek, life+topos—Greek, place, *Webster's Third New International Dictionary*, 1993, p. 219). "A biotope is a life space, more particularly a region in which the main environmental conditions and the life forms adapted to them are uniform. We may speak of the biotope of an animal species as the characteristic life space to which the species is adapted and whose effect the species undergoes" (p. 328). Van Geert uses the analogy of an island biotope metaphor to explain the development of the human cognitive system.

First, think of the island as an ecological system with a mix of plant and animal species engaged in complex interactions geared toward the survival of each species. "All these cognitive species depend on one another (some more directly than others), and it is this structure of interrelationships that keeps the cognitive system dynamically stable and self-maintaining" (p. 268). Second, the relative isolation of each cognitive island from other islands explains why each person's cognition has a unique ecosystem while maintaining many properties in common with that of other persons or surrounding islands. Species migration or behavioural communication among surrounding islands limits the development of each cognitive system to the ambient conditions (e.g., speech, learning patterns, etc) attendant in both sending and receiving the communication. Third, cognitive development is due to colonisation of processes from other islands as well as autonomous evolution of the island's ecosystem. Internal cognitive growth together with environmental stimulation establish different probability levels to chances of species survival. Fourth and last, many, though not all, of the cognitive species (individual capacities) are home grown from evolutionary older forms and not imported from other sources. Each person's sensorimotor skills have to be "reconstructed and adapted to the biotope as it is already evolved" (p. 269). Admitting the inadequacy of the island biotope metaphor to account for cognitive development, van Geert deserves credit for using a novel heuristic device to begin formulating better questions to aid in the search for understanding human cognitive development.

Building on van Geert's work it occurs to me that the biotope metaphor has an additional use. Pepper (1942) formulated a span of intellectual history consisting of six root metaphors used to model the universe.

> They are (a) *animism*, the notion that all nature is imbued with life; (b) *formism*, the Aristotelian concept that each organism has within it the seed of its structure, which will guide its development; (c) *mysticism*, the belief that a person may merge with nature or the universe to attain a higher level of being; (d) *mechanism*, the concept that all processes ,including those of human development may be understood as analogous to a machine; (e) *organicism*, the theory that all living matter, as organisms, may grow through the ingestion of nutriments and follow a developmental sequence; and finally, (f) *contextualism*, which is the view that the best approach to understand all human phenomena is to view them in their historical contextual environment and understanding their meaning. (Palombo, Bendicsen, & Koch, 2009, pp. xxxvi–xxxvii)

With advances in knowledge and theory construction a new hypothesis is suggested. I want to add a seventh root metaphor—*biotopism*, the view that human development is governed by non-linear dynamic systems principles.

In the following psychotherapy accounts, we shall see how knowledge about self-states or states of mind, secure and insecure attachment patterns, open and closed metaphors, the attachment–individuation process, cognition, and non-linear dynamic systems theory contribute to the overall understanding of the evolving transformational self process in adolescence.

Note

1.   "Because Piaget supported a constructivist explanation of knowledge, he
     has always rejected one-sided conceptualizations of development, such
     as nativism* or empiricism or information coming across solely through
     the social environment. The constructionist position is that the child,
     based on previous experiences and on already existing structures,
     actively pieces information together, bit by bit. The success and level of
     sophistication in this constructionist approach are dependent on the intel-
     lectual maturity and the underlying structure of the individual's mind.
     Social constructivism expands this notion to include the perspectives and
     the contributions of others, peers, parents, teachers—as an inevitable
     dimension of this knowledge-building process. Thus, development
     occurs through cooperative exchanges between subjects and their social
     world. Actually, Piaget's theory has been social constructivist since the
     beginning, but this fact has not been recognized until recently (Youniss
     and Damon, 1992)" (In Muuss, 1996, p. 168).

     *Nativism refers to the belief that an innate design guides development.
     My clarification.

PART IV
THE APPEARANCE OF THE TRANSFORMATIONAL SELF IN TWO CASES

CHAPTER ELEVEN

Two psychotherapies

Hurricane Girl

Reason for referral

D awn was sixteen years and nine months of age, Caucasian, and a high school junior' of Protestant faith, when a professional colleague who was treating Dawn's mother referred her. Dawn was depressed, very thin, underachieving, "boy crazy", and withdrawing from friends and school life. Beginning with her high school classes in the fall and spring semesters for the past three years, she had vomited in the morning and found it very hard to get out of bed to go to school. This has lasted for the first few weeks of each new term during which time she gradually found enough energy and momentum to get to school on time and not miss classes.

Background information

Dawn was the middle sibling in a sibship of five ranging in age from ten to twenty-one, with two younger and two older brothers. The family's socioeconomic status was in the upper middle class with both parents being professionals in different disciplines and progressing well in their respective careers. The marriage was the first for each parent having been high school and later college sweethearts. Both were high achievers and valued academic accomplishment.

The marriage lasted eighteen years before mother left one day, having kept the children home from school to help move. Mother filed for divorce a year earlier and no movement had taken place toward dissolving the union. Dawn was fourteen at the time of the separation and sixteen by the divorce. The divorce was bitter, the anger intense, the conflict ongoing with the children often forced to take sides. Mother seemed tired, depressed, and vulnerable from what she described as a marriage that had become progressively verbally abusive and un-healthy. She said it could easily have shifted into a domestic violence pattern if she did not finally act. The children divided the week living first with the mother and spending the second half of the week living with the father. Both parents live in the area so the children can go to the same schools. Father told a very different version as to the reasons for the failed marriage. He accused his wife of being unfaithful and falling away from the church. The respective parental stories and per-ceptions were so different, and the affects accompanying each were so intense that no effort was ever made to meet with the parents together, let alone attempt to reconcile the differences. Both, however, said that they loved their children and wanted what was best for them.

Dawn recalled her childhood as one of parents arguing and disagreeing, with all members growing fearful of Father. According to her, Father became intimidating, intrusive, and unapproachable. Mother was developing a victim/martyr stance until she "saw the light" and then began to prepare herself for the day when she would need to take the children and be self-sufficient. The extended families remained available to the children for emotional support. Once sepa-rated, Mother began to struggle financially, and the pressure to secure needed resources further strained an already overloaded system.

Dawn's childhood was remembered as one where she liked to be by herself, "in my own little world", as she put it. She enjoyed elemen-tary school, reading a lot and getting good grades. She felt her older brothers tended to be protective and her younger ones more playful and teasing. Everyone was angry or emotionally hurt by some event. Her brothers began to express anger by defying their father in passive aggressive ways. Because he pushed sports, they developed computer or musical interests, more in line with Mother's interests. According to Dawn, Mother pushed her into piano, ballet, and cheerleading

activities, things Mother did not get to do as a child. Dawn felt justi-
fied dropping out of these activities at the first opportunity because,
"They were forced on me". A kind of secret family life emerged which
excluded Father. Communication, certainly with respect to unpleasant
news, was diverted around Father. When he found out about baseball
tryouts, the deadline had passed. This had the effect of creating a
family within a family, with each family member knowing the value
of the motto, "Loose lips sink ships".

Increasingly, Dawn retreated into her own world finding ways to
differentiate by expressing her anger in making choices which would
displease Father, letting her grades slip, and in taking an intense interest in boys at age 13. She began going steady with a minority classmate, Marcus, in eighth grade. It was obvious she had selected a
soulmate in that he was depressed, came from a dysfunctional family,
was anhedonic, and ambitionless. A joyless and colourless relationship, both had grown overly dependent on each other. Also in eighth
grade Mother had taken to sleeping in Dawn's bedroom believing
Father would not come after Mother there. This protective measure
lasted about a year until the clandestine move. Dawn remembered
herself at this time being shy, nervous, constantly twirling her hair,
and rolling her fingers and hands together in a washing motion. She
sampled beer with peers, but found it too bitter.

With respect to sexual enlightenment, Dawn said she had a course
in family life education in school, and she was prepared for her
menses, having knowledge from both the course and through discussions with her mother. Mother and Dawn mutually agreed that Dawn
should be placed on birth control pills with the understanding that
father not know. Sexuality was not discussed to any appreciable
degree with female peers.

By her freshman year, aged 14, Dawn was more in touch with her
anger and began increasingly to turn it against herself. She wondered
if she was developing an eating disturbance as she lost interest in
food, found it very hard to get out of bed on school days, did not
participate in school activities, and had few friends. She felt depressed
and suicidal and early in her freshman year entertained suicidal
fantasies, at one point holding a razor and contemplating cutting
herself. Interestingly, she never turned to alcohol or drugs for relief
or escape. She began to see her Mother as weak and treated her
with utter contempt and disparagement whenever the opportunity

presented itself. Dawn was enraged with Father, but very careful to conceal it behind a mask of hostile compliance. She deeply resented having to live in two homes, and eventually her reluctant compliance turned into waxy indifference.

There did not seem to be a clear precipitant triggering the referral. Perhaps some issue, which became mobilised in Mother's own treatment, prompted the call.

First diagnostic session with Dawn and clinical impression

Dawn was alert, responsive, and engaging. It was readily apparent that she wanted to talk and was eager to use the experience of being alone with someone who was listening to her and only her. Maintaining good eye contact, she had the capacity for reflection and insight. Excited about examining and understanding her life, it was obvious that she welcomed and looked forward to the experience.

Dawn reported that she enjoyed her brothers and, like them, avoided sports. Even running in gym class made her feel awkward and self-conscious. She could not concentrate in school and lamented the slippage of her grades from As to Cs. Having a vivid fantasy life, she daydreamed a lot and often imagined herself in faraway places being adventurous. She found it hard to get to sleep and hard to wake up.

Dawn reported a recurring dream. "I am older, travelled a lot. But it was the first few days of my freshman year and I am walking down a hallway when an angry mob of people, some my friends, surround me and tear off my clothes. They hold me down naked on the floor while some abuse me. I see a window open, and suddenly, I could fly and flew right out of that window". Associations were "It was raining in the building. A guy I know throws me to the ground and all are hitting and kicking me. I lie on my back and just lie there. In another version I have wings everyone can see, and sometimes it is not raining".

At this point Dawn reported that she has a secret diary that she writes in daily. She wonders if Mother will read it without her permission. She wonders why her Father is so hypocritical. "Why is he always so angry, and how can someone be so religious and still put his children down and have such a temper?" She also wonders why her Mother is so disorganised. "Why can't she cook us regular meals, why is she always broke, and why is she such a slob?" She could find nothing positive whatsoever to say about either parent.

Treatment plan

Both parents needed to approve of me before treatment began, and they shared the expense equally. It was agreed that I would involve each parent, separately, but equally, in Dawn's progress. She was seen on a weekly basis, and parents were seen alone on alternating months to assure that there was continuity between homes and that the parents did not use her as an agent to continue their ongoing battles. Both parents were cooperative and worked surprisingly well on her behalf to keep her out of the middle in their quarrels. Consistent participation in treatment was facilitated by the parents' regular and conscientious transportation of her to the office.

Course of treatment

The first year focused on three themes: exploring the vicissitudes and the meaning of Dawn's intense relationship with Marcus, discovering her role in exacerbating the conflict between her parents, and understanding the root causes of her depression. She was well aware of the mutual needs that were met in her relationship with Marcus, now beginning its fourth year. She grew to appreciate that as she changed, Marcus would probably not and so toward the end of the first year, the mutuality became discordant, and he was seen as an anchor around her neck. Friends and family validated this perception for her. Birth control was conscientiously practiced, discussed with her Mother and still kept secret from her Father.

It was a surprise to Dawn, when she became aware, that she was able, with so little effort, to inject such great turbulence into the already volatile parental relationship. She had discovered just what to say to each to stimulate rage and retaliation. Her ability to stop that instigating behaviour pleased her and made her feel more differentiated and in better control. In fact, the level of parental conflict did appreciably diminish when her contribution was removed.

Dawn's depression was seen as due, in large part, to the years of family stress. Her recurring dream was understood as a representation of her struggle within her family to survive and individuate. The fact that it always ended with her escaping suggested potential for liberation from stressful family life, hopefulness, and control over her future.

The second year saw Dawn come to a decision to break up with Marcus. She handled the matter sensitively, but with dispatch and resolve. Marcus accepted her decision saying that he knew their relationship would not last, even though he still hung around her Mother's house with his second family, having made friends with her brothers. She had found a second boyfriend, Anthony, who was a better match. Anthony was also a classmate, as well as from her church and an aggressive A student with clear plans for college and career; in short, the opposite of Marcus. The quality of interaction was quite different, with the new couple engaging enthusiastically in age appropriate interests and activities. Quite reflective, she used interpretation well and was a purposeful participant for virtually the entire treatment. She was quite conscious that her choice of a new boyfriend was a function of her lifting depression and her resultant growing capacity to enjoy more of life.

Unable to talk with either parent, Dawn asked the therapist many personal questions (Eissler, 1953; Gibson, 2012; Hoffman, 2009; Palombo, 1987; Quillman, 2012; Raines, 1996; Weiss, 1964). Do you have children? What is it like to be one of your children? What would your children say? Do you get angry? How do you let your anger out? What do you do when you get angry? A technical question emerged as to what are suitable boundaries to revealing personal information. (For self-psychologists this question would be of lesser concern.) What information could be shared consistent with sound clinical judgment and treatment considerations? On the other hand, how would complete withholding be understood? A careful and selective sharing was decided upon, such as with the question, "How do you express your anger?" I decided to answer that one by saying, "I think about it and tell certain people I am angry after I decide how they might handle it. I also exercise; I play racquetball". Becoming round-eyed, she reacted with amazement and smiled. This was a revelation, as if to say, "So this is how normal people do this!" She had never broached this subject with anyone and used this new information as a catalyst to finally approach her Father in meaningful communication.

As treatment unfolded, Dawn found parallels to her life circumstances in movies and books. A vignette accompanied virtually every facet of her changing life from class. For example, she was developing kitchen competence in home economics class; she ate what she prepared, causing her to marvel and filling her with satisfaction and accomplishment. In film class she was developing widening understandings about life, which add to her knowledge about how people cope and function. She read Sylvia Plath's *The Bell Jar* and said, "You know she was depressed and suicidal. I was Sylvia Plath Junior". She contrasted Marcus with Anthony by employing a nature story she saw on television. "A male rhino wouldn't mate with any of the female rhinos. The female rhinos didn't like him and butted him. He was a loser like Marcus". As she reflected on the interaction amongst the rhinos, she was obviously impressed with the power of the female rhino. But, what was more significant to Dawn was the ability of the female rhino to control its circumstances.

At the midpoint of her second year in treatment, Dawn's grades were improving; she was contemplating life after high school, and was working on college planning. She wanted to attend a college close to the one Anthony will attend, but her ambivalence about leaving home was emerging. She was slow and hesitant about exploring colleges, completing applications, securing funding, and taking the American College Test (ACTs). With respect to countertransference, at this point I found myself becoming parental, urging her to seek out financial resources, meet with her high school counsellor, and otherwise get about and complete the business of applying to college. Because this felt so distinctly paternal, I began working with Father in our sessions to help him think about and define his role in the college application process. Her procrastination and lack of energy for this major transition in her life has been extensively examined. It paralleled her reluctance to get a job, even after she had an earlier successful job as a clerk in a department store. Her worldview was changing. Just how bad was her family?

In the nineteenth month, to Dawn's surprise, Father's positive qualities were now emerging. She noticed that his home was orderly, neat, and clean. He was good at budgeting and managing money. He has a good memory and keeps promises. Mother was fun to go shopping with, and they have the same things in common such as art, pets, and crafts. Mother was now more interesting and Dawn liked to discuss literature with her. Dawn found the courage to talk with her Father and even disagree with him on current world events. To her amazement she was neither devoured nor dismissed. From a self-psychological perspective, she experienced a freeing up and maturation in the idealising parental imago pole of the tri-polar self.

At the twenty-one-month mark in treatment, Dawn mentioned that she felt like screaming in the school cafeteria the other day, but rushed to assure me that she had not. She had read a novel where a woman was in a support group, and in order to emotionally free herself, was encouraged to scream. "You know women need support groups and letting out that force within you is healthy". In securing her permission to tell her story and in discussing its presentation, she said impulsively, "Call me Hurricane Girl", referring to the urge to scream. But she soon questioned that choice saying essentially that we needed something more decorous. She selected the pseudonym Dawn because, "It was the name my Mother wanted to give me, but she was overruled by my Father".

Summary

Dawn has been able to find and use self-objects to facilitate the passage from despair to fulfilment. Her self-narrative was being constructed in the intersubjective space between historical reality and the creation of personal meaning. It is a story that is increasingly coherent and self-enhancing. Defences are more mature and self-esteem and self-worth are more positive. Object choice was now developmentally appropriate and served the self-object functions of regulating self-esteem and confirming personal worth. Her differentiation trajectory was not about traditional male autonomy, but rather about being embedded in facilitating attachments, on her own terms, that were affirming and validating. Her original secure attachment has allowed her to recreate and use that state in a healing psychotherapy.

Dawn represents an example of the secure transformational self. Her early "average expectable environment" equipped her with an adaptive flexibility, that enabled her to withstand the stress of later family dysfunction. Use of new open metaphorical self-references, such as "female rhino" and "Hurricane Girl", signal passage into the intermediate developmental space between adolescence and young adulthood. She probably fits best into Offer's (1980) surgent growth pattern.

Doctors (2000) suggests that in secure attachments, individuation is facilitated by comforting, sustaining internal representations of the mother. Ambivalence toward the primary maternal figure was moderated by the fundamentally secure base which provided a platform for weathering subsequent stress associated with the divorce and normative individuation demands.

With the lifting of Dawn's depression, the question remained as to her vulnerability. As her self transformed into a more cohesive self-state, her resilience and ability to deal with ambivalence will continue to improve. Her increasing self-awareness of, and confidence in, having potentialities with attendant competencies will guide her development.

What is the nature of the attachment to the therapist? The therapist has the belief that he exists in a stable way for Dawn outside the hour and that there is a genuine and useable therapeutic relationship that exists over time. Genuineness refers to depth, substance, continuity, meaningfulness, and mutual attunement. Abstract ideas and concepts are produced and tied to life issues and dilemmas. Attachments outside of therapy are stable and predictable.

Ten years post treatment found Dawn graduated from college, married with one child, teaching high school social studies and history. She was enjoying her relationships and her career and maintaining functional relationships with both parents and siblings.

Sunshine

Reason for referral

Mesia was fourteen years and eleven months of age, African–American and a high school freshman of Protestant faith, when she was referred for treatment by the foster care department of a child welfare agency. The referral followed a second psychiatric hospitalisation, this one for depression and a suicidal gesture involving ingesting fifteen aspirin and sinus medication tablets over a six-hour time frame.

Background information

Mesia was the eldest of five siblings born to mother, Ms R, by three, possibly four different fathers. Mesia knew her birth father marginally who was in and out of her life until he finally abandoned her and her mother altogether when Mesia was seven. Ms R was married and divorced to the father of the two youngest siblings, Mr R. Mesia was between the ages of four to seven when this stepfather was the paternal head of the family. A former drug addict, Mr R fell back into drug usage and distribution from the house leading directly to the destruction of the family. The struggling family, characterised by shifting living and financial circumstances, grew progressively more dysfunctional and turbulent. Mother, Ms R, was a high school graduate who had earned a certificate in business administration from a junior college; she had strong potential for a promising career in office administration. However, while successful in landing good positions, she could never pass the probationary employment phase because she was too opinionated and had difficulty working cooperatively with office colleagues. A substance user in high school, she moved into abusing drugs and became progressively more unstable as she struggled to keep herself and family together.

When Mesia was eight her Mother dropped her and her six-year-old sister off at the maternal grandmother's house saying she could no longer care for them. At this point Mother reported that she was thoroughly depleted and in a panic. Bereft of any resources or support network, she found herself riding about in a cab with her five children with no money to pay the fare. Her only thought was to reach her mother and beseech her to take her two oldest children. Grandmother and Mother argued; Grandmother paid for the cab and Mother, with the three younger children, continued in the cab and were taken to stay at a friend's house. The Grandmother reluctantly took in the girls and then called the state family welfare department whereupon the two siblings were taken to an emergency shelter.

At this point the Grandmother was retired; her husband had passed away three years earlier and she had been raising a second family for about a year. Grandmother had a daughter and a son who between them had eight children. With the drug related murder of the son when Mesia was seven, Grandmother suddenly found herself raising a second family of three grandchildren and was unable to extend herself further to care for any other grandchildren. A second catastrophe struck when Mesia was eleven; her mother, aged thirty-three, died of sudden heart failure.

While Grandmother deeply lamented the loss of her only two children, she was also critical of her children for falling into drug cultures, failing as parents, and leaving her with a second family to raise. Very devoted to her grandchildren's welfare, she, nevertheless, felt overwhelmed, exhausted, and saw the world as increasingly threatening. With escalating demands being made on her, she became irritable, hostile, and resentful. Easily frustrated, she was at risk of becoming abusive.

Mesia reacted to her mother's death in a kind of stoic manner by tending to idealise her while remembering how frightened she could get by strangers coming and going at all hours dealing drugs. She lamented the fact that Mother was not stronger and wished things could have been different.

Sadly, between the ages of eight and eleven, Mesia found herself in no less than twelve different living situations, some back with her mother, some with her Grandmother, some with her sister, and some in foster care. This pattern continued until the first hospitalisation at the age of ten for one month. This was due to repeated running away, endangering herself, and being picked up by police. "I didn't respond well to authority", Mesia said. Diagnosis was major depression, recurrent with a rule out of Bipolar I. She struggled with inner turmoil from rejection by her natural family and fear of abandonment. Feelings of inadequacy, low self-esteem, and poor interpersonal skills left her vulnerable to rage reactions and impulsive, aggressive acting out behaviours. Her notable strength was her ability to do well in school, due in part to an average to above average IQ. Following this hospitalisation, the Grandmother took in Mesia. From the age of eleven until the age of seventeen years and nine months Mesia lived with her various siblings and cousins together at Grandmother's house. A second hospitalisation occurred when she was fourteen and into the third year of living with Grandmother and her reconstituted family. This hospitalisation also lasted one month and again the diagnosis was the same. However, the recommendation was for placement in a group home where she could benefit from the added structure and limit setting. With Grandmother agreeing to Mesia and her sister's return, this recommendation was not implemented. Grandmother was adamantly opposed to out of home placement, believing devoutly in the sanctity of the family.

The years spent living with Grandmother were filled with escalating stress and conflict related to complying with Grandmother's living expectations, the stress of adjusting to high school, and mourning the loss of her Mother and Uncle. Mesia and Grandmother had very different perceptions and understandings about each other's role in generating stress and no progress was ever made on reconciling these sharply discordant attitudes.

First diagnostic session with Grandmother and clinical impression

I was the next in a long line of professionals and paraprofessionals Grandmother had seen over the past five years because some of the grandchildren had special needs, and she had become a licensed foster parent in order to receive financial support. With this involvement in foster care in the state child welfare system, she had to demonstrate her fitness to parent her grandchildren because of the monthly subsidies she was receiving. She had to take a psychological examination, subject her home to a licensing study, and attend parenting classes. She took it as highly intrusive, demeaning, and insulting that her parental fitness was being questioned. After all, they were her grandchildren, and if she did not need the financial support, who would know or care anything about her parenting? In addition, three of her grandchildren were in treatment and two made abuse charges against her. Because therapists are mandated reporters and had to file the complaints, she believed the therapists and the system were aligning with the grandchildren against her.

She was quite startled to see me, a white clinician, as she had somehow been led to believe her granddaughter's therapist was African–American. A short, stocky woman, she walked carefully into the office in a heightened state of alertness. Thoroughly enraged at the point I met her, she spent the entire first session venting her anger and expecting me to tell her that she needed therapy, as other clinicians had. A heavy smoker, she had difficulty breathing, especially when under stress.

She felt exhausted and alone in the cavernous, unsympathetic system and needed an ally. She impressed me as articulate, fiercely committed, and yet very vulnerable. In such a frustrated, depleted state it seemed entirely possible she could become abusive (certainly verbally) to her grandchildren. I listened and absorbed her poignant story. I suggested that she, in her heroic devotion to her grandchildren, was ignoring her own very legitimate needs and that this state of affairs could not continue. Furthermore, I stated that she could benefit from a regular periodic consultation for herself where she could feel someone was there just for her. She accepted and we met on a monthly basis for the duration of the treatment experience.

First diagnostic session with Mesia and impression

Mesia was articulate, seemed to have average intelligence and reasoning abilities, maintained good eye contact and was able to form a solid therapeutic alliance. She was appropriately concerned about her garb, make-up, nails, etc. Of average height, weight, and appearance for her age, she was alert and responsive. While functioning with a solid sense of femininity, one, nevertheless, had the sense that her overall integration was fragile. She seemed to have many strengths and was able to convey to this therapist that she could use and profit from a therapeutic relationship.

Mesia spoke of how unfair things were at Grandmother's. Grandmother yelled a lot, was overly strict, made demands, and was always negative. She never gave in to see things from Mesia's point of view. If only she could have lived with her Mother. At least there she had more freedom and could do what she wanted.

Deficits in self-processes included chronic vulnerability to fragmentation anxiety. Stress exposed the fragile state of self-cohesion with poor restoration ability. Regulatory capacities were unable to channel anger in healthy ways. Mesias' self-object milieu was unreliable, often unavailable and, when available, was seriously misattuned to her needs. Other processes that appeared compromised were judgment, impulse regulation and control, modulation of affect, object relations, self-esteem regulation, and mastery. Certain cognitive immaturities were evident as Mesia could not figure out why she was so sleepy during school after saying she stayed up late at night, why teachers picked on her, etc. Dependency needs were strong and manifested in a sense of helplessness and in an inability to check the forward progression of conflict among family members. Her school functioning deportment was often challenging and aggressive to certain teachers. When given consequences for her misbehaviour, she projected blame on to the teacher. She was unaccepting of authority in any form from anyone. "Grandmother is a control freak. She cooks for us; she lays out clean clothes in the morning on our beds for us to wear to school. I can't make any choices. She makes all the decisions. So we start to argue", Mesia said. Her sense of self-esteem was more tied to need satisfaction rather than her social standing with peers. She had not yet internalised a motive for learning and achieving in school. She could not link age appropriate self-imposed sacrifice today for greater rewards and satisfactions tomorrow. She demonstrated a marginal sense of internal regulation and self-control. Her ego ideal was to become a medical doctor in order to help others who are malnourished. Her superego functioning was intact in that she was neither devious nor manipulative with authority figures and Grandmother, but rather concerned about being a good example to her younger sister and brothers. While she experimented briefly with smoking and marijuana, she never progressed to abusing drugs or alcohol and now is abstinent.

Treatment plan

It was determined that Mesia needed to be seen in at least weekly treatment. Because she was responsible for transporting herself to the office after school (two busses, with one transfer, lasting over an hour), weekly sessions were agreed upon as realistic. The goals of treatment were agreed upon as relieving depression, mourning the loss of her mother and uncle, reducing the family conflict, and, in general, getting back on the developmental track.

As mentioned, Grandmother was seen in monthly consultation. The main goal of consultation was to help Grandmother improve parenting strategies by being less reactive to Mesia and disengaging from the pattern of spiralling verbal conflict.

Course of treatment

Treatment began with three focal themes: to improve the relationship between Mesia and Grandmother, to mourn the loss of Mother, to understand the impact of this loss on Mesia's functioning, and to support the taking of psychotropic medication. The struggle to get Mesia to comply with routine house rules and living expectations, as did the other children, has been the monolithic problem for Grandmother. This struggle became enmeshed with other issues such as the taking of Depakote and Prozac. She soon resisted regular doses as she complained that they made her feel fat, drowsy, dizzy, and nauseated. In fact she was noticeably gaining weight. By the twelfth month of treatment she was self-medicating and soon thereafter stopped taking both medications altogether. During this time frame she began spending weekends with her Mother's best friend and her children. This family bore some parallels to life with Mother in that the friend struggled financially, there was no consistent, paternal figure, and substances were occasionally used. She would leave the house not telling Grandmother where she was going and returned as she pleased. Grandmother knew this friend of her daughter's and eventually communicated with her and established some measure of agreement that Mesia needed this relationship and did not oppose it. Also, Mesia developed a relationship with Tyrone; Grandmother disapproved of this boyfriend believing that Tyrone exploited Mesia and was turning her toward additional contrariness and defiance. Conflictual turbulence frequently flared up resulting in heightened stress levels for all parties in the family. These were extremely unpleasant experiences eventually involving the police and neighbours.

Attendance at the weekly sessions began to be tested early in our relationship. Mesia would not show, apologise and then reschedule, and then might or might not show. Participation slacked off for weeks; even months at a time, as her interest in after school activities and involvement with her boyfriend were all attractive alternatives to treatment. In the countertransference, I grew at points to feel useless and expendable with Mesia, while feeling useful and helpful to Grandmother. Criteria for keeping the case active in the clinic had to be stretched. Grandmother, however, continued to appear monthly as planned.

Mesia demonstrated a solid ability to explore and reflect on her life with Mother and her current situation, but the process had no carryover effect. Her life went on unmodified. This therapist grew to feel ineffectual with respect to helping her, but felt useful helping Grandmother relieve some of her stress while periodically renewing her focus on the parenting strategy. At points it felt as if Mesia had dropped out of treatment, but then she would surface again.

Mesia was sexually active with Tyrone. She learned sexual enlightenment from a family life education course in school, through extensive discussions with female peers, and from a public health clinic, which placed her on birth control pills. She knew all about pregnancy and was not going to end up like her Mother. This was a source of conflict between Grandmother and Mesia as Grandmother insisted on talking with the clinic staff who refused, citing confidentiality requirements.

At about the two-year mark, Mesia became pregnant, had an abortion and struggled with her disappointment and feelings of abandonment by Tyrone. She used therapy to process this event, after the fact, stating that she was careless with birth control and that it was never her intention to carry the pregnancy to term. She said further that the birth control measures she used were unreliable and declared that she was not going to repeat her Mother's mistakes. In fact, she stopped taking the pill and on occasion did not insist that Tyrone use a condom. Finishing high school was important and her thoughts were always to some degree pointed toward college. She began to invest in another relationship with James whom she met near her Mother's friend's house and they became close. She believed that James was involved in a gang and a drug culture. She saw potential in James and encouraged him to turn away from this negative life. Some months later James was killed in a drive by shooting, which she mourned very hard.

Then she began to decrease her participation again, while staying in telephone contact. Grandmother said Mr B would not release her from treatment because she had not finished the work she agreed to undertake. She met and asked to be released stating she got what she wanted from treatment, thank you. I said that because Grandmother and she have such different perceptions of matters could we meet, the three of us, and take stock? She agreed and the first such meeting, while tension filled with charges and counter-charges hurled back and forth, left me feeling, in retrospect unrealistically, that we could profitably meet again. A second meeting was scheduled which ended poorly in that the arguing flared up with intensity and Mesia left the room. We were never able to meet again as a threesome. In hindsight it was unrealistic to think such meetings could be successful. There had never been any movement between Grandmother and Mesia with respect to coming closer together. Grandmother saw Mesia as selfish, loud, volatile, and easily given to temper tantrums; Mesia saw herself as sensitive, kind, generous, and compassionate. Mesia saw Grand-mother as insulting, unreasonably strict, and abusive; Grandmother saw herself as reasonable, a survivor, devoted to her children's welfare, and unwilling to give up control of her house.

In the third year of treatment, Mesia began planning for her post high school life. After initially considering college, she began to focus on the armed services. After exploring this option, this route was abandoned, and she returned to her dream of going to college. Frustrated with her Grandmother and conflicting recommendations in the planning process, she asked about returning to becoming a foster child as a way to assure she could access resources. I invited her to think about the study expectations, the volume of homework, unstructured dormitory life, and all the distractions and temptations. Much self-discipline would be required. Was she ready? Was she strong enough to be a successful student away from home? Could she make use of the supports, as unstable as they were? I understood my function as one of encouraging her to make a realistic self-appraisal of what plan would be in her best interest.

By the third year of treatment, matters had reached a stalemate and I was seriously considering closing the case. Mesia had missed two and a half months worth of sessions and the level of conflict at home had risen to earlier levels and was taking a serious toll on Grandmother's physical health. During the previous session in mid December, she expressed the desire to return to the State's guardianship as a way to secure tuition money for college and assure that her post high school planning was firm. Grandmother had declared that she had to leave upon graduation as the level of discord at home had reached unbearable proportions. In the ensuing two and a half months, I endeavoured to explore this option and connect Mesia with a church based college resource, all to no avail. This was the state of affairs when Grandmother called me to say that after yet another intense argument Mesia had done something unusual: she ran away to a group home. Leaving home for unspecified periods of time to unknown destinations were *de rigueur*, but to a group home!

I called the group home to learn that Mesia wanted to see me. A session was arranged which she kept. It was learned from her that she left home because she could not tolerate the constant negativity and insults. It was an unhealthy atmosphere. Undoubtedly having thought this out, she said she left to prevent any more damage to Grandmother's health, to set a positive example for her sister, and to try to gain assistance in going off to college. The armed services were no longer the first choice, as a way to secure a college education, because of the magnitude of the six-year commitment required. She left also, because others she consulted with encouraged her to go off to college as a way to emancipate and disentangle herself from the never-ending conflictual family enmeshment.

In a subsequent staffing I called with all interested parties, a realistic plan was formulated. Rather than persist in planning to go off to a four year out of state college, it was agreed that she would participate in a life skills transitional living program, work part time, and attend a local college full time. She needed to test herself in a positive milieu. Could she stay organised and focused? Could she be self-regulating and self-disciplined enough to attend to her homework properly, keep appointments, be on time, and so on? Parenthetically, enlisting in the armed services was occasionally thought of as an option, but was now a distant second choice. It was a remarkable meeting in that she was able to build on her accomplishments, reshape her aspirations in full cooperation with the planning process and package a set of resources for herself. Her ability to enlist facilitating self-objects at this critical juncture in her life speaks to the emergence of her transformed self.

How can this event be understood? Had she experienced an epiphany? I was surprised to hear her tell of how she loved her Grandmother, but could not live with her any more. At this time and with considerable effort, Mesia empathetically helped her grand-mother acquire a major kitchen appliance, through the department store she worked at part time, using her discount. Her ability to be a self-object, as opposed to using self-objects suggested she was getting on the developmental track and was transforming herself. Her ego ideal was being reshaped, now more concordant with a realistic, consensually validated assessment of her capacities.

In subsequent sessions, Mesia spontaneously sprinkled the words sunny and sunshine in her verbalisations. As we reviewed events and discussed the pros and cons of writing up and sharing an account of her three year psychotherapy, she said, "I feel like changing my name to Sunshine . . . I feel sunny, not cloudy". She became playful with the words sunny and cloudy. She used them metaphorically to refer to her moods as well as to characterise her past and current experiences. In one of our last sessions she said, "Sometimes I shine. Sometimes when the sun's not out it's cold and I feel cold. Sometimes when it's out I feel happy. It stands for my moods".

Mesia, when reading this record, said she felt overwhelmed, yet pleased with herself for getting this far. "I've really been through a lot. You tend to forget what you've been through". She grew reflective about her mother. She remembered a sudden family gathering at Grandmother's house. "I knew it was going to be something bad, but I thought it was about my baby brother, who had been sick". Her birth father, whom she saw rarely, and the father of her sister came to her and, together, took her into a room. "It was kinda strange to see my Father. My Father told me that my mother died suddenly of a heart attack. He held me. I cried and got hysterical. I was devastated. I slept a lot. Even on the way to the funeral, I went to sleep in the car".

With respect to why she had such conflict with Grandmother, Mesia said, "I always thought I was the mother. My Mother was doing her thing and I took over being the mother. I used to care for my sister and brothers. I cooked for them and dressed them. When I was seven or eight, I could peel potatoes, make sandwiches, and cook noodles. I wasn't too good at opening cans". "I bet you thought you were a good mother", I said. She agreed and we immediately understood that to lose her Mother and then to give up mother's role was expecting too much. "It was my job to take care of my sister and brother. I thought I had to do this. I got angry. I got in my Grandmother's face and we argued over who was in charge".

Summary

At the point of beginning treatment, Mesia was experiencing a developmental lag in that this fifteen-year-old seemed emotionally a mid-latency child. The early data suggested a mother and child existing in an increasing state of misattunement resulting in an insecure attachment. It is reasonable to assume that fixations in certain sectors of development occurred after Mother's abandonment of Mesia at age eight and her subsequent death when Mesia was aged eleven. This traumata, plus the dysfunctional/criminal family of origin circumstances, had contributed to the establishment of an immature, pseudo-sophisticated, highly vulnerable individual who was regression prone and clinically depressed. The unexpected death of Mother had been a great sadness; it was overwhelming for Mesia and constituted a major organiser for her as she struggled to mourn this enormous loss. When Grandmother disciplined Mesia, Mesia would say that she knew her Mother's friend treated her children better than her Grandmother treats her. Unresolved mourning acted as a filter through which she attempted to understand what was happening to her. It complicated and intensified her reactions to being disciplined. She understood consequences for misbehaviour, not as discipline, but as deprivation, denying her the opportunity to mother, thereby disrupting the metaphoric nurturing tie to mother.

The hostile, conflictual relationship with Grandmother cannot be understood in only an intrapsychic framework. It must be contextualised and seen as a part of the fabric of social life for impoverished, inner city, African–American female adolescents. In this context, vitriolic exchanges between mother and daughter are commonplace. The easy verbal, sometimes violent, combativeness amongst female peers, usually in triadic contests over romantic relationships with boys, is seen as an aspect of a larger normative crisis. The adaptation to the cultural dissonance between Africentric *vs.* Eurocentric experiences, along with learning to cope with the stress of living in a racist society, are seen by most social researchers of minority life as a specific survival skill that, when acquired, confers healthy resiliency (Stevens, 1997).

Mesia existed very much as a function of the environment and, consequently, was reactive; when under stress she could react impulsively and in a self-harmful manner. The therapeutic task was understood as providing her with a reliable self-object, getting her on the developmental track, and strengthening coping capacities for more age appropriate functioning.

At the current point in treatment, three years later, it is apparent that enhanced structuralisation has occurred in a significant way. Adaptive functions and self-esteem are strengthened. Mesia is feeling actualised and empowered. She feels a budding sense of mastery and a push for individuation. She is regulating her impulses and modulating affect better. I do not believe this is sudden change, but rather has been embryonic. In a facilitating environment, she will be able to consolidate her gains in an incremental manner and so strengthen her self-cohesion. Having formulated a plan for her future, she feels transformed and capable of steering her life course. She fits best into Offer's (1980) tumultuous growth pattern.

Doctors (2000) reminds us that severe ambivalence towards the primary care-giver is an indication of pathology in the attachment process. Ainsworth, Blehar, Waters, and Wall (1978 in Doctors) maintain that adolescent turmoil is not normative, but is a function of insecure attachment. Mesia's primary care-giver, Grandmother, frustrated Mesia's normal self-object longings. In Mesia's case her insecure attachment impeded and frustrated individuation. Mesia's internal representations of her Mother were insufficient to exert a soothing, comforting presence in Mother's absence.

Mesia represents an example of the insecure transformational self. Her self-characterisation as Sunshine speaks to increased reflection and differentiation, all parts of the transformational self. Resonating with the "affection is warmth" metaphor, she said, "Sometimes I shine. Sometimes when the sun's not out it's cold and I feel cold. Sometimes when it's out I feel happy. It stands for my moods". While these comments speak to a better modulated affective life, they also suggest a longing for mutually responsive relationships. Does Mesia know at some level that she functions best in a structured milieu and that she will need to have facilitating self-objects available, such as in the armed services? She had no associations to the name Mesia, but I gathered it was identified with something rather mysterious and adventurous.

What was the nature of the attachment to the therapist? It is interesting to note that at points of crisis and trauma in Mesia's life, the therapist was one of the last people to know. The therapist was never seen as a resource in terms of anticipating difficulties or solving problems. No abstract ideas were introduced and life dilemmas were concretised. It was out of sight, out of mind, or so it seemed. *Pari passu*, a sense of immediacy, in terms of the situational usefulness of the therapist, seemed present. During the session a high level of engagement seemed possible, but between sessions, I wondered if the therapist was remembered; does our work exist in her mind?

Ten years post treatment, found that Mesia had signed up for the support section of the US Air Force, specifically food service. She was married to a fellow service man, in a marriage with periodic turbulence, but overall both maintaining a long term commitment to each other.

PART V
SYNOPSIS

CHAPTER TWELVE

The transformational self: gateway to young adulthood

A s T. S. Eliot (1943) reminds us, the end is always to be found in the beginning. So I will end with 1) a digest of the main points of my thesis and invite your opinion as to how well I assembled a case to support it, and 2) an offering of a suggested answer to the question I posed in Chapter One, "When does adolescence end?"

A reviewer suggested I find the "red thread" that will link these disparate domains of knowledge into a coherent unity. I do not think the matter is that simple. Rather, a fabric of red threads woven into a conceptual integration of the components of the transformational self might be more realistic. I will begin with a detailed elaboration of my general thesis and conclude with brief comments about the potential usefulness of my formulation.

General thesis (Chapter One)

I now turn to a summary of the main points of my thesis.

With the proliferation of interpersonal and intrapsychic psychological theories vigorously competing for the attention of students and veteran clinicians alike, confusion abounds. The clinician lacks an overarching framework resulting in the very real risk of incoherence.

The default position is to turn toward theoretical eclecticism. I am proposing an alternative to this form of reductionism. I believe it is possible to weave together a compatible set of interlocking theories that would yield both satisfying explanatory power and an efficacious sense of coherence. That set would include neuroscience research findings, non-linear dynamic systems theory, linguistic metaphor theory, contemporary psychoanalytic developmental theory, attachment theory, self psychology cognition, and relational theory.

The aforementioned set of domains of knowledge constitutes an explanatory synergy I label regulation theory. In formulating criteria for the transition from late adolescence into young adulthood, regulation theory allows for movement away from the static listing of developmental tasks to the dynamic analysis of interactional processes. It privileges neuroscience research findings as a dominant thread to harness and magnify the existing explanatory potential of the popular contemporary psychological theories.

Embodied metaphor is a key component in regulation theory. I explicate the discovery of self-referencing metaphor and its unfolding significance in the personal psychological transformation of teenagers into better regulated young adults.

I illustrate the multiple usefulness of regulation theory in its application to understanding better a significant contemporary cultural phenomenon, the interactional nature of young adults returning home, to case formulation in the treatment of two adolescent girls and to development from a psychoanalytic perspective in which activation of the transformational self, a phase specific dimension of the neural self, illuminates the dynamics associated with the transition from late adolescence to young adulthood.

Conceptual integration—regulation theory

Regulation theory has been referenced five times in this monograph: once, in the functional aspects of the transformational self (Chapters Three and Four), second, as an aspect of Coppolillo's model of adolescence (Chapter Five), third, in the context of Fonagy's hypothesis that the interpersonal integrative mechanism is a regulatory mechanism for the appraisal and reorganisation of mental contents (Chapter Seven), fourth, as Schore's belief that attachment theory is actually an affect state regulation theory (Chapter Eight), and fifth, as an organising feature in the use of non-linear dynamic systems to describe dimensions of the transformational self (Chapter Nine). I observe that a distinct trend in the study of human brain/mind processes and human behaviour/motivation dynamics is developing which is to turn to regulation theory[1,2] as an organising concept in the study of interactional system components. What gets regulated? How does the "what" become regulated and maintain regulation? How is that state of regulation disturbed and restored? As our knowledge domains expand, complexity certainly will increase, and it will become necessary to answer these questions from the perspective of integrating these discrete domains. The application of regulation theory from an integration of interdisciplinary knowledge constructs is becoming commonplace. As an example, I cite Daniel Hill (2010) and his contribution to understanding the mindset of fundamentalist extremists.

> Regulation theory is an interdisciplinary approach to the body-brain-mind that integrates attachment theory, neurobiology, psychoanalysis, psychiatry, cognitive science, evolutionary biology, and infant developmental psychology. The theory provides an understanding of how mental states are organized around affect regulation, which involves the modulation of levels of arousal and maintenance of the organism in a homeostatic state in which the brain-mind can function optimally. The theory takes seriously the idea that the mind, brain, and body are mutually influencing subsystems of the organism. To function adaptively, the organism must be regulated. The regulation of affect is the regulation of the organism. The capacity to regulate affect is developed in the attachment relationship to the caretaker. Patterns of affect regulation are activated each time one is involved in an attachment relationship. (Hill, 2010, pp. 80–81)

Hill goes on to apply regulation theory to what I have already discussed with respect to secure and insecure attachments as states of optimal regulation and dysregulation respectively and return to the homeostatic state as an example of adaptive flexibility, and so on. Regulation theory, as described, has become today's intellectual trend, a *zeitgeist*, if you will. The point I want to make is that the integration of interdisciplinary knowledge is necessary to obtain the fullest understanding of the transformational self.

The transformational self synthesis

Self psychology (Chapter Three)

Kohut's self psychology is considered the framework that broke the decades long hegemony of ego psychology. Fresh conceptualisations such as the tripolar self, self-objects, the self-object milieu, transmuting internalisation, transformations of narcissism, and the contemporary understanding of human needs leading to reconfigured transferences have led to a way to think about the human experience that is more consistent with postmodern, social constructivist philosophy. I will not review the essentials of self psychology here, but refer the reader to Chapter Three for some of its dimensions that have relevance for the transformational self.

However, I do want to draw a connection to the goodness of fit with respect to concepts from other knowledge domains and self psychology. Relational theory, the need for self-objects throughout life, the attachment–individuation process, complexity theory, modern metaphor theory, the neural self, and Greenspan and Shanker's developmental model form a complicated, but valuable explanatory synergy that can help further a coherent construct of human functioning.

In addition, the self of self psychology, the narcissistic/cohesive self, is of heuristic usefulness in that its dynamics fit within the morphology of the neural self. Borrowing from Stern (1985, p. 14), if you will, the self of self psychology breathes psychological life into the empirical self. Both are dimensions of the neural self, of which the transformational self is the adolescent–young adult developmental variant. In this Synopsis, see the section on "When does adolescence end?" for context.

The contribution from attachment theory (Chapters Four, Five, Seven, and Eight)

Siegel (1999) states, "Repeated experiences become encoded in implicit memory as expectations and then as mental models or schemas of attachment, which serve to help the child feel an internal sense of what John Bowlby called a 'secure base' in the world" (Siegel, 1999, p. 67). The attachment self (Wallin, 2007) has four components, consisting of somatic, emotional, representational, and reflective/

mindful dimensions that combine to form an enduring attachment style (Main, Kaplan, & Cassidy, 1985). I maintain that the attachment self serves as a conceptual bridge to the neural self. The outcome of the attachment process is seen not as attaining autonomy, but rather from an "attachment–individuation" perspective (Lyons-Ruth, 1991 in Doctors, 2000); it is seen as repositioning oneself in terms of maintaining important family relationships in a mutually reconfigured manner. In this perspective, significant relationships undergo a re-evaluation and renewal. From a self psychology perspective, these significant relationships, understood as self-objects, are needed throughout one's life in order to maintain self cohesion, vigour, and adaptability/resilience.

Given our current state of attachment knowledge (Wallin, 2007), two attachment styles can be predicted with some certainty, the secure and the insecure. In the case of Dawn, a secure attachment base is suggested that has allowed her to move forward in development with what can be called a surgent growth trajectory (Offer, 1980). In the case of Mesia, her turbulent, unstable, and unpredictable developmental experience suggests an insecure attachment pattern configured in a tumultuous growth pattern (Offer, 1980).

Some elaboration of Doctors' (2000) position on attachment–individuation is in order because of its synchronous extension of the nature of the attachment process in adolescent development. When adolescent turmoil occurs, it

> is better understood as attachment–individuation difficulties than as normative adolescent separation distress. With this shift, a clearer distinction between healthy and pathological development becomes possible. The clinical presentation of (a) extreme ambivalence towards parents and (b) dramatic symptoms that often contain concretized expressions of developmental needs and intersubjectively discordant responses to those needs ... can be recognized as signifying disordered attachment processes rather than normal adolescent separation issues. Attention is thereby drawn to the nature of the adolescent's inner ties and to the clinical problem of enhancing relational security and developing the various functional capacities that are ordinarily the natural sequelae of secure attachment so that normative individuation may proceed. Individuation continues to be recognized as accelerating in adolescence but is recast as drawing on and contributing to sufficiently secure attachment. (p. 14)

In each psychotherapy case treatment was envisioned as a process of understanding the nature of the attachment, creating a shared, cohesive narrative, and reacquiring the use of functional self-objects embedded in women's need for affiliation and caring relationships (Gilligan, 1982, 1987; Chodorow, 1978). Each adolescent believed she could become different and began the process of transforming herself.

Attachment–individuation offers a conceptual validation for my belief that the appearance of the transformational self heralds the need for mutual re-connection throughout life, but especially during the transition from late adolescence into young adulthood.

Contemporary psychoanalytic developmental theory (Chapter Five)

Infant research is busy exploring the yield from neurobiological research and working them into modifications of contemporary, psychoanalytic developmental theory. I favour and cite the work of Greenspan and Shanker (2004) who promote a non-teleological evolutionary perspective integrated with neurobiological research findings in the formation of their lifespan developmental framework In addition, their model is non-deterministic, anchored in attachment theory with the conviction that the intergenerational transmission of interactive affective laden cultural experiences fosters symbolic expression enabling humans to reach ever more complex forms of development (Greenspan & Shanker, 2004, pp. 97–102). They generate from these domains the hypothesis that the role of emotions has evolved through our human ancestors over millions of years into a succession of more complex interactive emotional signals. They maintain that, "The origins of symbolic thinking and speaking depend heavily on the social transmission of cultural practices that were not genetically determined but were passed down and thus learned anew by each generation in the evolutionary history of humans" (pp. 2–3). While genetics may serve as a switching device using so called regulator genes in influencing gene expression and behaviour, environmental variability may play a far more influential role in the developmental capacities of human behaviours. The brain develops new pathways of learning due to the cumulative enrichment of experiences of previous generations. They marshal data to support their contention that the growth of ever more complex societies and cultures, and human survival itself, depends on the capacities for intimacy, empathy, reflective thinking, and a shared sense of humanity and reality. They contend that these capacities are derived from the differentiation of emotional symbol formation leading to symbol usage in metaphor and language. In addition, they posit the concept of dual coding of experience in which experience is coded according to both its physical and affective properties, leading to the physiological states of discriminating emotions in an unfolding consciousness. Subsequently, these dual codings get organised into patterns of experience. "For example, a baby touches its caregiver and registers both a physical sensation and pleasure" (Greenspan & Shanker, 2004, p. 288). I believe the efforts of Greenspan and Shanker constitute the leading edge of thinking on the subject of empirically constructed developmental models oriented towards the contemporary psychoanalytic framework.

There are contrary opinions on the value of the sequential phase developmental model. For example, Galatzer-Levy (2004) embraces a postmodern perspective in which all development is seen through the lens of non-linear dynamic systems theory or complexity theory. Through this lens development is seen as discontinuous with unpredictable episodes of surgent activity and periods of inactivity or stagnation. This view is the antithesis of the sequential phase model and is explained "nicely" through complexity theory. It fits the micro or divergent, multiple, individual pathways that Thelen and Smith (1994) have described for cognition and locomotion. Are the treasured, venerable positivist models now to be discarded?

I believe there is value in finding an accommodation between both perspectives. The view from above, the global view, has merit from an averaging standpoint. Developmental benchmarks remain useful, if inexact and imprecise, markers that help to anchor educational and mental health professionals in devising educational and treatment strategies and tactical interventions. How else can we determine if one is on or off the developmental track? However, those who embrace the micro view from below do not generally value concepts such as tracks, normality, or developmental benchmarks. Moving away from sequential phase thinking, these postmodern interventionists believe that change can be understood as manifestations of naturally occurring variables within the complex adaptive system that do not require a theory of motivation. This stance suggests "an approach to therapeutics in which the major work of the analyst is to provide an environment in which the development can resume in safety, rather than an attempt to achieve any particular developmental aim" (Galatzer-Levy, 2004, p. 436).

Can the views from above and below coexist without fostering confusion? Both views have followings that have to be negotiated in professional activities. Completely orthodox examples of pure practice of either viewpoint probably do not exist. As Hoffman (2009) wisely suggests, "For my own and others' writings showing that various theorists commonly regarded as 'relational' or 'intersubjectivist' are, at least sometimes, if not more generally, objectivist in their thinking" (p. 629).

Relational theory (Chapter 5)

What is relational theory? Relational theory:

> involves efforts to conceive of the two-person field as comprised of not only an overt interaction but also the internal world and the inner experiences, conscious and unconscious, of both participants. It is in this way that the relational perspective integrates one-and two-person psychologies. The focus on the experiential worlds of two people in interaction leads to this point of view being characterized, with variations on the theme as "intersubjective" (Benjamin 1988; Stolorow & Atwood, 1992). Relational analysts look to the analytic interaction itself, the interweaving of transference and countertransference, as the site of the interaction in psychoanalysis. For purposes of exposition, one can speak of the internal worlds of two people who then engage on an overt interaction (see Stern (1995) for an elaboration of such a model). This way of looking at the analytic interaction, however, artificially divides the internal from the external world. To speak of the patient for the moment, it is more adequate to say that the manifestation of the patient's internal world is always under the influence of the analyst's presence and behaviour. The analyst's behaviour, however, is also under the influence of the patient's presence and behaviour. Each person evokes certain reactions in the other, selectively attunes to certain aspects of the other, and so on. So, ultimately, we have an intermingling of two subjective worlds, and of internal and external realms, in a way that makes it impossible to draw sharp lines of distinction between who's who, and what was pre-existing in the patient's internal object world and what was evoked by the analyst. Relational analysts work and act in this complex and ambiguous interpersonal and intersubjective field. Mutual influence is taken for granted between patient and analyst, but the relationship is seen as

asymmetrical, with the analyst having primary responsibility for fostering an analytic inquiry into the interaction (Aron, 1996). As patient and analyst together engage in a dialectical process of action and reflection with each other, rigid and constricting patterns in their intrapsychic/interpersonal worlds are loosened up, and possibilities for change emerge. (Altman, Briggs, Frankel, Gensler, & Pantone, 2002, p. 9)

As mentioned in Chapter Five relational theory is most consistent with postmodern, social constructivist philosophy. See Appendix Two for details. While the quest for theoretical homogeneity may be desirable, it is probably not attainable. A major social constructivist thinker, Hoffman (2009), declares, "For my own and others' writings showing that various theorists commonly regarded as 'relational' or 'intersubjectivist' are, at least sometimes, if not more generally, objectivist in their thinking" (p. 629). It must be mentioned that while relational theory offers neither a self-construct, nor a developmental model (Palombo, Bendicsen, & Koch, 2009, p. 236), it is, nevertheless, one of the necessary red threads. If relational theory is not a dominant thread from a theoretical perspective on development, it nevertheless provides a useful clinical perspective consistent with the greater red fabric of this monologue. The two psychotherapies are not cited as examples of relational work, but contain elements of it in the overall assessment of the processes.

The contribution from the linguistic theory of metaphor (Chapter Six)

Modern metaphor theory has been revolutionised and, consequently, is quite different from traditional Aristotelian thinking about metaphor. Contemporary metaphor (Lakoff & Johnson, 1980/2003) is tightly linked to neurobiological research findings and considered to be embodiments of brain processes. These processes can be demonstrated through computerised laboratory experiments of primary metaphors, such as "affection is warmth". Metaphor is less about words and language and more about overlapping concepts tied to functional aspects of body processes. The basis for imagination is the brain's ability to take our physical experience and use it metaphorically.

Distinctions between open and closed types of metaphor (Modell, 1997) have been proposed. The open type facilitates meaning exchange through recontextualisation of affects associated with experience. "It is important to understand that meaning cannot simply be created once with the expectation that it will remain forever unchanged. Meaning systems must be constantly maintained and amended so that the content will fit with the context and experience of the present. The processes of the self must therefore be active in creating and altering meaning throughout life" (Saari, 1993). The closed type inhibits meaning transfer and therefore limits growth potential.

In thinking about late adolescence through embodied metaphor, a clinical advantage presents itself. It seems that the advent of self-referencing metaphors in adolescent psychotherapy suggests the attainment of gains that may herald the beginning of the end of the psychotherapy. I am thinking here of efficacy needs and the urge to mastery in one's environment (Wolf, 1988).

Each client had created a different "state of mind with respect to attachment" and managed to find a place in the world of work in alignment with their respective, maturing ego ideals that validated strivings for meaningful interaction with affirming self-objects.

The contribution from neurobiology (Chapter Eight)

The "Decade of the Brain" presented an opportunity to reveal various heretofore unknown workings of the mind. Among these workings, of relevance to the transformational self, was the discovery of the late maturation of the prefrontal cortex (along with its extensive neural interconnectivity), the neurobiological underpinnings to the attachment process and to states of mind (Siegel, 1999). The "Decade of the Brain" enlarged our understanding about memory, consciousness, cognition, affect, and fostered hypotheses on the nature of the self. Among the most useful has been that of Feinberg (2009) and his neural self concept defined "essentially by its coherence: *a unity of consciousness in perception and action that persists in time*" (p. xi). Feinberg's neural self is located within his concept of the integrative system that accounts for internal and external perception, cognition, and self-awareness. Feinberg's emphasis on the neural self's coherence compliments the narcissistic self with its emphasis on cohesion.

Some clarification is required between the use of the adjectives "coherent" and "cohesive" when referring to the nature of the self. (I am indebted to Joe Palombo for this clarification in a personal communication dated August 23, 2011) Kohut customarily uses "cohesive" to refer to the self's stability, strength, and firmness (1971, 1977, 1984). Kohut also uses "cohesive" to refer to a developmental phase as in "the stage of the cohesive self" (1971, p. 32). On at least one occasion Kohut seems to use coherent and cohesive synonymously, "Still, if the self is healthy, firmly coherent, and of normal strength, then it will not spontaneously become the focus of our empathic (or introspective) attention" (1977, p. 97).

Again let me reference Feinberg's (2009) neural self concept defined "essentially by its coherence: *a unity of consciousness in perception and action that persists in time*" (p. xi). From an attachment theory perspective, Wallin (2007, p. 133) states,

> The investigations of Main, Fonagy, and others confirm that the capacity to reflect coherently upon experience—rather than being embedded in it or defensively dissociated from it—is a marker of both our own attachment security and our ability to raise children (and perhaps patients) who will also be secure. As in the Adult Attachment Interview of a secure adult, this capacity for a "reflective" or "mentalizing" stance (I use the terms interchangeably) is manifested in a coherent account of experience that, in turn, reveals a coherent self. By that I mean a self that (1) makes sense rather than being riddled with inconsistencies; (2) hangs together as an integrated whole rather than being fractured by dissociations and disavowals; and (3) is capable of collaboration with other selves. Following the lead of Daniel Siegel (2006), I would suggest that a coherent self is also one that is stable, adaptive, flexible, and energized.

To be consistent with Palombo's clarification guidelines, I propose the following distinction. Cohesiveness is a quality that is inherent in both animate and inanimate objects and, consequently, refers to a property of that object. Selves, therefore, can have more or less of the cohesive property. From the standpoint of a subjective experience, we can speak of ourselves feeling cohesive. "Coherence" applies to linguistic expression and a course of reasoning. The discourse and arguments people propound may be judged to be more or less coherent or incoherent. Consequently, a narrative may be coherent, but not cohesive, unless cohesion is used metaphorically. "Coherence" refers to the logical relation of parts, for example, of a narrative, that affords comprehension or recognition (*Webster's Third International Dictionary*, 1993, p. 218). "Coherence" is not something people experience unless one uses the term to refer to the content of what the self is attempting to process.

Rather, "coherence", or lack thereof, is a judgment about what people say. Feinberg, Wallin, and Fonagy appear to use the adjective "coherent" correctly. Siegel and Kohut, in the one example cited, appear to not use "coherent" correctly, but with Kohut we must remember that English was his second language.

The neural self, as a complex adaptive system, is a repeatedly reconstructed biological state that endows our experience with subjectivity and that depends upon the continuous reactivation of images about our identity and our body (Damasio, 1994). In addition, the neural self emerges as a result of right hemisphere maturation. It is a body self through the gradual differentiation of mutual co-regulation of state and affective experience between the care-giver and the self (Schore, 2002).

The neural self can be thought of as a nested or compositional hierarchy in which lower elements are contained or nested within the higher parts to create increasingly complex wholes called holons. Either the entire self-structure or any part may be called a holon. Control or constraint is decentralised and is embodied within the organism and each of the holons so that collective action creates emergent properties at higher levels which exercises constraint at lower levels. In the hierarchy of our conscious awareness, it is *meaning* that provides the constraint that pulls the mind together to form the core of the neural self. The greater the degree of constraint over nested parts (neurons and neuronal assemblies) within the hierarchy, the greater a behaviour is purposive and therefore conscious. In other words, "At the lowest level of the hierarchy the individual cells do not care or know why they do what they do. It is only through the constraint at the higher order purpose of the act that the cells are bound into meaningful action" (Feinberg, 2009, p. 180). The transformational self is ever-changing and gets organised into a state of mind, a coherent neural self when a self-referencing metaphor generates excitement and a level of meaning that pulls the self into purposive action.

"State of mind" is a term coined by Siegel (1999) to advance his interpersonal neurobiological hypothesis. A state of mind can be defined as the total pattern of activations in the brain at a particular moment in time. Such a state involves a clustering of functionally synergistic, cohesive processes that can become a remembered brain activity configuration or neural net profile. States of mind can become traits of the individual that influence both internal and interpersonal processes (pp. 208–210).

I want to review how states of mind are organised. For our purpose, the transformational self, the psychological part of the biological neural self, can become activated when an embodied metaphoric self-reference appears creating a new energy potential. This energy potential acquires an affective signature or charge, becomes differentiated as a clustering process of ideational dynamics, is reinforced through long term potentiation (repeated firing patterns of synchronous neural assemblies), and a state of mind is mobilised. The degree to which this clustering is useful, repeated, and effective determines the state's cohesiveness. Dysfunction can be explained by certain self-states coming into conflict with each other or functioning in an anti-synergistic (entropic), asymmetrical manner.

With the acquisition of self-referencing metaphor and shift in self-representation, the late adolescent undergoes a threat to her homeostasis. This threat can be either negative or positive in terms of its outcome; but nevertheless, it is a real disturbance to the individual's equilibrium. The manner by which this is resolved speaks to the adaptive nature of the individual.

Conceptualised in self-referencing metaphor and expressed in idealised dimensions, the late adolescent reconfigured self-state becomes a true developmental potentiality evidenced by the use of different self (and other) representations.

The contribution from non-linear dynamic systems theory
(Chapter Nine)

The brain's functioning can be thought of in terms of non-linear dynamic systems theory or complexity theory. As such it is an open system highly sensitive to environmental as well as internal perturbations. Strengthened synaptic connections are reinforced patterns of interaction alternately thought of as states of activation or attractors. Attractor states are stabile forms of repeated interaction which give the system shape, firmness, and therefore some measure of predictability. From complexity theory come three principles that deepen our understanding of many aspects of the brain's functioning from emotions to human relationships.

First, complex systems possess an inherent orderliness called a self-organisation. Second, complex systems are non-linear in that a small input can generate a disproportionately large outcome. Third, complex systems have emergent patterns with recursive features. In other words, as our states of mind flow in a dynamic of progressive differentiation, the self-organisation emerges ever anew while re-experiencing those features which convey the continuity of self identity (Siegel, 1999).

The application of complexity theory with its emphasis on recip-rocal causality allows for an expanded way to think about brain/mind/body processes. The utility of this enhanced explanatory power offers vistas into the construction of developmental models that are closer to real experience, where states replace stages. These models are, consequently, more relevant than earlier frameworks.

The contribution from cognition (Chapter Ten)

The beginning and ending of adolescence can now be thought of in bio-logical terms, puberty, and prefrontal cortical maturation, respectively. With the maturation of the prefrontal cortex and its enlarged neural interconnectivity, the brain's full executive potential comes on line, allowing for "mature" goal directed behaviour. These biological book-ends may not, however, be consonant with the psychology of adoles-cence. Some researchers maintain that the psychology of adolescence precedes its biology, that is, puberty. For the purposes of this mono-graph, I take the position that adolescence will be defined as that devel-opmental period between puberty and prefrontal cortical maturation. I will refer to this period as adolescence proper. To understand the psychology of adolescence, as well as cognition beyond adolescence within these biological parameters, we must look to regulation theory.

Formal operational thought, a higher order equilibrium state, char-acterises the nature of cognitive potential available to adolescents. For Piaget, intellectual development is a process of adaptation to chang-ing reality. As new information is acquired, current schemas of under-standing are dislocated resulting in a disruption to the existing cognitive homeostasis. Fresh information, in our case, in the form of new metaphorically organised self-representations, must either be accommodated and/or assimilated into a revised cognitive equilib-rium. The healthy mind will not tolerate the associated cognitive dissonance, or cognitive conflict, and so must struggle to integrate the new schemas. This constitutes a motivational urge, a progressive adaptive force for change and growth.[3]

There does exist a conceptual dissonance between the Piagetian framework and neurobiological research findings which does not support the concept of a single set of cognitive skills emerging in step wise fashion in adolescence. Rather, the findings suggest an unevenness among separate maturational processes that contribute overall to the enhanced speed and accuracy of performance in cognitive tasks. Considering that both frameworks base their formulations on empirical data, the different hypotheses (the view from above *vs.* the view from below) may reflect a paradigm shift (Kuhn, 1962) rather than an invalidation of one over the other. In other words, the organismic metaphor gives way to the biotope metaphor.

Another significant contribution from the neurobiology of cognition relates to the concept of hot cognitions. Hot cognitions are emotionally biased brain activity that can override rational thinking, leading to risky behaviour. There may be a dimension of hot cognition in the formation of the transformational self in that the emergence of one or more self-referencing metaphors may lead to taking risks in the sense of testing new identities and self-capacities.

Post formal operational thought models expand possibilities for additional cognitive development. The traditional Piagetian framework formulating adolescent/young adult cognition is yielding to a paradigm of contextualism and relativism. This direction is compatible with postmodern philosophy and, consequently, contributes more pressure toward synergistic possibilities.

Psychotherapies of two adolescent girls (Chapter Eleven)

Process

These psychotherapy records are also biographical accounts in that each client has approved of these editions of their lives. Both Dawn and Mesia were enthusiastic about sharing these accounts of their transformed lives. Both expressed the thought that it would be good if others could profit from what they went through and resolved.

The paths that the late adolescent lives of Dawn and Mesia took can be more clearly understood through the use of the concept of the transformational self. For Dawn, the data suggested that the early positive state of the parent's marriage facilitated an average mother–child attunement experience resulting in a secure attachment. The capacity for open metaphor facilitated maturation of innate strengths and promoted resilience. Later, as her parent's marriage deteriorated, ending in divorce, Mother was increasingly preoccupied and less available, but a useful self-object, nevertheless. Dawn's extended family environment was stable, supportive, and responsive.

In Mesia's case, an increasingly unstable mother–child misattunement experience is hypothesised, as Mother became progressively involved in drugs and criminal life. Mesia's environment was marginal, sometimes disorganised, impoverished, and violent. Her mother's death left Mesia, at the age of eleven, unable to use self-objects resulting in a pseudo self-sufficiency, a brittle self easily given to depression, fragmentation, and rage reactions. The extended family was less reliable and dependable. The lack of capacity for open metaphor further explains its defensive nature.

Theoretical formulations

In the two psychotherapy cases, note the use of metaphors to self-characterise the advent of the transformational self. With a non-linear dynamic systems approach to recreated states of mind, it is assumed that the new, repeated self-referencing metaphor functions as an attractor and exerts a disproportionate impact through long term potentiation on the reconfigured, young adult self image. The new self-referencing metaphor is contained in autonoetic consciousness and becomes a stable self-representation. The stabilisation of the self representation(s) occurs, not exclusively, but especially, through the opportunity to continuously express itself via interactive self–self-object experiences, notably those of employment and the world of work. The opportunity to be mentored (receiving mentoring) and to be a mentor (giving mentoring) is a powerful way to operationalise efficacy needs.

Wolf (1988) writes about the self–self-object experience as one customarily thought of as "the self as the recipient of some action of the self object. Even when these actions of the selfobject were somehow evoked by the self having made its needs known, these selfobject experiences focused primarily on the selfobject as the actor and the self as acted upon". However, "there is another group of phenomenon that proceed in the opposite direction, that is, phenomenon characterized by the self as the actor and the selfobject as the acted upon". Because of "the self's experience of being an effective agent in influencing the object, one might call these phenomenon efficacy experiences". It has been suggested that the experiencing of such reciprocating pheno-menon mobilises a feeling of effectance, competence, or mastery (Lichtenberg, 1983; White, 1959), or, in other words, the feeling of being an effective agent in the conduct of one's affairs. It is the feeling of, "I am somebody" (Wolf, 1988, pp. 60–61). That feeling must surely be registered as a narcissistic enhancement, a feeling of "competence pleasure", and act as an adhesive in the formation of new self-referencing metaphors.

Assessing clinical efficacy: coherence criterion method (Chapter Two)

In Chapter Two, I mentioned that Palombo's (1991) coherence crite-rion of coherence, consistence, and completeness, would be used, to the degree possible, to assess efficacy in these psychotherapies. In the absence of long term follow up and study, it is only possible to hint at the nature of the meaning created for these clients through the treat-ment process.

For Dawn the new self-referencing metaphors were liberating and helped her to find her voice. The potential to convert this sense of liberation was represented in the different ways she viewed her parents and the choice of vocation. The open metaphor mode suggests an ability to metabolise the metaphor's significance as a psychological nutrient. Dawn's surgent growth pattern suggests that a sense of consistency and a sense of completeness accompanied this new self-referencing meaning.

For Mesia the new self-referencing metaphors reflected getting in touch with her affective life and the larger world of feeling better inte-grated and functioning in a more cohesive manner. She was able to get back on the developmental track, eventually formulate and execute life plans. Her tumultuous growth pattern suggests that the meaning of her self-referencing metaphors were unstable, foreclosed at times, but with her selection of vocation, guiding, and shaping.

Assessing clinical efficacy: social comparison method (Chapter Two)

In the social comparison method, treatment efficacy is assessed by com-paring the level of client functioning to that of normal peers. I will rely on Offer, Ostrov, and Howard's (1981) and Offer and Sabshin's (1984, pp. 76–107) definition of normal adolescence as a frame of reference.

Recognising that the Offer and colleagues data from the 1981 study is more than thirty years old, that it was gathered from 1385 adolescents rated as "average" from ten rural, urban, and suburban high schools in the US, and that the subjects were mostly white from working class, middle class, and upper class family/economic circumstances (1981, pp. 30–39), it nevertheless offers a useful baseline for answering this question. Obviously missing is data from adolescents from minority, under-privileged circumstances and from those in developing countries. The analysis of data, gathered from a standardised self-response questionnaire, was cross-sectioned into five types of selves: the psychological self, the social self, the sexual self, the familial self, and the coping self. Criteria for successful functioning in each of these selves were established. Dawn clearly demonstrated symptom improvement in that her depression lifted; she had energy available that she could focus on purposeful activities, and she viewed her family relationships in a more realistic manner. In Dawn's case improvement in each of the five selves was clearly evident. Where Dawn tended to internalise her dysfunction, Mesia externalised it. Mesia's intense ambivalence towards her grandmother lessened. Mesia's life took on a stable dimension not heretofore seen. She continued this stability by joining the US Air Force and embedding herself in a functional self-object matrix. In Mesia's case improvement was more dramatic with most improvement registered in the areas of the family and coping selves.

Gender empowerment

In presenting this material to my study group some members questioned why I do not feature the two psychotherapy cases from a gender empowerment perspective. It is a legitimate question, but one that introduces yet another red thread, a very large red thread, into the already expanding weave. Gutierrez (2001) defines empowerment as, "Empowerment is the process of increasing personal, interpersonal or political power so that individuals can take action to improve their lives" (p. 210). Empowerment is often associated with helping disadvantaged segments of the population, grass roots community organising, political action, and legislative advocacy, dimensions of social work activism practice that historically defined the early nature of the social work profession. Empowerment is seen as being in conflict with the protective intervention, beneficence, quantifiable research practice, and individual clinical practice counter movements (Urdang, 2008, pp. 23–29, 562–563). Empowerment is now related to a strengths (Saleebey, 2006) perspective. It is also related to a resilience, defined as "successful adaptation despite adversity", perspective with emphasis on risk and protective factors (Fraser, Kirkby, & Smokowski, 2004, p. 23). To this mix must be added a problem/solution focused intervention model and ecological theory, among still other dimensions.

Introducing the subject of empowerment at this point in our journey is like tasting a mulligatawny stew for the first time. While empowerment is a valid question, its implications for this monograph take on kaleidoscopic proportions; I will defer to the social activist experts. I need to view empowerment as an internal, intrapsychic dimension of developmental passage in which the neural self emerges resilient and renewed in young adulthood. In my view each client experienced a therapeutic sense of strengthened coping capacity that enabled them to feel empowered and liberated. Each pathway was different, of course, but for each client, a sense of direction emerged with the formation of the transformational self. In other words, activated, self-referencing metaphor became the pathway to personal metamorphosis.

When does adolescence end? (Chapters One and Ten)

This journey started with the hope that fresh answers to this decades old question could be generated from a contemporary, psychoanalytic, developmental psychology perspective. Complicating matters has been the continual broadening or elongation of adolescence. I have tried to confine adolescence to that developmental period between puberty and prefrontal cortical maturation, and labelled it as adolescence proper. It has been demonstrated that cultural conditioning continues to drive this issue as suggested by the Arnett (2004) proposition entitled: emerging adulthood. The emerging adulthood stage is interposed between adolescence and adulthood as a way to explain the delay in making lifelong commitments traditionally characteristic of adulthood. A psychological profile accompanies those in emerging adulthood consisting of identity exploration, instability, self-focus, feeling in between, and a reflective element, a kind of poetic musing he calls a "sense of possibilities". What can be said of this clustering of dynamics? I believe that the attempt to create a new developmental phase, emerging adulthood, is taking too great a conceptual leap. The cluster of dynamics seems consistent with those associated with adolescence and not sufficiently distinctive to justify a new phase. Of course, not everyone agrees with my position. Harter (2012) has accepted Arnett's proposition and has begun to research associated self representations (pp. 131–157).

In addition, Erikson's (1958) concept of the psychosocial moratorium (pp. 43, 100–104) contains adequate conceptual power to clarify the prolongation of the adolescent phase. In Erikson's words, a moratorium is "a span of time after they have ceased being children, but before their deeds and works count toward a future identity" (p. 43). A variety of moratoria are possible. The adolescent may not "*know* that they are marking time before they come to their crossroad, which they often do in their late twenties, belated just because they gave their all to the temporary subject of devotion"(p. 43), as was the case for Martin Luther. Of course, adolescents may chose to suspend their development for many reasons, some in the service of healthy "identity" consolidation, others in the cause of more pathological "identity confusion" (Erikson, 1950, pp. 261–263). At this point I want to call upon family systems theorists who hold to an alternate perspective to the traditional way of thinking as being on or off track developmentally.

> Our classification of life-cycle stages of American middle class families in the beginning of the 21st century highlights our view that the central underlying processes to be negotiated are the expansion, contraction and realignment of the relationship system to support the entry, exit, and development of family members in a functional way. Generally speaking, major life-cycle transitions require a fundamental change in the system itself rather than just incremental changes or rearrangements of the system, which go on continually throughout life. We do not see individual or family stages as "inherently" age related (e.g., Levinson, 1978) or dependent on the structure of the traditional family (e.g., Duvall, 1977). Nor do we view healthy maturation as requiring a single sequential pathway through marriage and child rearing. We hold a pluralistic view, recognizing many valid, healthy options and relationships over the course of life, in contrast to traditional views that not marrying is an "immature" choice or that women who do not have children are unfulfilled. (McGoldrick & Carter, 2003, p. 384)

The family system theorists add a valuable dimension to this discussion. Their pluralistic viewpoint is consistent with postmodern, social constructivist philosophy. This position is essentially congruent with the stance I take with respect to formulating an answer to our fundamental question, "When does adolescence end?" The joining of biological, cultural, economic and psychological determinants create multiple, highly varied temporal pathways for developmental progression. The maturation of the prefrontal cortex coupled with the appearance of self-referencing metaphors makes it possible to say, adolescence proper ends with the instantiation (activation) of the transformational self.

One more ingredient remains to be factored in—the individual developmental context of the transformational self. The reader will recall in Chapter Three that I established a self-system that locates the neural selves or states of mind in a developmental context with: 1) Kohut's cohesive self as the supra-ordinate structure, the psychological self-abstraction; and 2) Greenspan's model as the sub-ordinate structure, the empirical, neurobiological, (dual coded, with companion affective and cognitive dimensions) functional, developmental trajectory of the attachment–individuation process. The transformational self positions itself within this self-system at a temporal moment at the juncture between adolescence and adulthood. The transformational self is a "... *unity of consciousness in perception and action that persists in time*" (Feinberg, 2009, p. xi). Its dynamic properties include:

1. the actualisation of the individual's aspirations in alignment with talents and competencies organized by the ego-ideal (or the idealised parental imago)
2. the emergence of a reconfigured self-state buttressed with new, embodied metaphorical self-references organised within an enlarged belief system
3. an enhanced meaning making capacity with synergistic potential for guiding behaviour
4. the shaping of a set of consistent coping processes and living skills for the handling of anxiety and associated affects that are resilient and adaptive and for the enhancement and protection of the self-system,
5. the regulation of the operation of the transformational self within the self-system, formulated through the use of non-linear dynamic system processes, and

6.   the impact of the respective neural selves within the developmental line, a force for the entire life cycle.

Concluding comments

In these pages I have attempted to generate a new procedure for accomplishing an end or solving a (psychological) problem, a developmental algorithm (*Webster's Third New International Dictionary*, 1993, pp. 56a, 52), if you will. The problem relates to determining the conditions in contemporary society by which it may be said that an adolescent is transforming into a young adult. The solution lies in weaving together concepts from modern metaphor theory, attachment theory, self psychology, neurobiological research findings, contemporary psychoanalytic developmental psychology, and complexity theory in the context of psychotherapy to create a composite, coherent understanding of the processes.

I have proposed a two pronged effort. First, the formulation of the transformational self was designed to unify a splintered field of contributions about the nature of contemporary thought in psychoanalytic developmental psychology. This formulation attempts to integrate diverse schools into a coherent formulation, given the current extent of our knowledge. It is hoped that this effort will offer enhanced explanatory power, generate a useful set of hypotheses that await confirmation, and, otherwise, focus the ensuing discussion. I have labelled the matrix of interdisciplinary processes regulation theory which accounts for the structural and functional aspects of transitioning from late adolescence to young adulthood.

Second, I apply regulation theory to two psychotherapy cases to demonstrate its operational usefulness from both diagnostic and treatment perspectives and, in so doing, illustrate its enhanced explanatory power for describing the dynamic processes.

The transformational self is a reconfigured metaphorical, neural, self-state constructed from the innate need for individuation through attachment. The organisation and stabilisation of the transformational self is the gateway to a self-actualised adulthood.

One of my reviewers, my daughter-in-law, Elizabeth, asked a vital question, "If one can acquire a transformational self, can one lose it?" Also a colleague, Rita Sussman inquired, "Suppose one never acquires a transformational self?" Well . . . those must be subjects for a second monograph.

Notes

1.

(from Freud, 1895a, p. 324)

In this schematic depiction of the neuronal brain/mind functionality Freud put forward a hypothesis of the ego as a regulatory organisation responsible for defensive functions involving inhibiting and alternately facilitating the movement of energy among neurons (Freud, 1895a, pp. 322–324).

In the *Project for a Scientific Psychology* (1895a) Freud postulated an integrated model of the mind based on the recent discoveries of neurons (1892) and synaptic transmission of impulses. The limited neurophysiology of his day and Freud's inability to make the conceptual leap to explain both defence and pathological repression in mechanical terms did not permit Freud to complete the *Project* (Sulloway, 1979, p. 126). However, it framed ideas which were to pave the way for his subsequent psychoanalytic discoveries. Using what would later come to be known as the economic and dynamic hypotheses and the principle of constancy, he outlined a regulatory system of the mind with an executive role for the ego.

The early ego in this pre-psychoanalytic period operated on a conscious level with three functions: to stabilise the movement of energy, to establish the predominance of secondary process over primary process, and to test reality. Only with the publication of the *Ego and the Id* (1923b) did the ego assume its full role in its conscious and unconscious interactions with the id, the superego, and ego-ideal (Quinodoz, 2005, p. 27).

Freud sent off the first three portions of the *Project* to his close collaborator, Wilhelm Fleiss, but kept the fourth. Unhappy with his inability to solve the core riddle of repression, Freud kept and apparently destroyed the last part. Freud asked Fleiss to destroy the paper, but Fleiss kept all his correspondence with Freud. In 1950, two decades after Fleiss' death and one decade after Freud's death, Fleiss' widow released her husband's papers for publication (Sulloway, 1979, pp. 118–119).

2. As of this writing, regulation theory with its multiple meanings and dimensions appears to be a theory in search of unification. To this conceptual mix of developmental features we need to add the "hidden regulators" of Hofer (1995) and Polan and Hofer (1999). Drawing on findings from attachment/separation research on rat pups and their mothers (dams), they suggest that "hidden regulators" are operating that constitute component psychobiological processes governing the pup–dam relationship as a whole. These processes once separated deepen the understanding of Bowlby's central contention that infant–mother proximity in altricial (slowly developing) mammals is a motivational system in its own right. These "hidden regulators" operating in concert include thermal, olfactory, tactile (ventral to ventral proximity), and sucking/milk flow components. Compromising any one of these components alters significantly the developmental trajectory of the pup. Additionally, the work of Greenspan and Shanker (2004) reference the regulation process as follows: "How does environmental variability interact with genetic variability in the development of a range of human capacities? For some capacities, the genetic structure may set the constraints, and environmental experiences may operate more like a switch—turning on or off certain 'regulator' genes, which in turn, influence gene expression and behavior" (p. 4).

3. "Assimilation and accommodation are the polar constituents of *adaptation*. . . . It is clear that the Piagetian adaptation function . . . is an iterative function. It takes current knowledge and an experience whose meaning is based on that knowledge as its input. As its output, it produces new knowledge and new experiences that are a function of the altered knowledge state. The production of new experiences and not just new knowledge is essential; adaptation takes place in the form of action. Action entails personal knowledge and experiences that from the interface between the person's knowledge and the reality touched upon in that action. It may take a while, of course, before a current experience, such as cognitive conflict, is transformed into new consolidated knowledge" (van Geert, 1994, p. 17).

Comparing and contrasting ego psychology with self-psychology

Dimensions	Ego psychology	Self-psychology
Definition	The ego is a coherent organisation of mental processes. The ego's executive function mediates among the id, the superego, and reality. Hartmann said that the ego existed in rudimentary form at birth. Before that Freud and others said the ego was neutralised id.	The self is the primary psychic constellation, the independent centre of experience and initiative and the main motivating agency OR our sense of being an independent centre of initiative and perception, integrated with our most central ambitions and ideals and with our experience that our body and mind form a unit in space and a continuum in time.
Evolution of component parts	Undifferentiated id→ego matrix→Id→ego→superego and→ego ideal.	Grandiose self→idealised parent imago→and twinship.
Object relations and narcissism	One line of development: autoerotism→primary narcissism→object love→secondary narcissism. Narcissism is the reinvestment of libido back into the ego using the metaphor of a "u" tube.	Two separate lines of development: object relations and narcissism.
Anxiety	Arising from intrapsychic conflict; types of anxiety can be loosely associated with each of the libidinal psychosexual phases: annihilation anxiety, (stranger anxiety), loss of the object (or separation anxiety), loss of the object's love, castration anxiety, superego anxiety, or guilt.	Arising from loss of contact with the self or objects; types of anxiety can associated with each pole of the tripolar self OR according to self states, such as disintegration anxiety (fragmentation of the self), depletion anxiety (self-perception of emptiness), and diffusion anxiety (weak self boundaries with biological substrate, as in panic disorder).

Dimensions	Ego psychology	Self-psychology
Defences	Organised according to developmental model thinking.	Defensive and compensatory structures; Splitting and disavowal are as prominent as repression. All defences are forms of disavowal.
Drives	Libido and aggression: Mastery (White); Individuation (Richmond & Sklansky).	No drives, but Kohut believed in an inner biological growth force pushing the individual toward completion of maturational tasks and development of a cohesive self.
Oedipus	Core—emphasis on guilt.	Peripheral—emphasis on shame.
Existential concerns	"Guilty Man"—Man as pleasure-seeking who struggles with conflicts that arise between desires and prohibitions.	"Tragic Man"—Man as struggling with empathic failures in attempts to achieve self-cohesion and self-realisation. Search for meaning in life.
Understanding/ knowing	Through insight.	Through empathy.
Narcissistic end point(s)	Ego ideal.	Creativity, humour, empathy, self-calming and regulatory capacity, wisdom, and an acceptance of the finality of life.
What propels development	The drives seek discharge in a steady state of tension reduction.	Optimal frustration, the wish to be responded to in a facilitating environment.
Psychopathology	More conflictual model, pre-Oedipal (psychotic, borderline, narcissistic—Kernberg) and Oedipal, the neuroses (hysterical, phobic, obsessive-compulsive, and depressive).	More deficit model, primary (from *DSM-IV-TR* and include the psychoses, borderline states, narcissistic behaviour disorders, and narcissistic personality disorder) and secondary disorders (reaction of a structurally undamaged self to the vicissitudes of life) and the character types (mirror-hungry, ideal-hungry, alter-ego-hungry, merger-hungry, and contact-shunning personalities).

Dimensions	Ego psychology	Self-psychology
Normal growth	Growth is the process by which the ego becomes progressively differentiated and organised. An early apparatus of primary autonomy exists outside of conflict to create an innate ego constitution. Organisation proceeds within the reciprocal relationship of the mother–infant dyad in which communication takes place via affective interchange. Adaptation, in which the self modifies in response to the environment and conversely, the environment is modified to accommodate the self, takes place in an average expectable environment. Regression and progression are normal dimensions of growth.	Growth occurs via transmuting internalisation—the process of transformation by which a function formerly performed by another (self-object) is taken into the self through optimal mirroring, interaction, and frustration. Microinternalisations refers to the metabolism of multiple and frequent psychological nutrients. A self-object can also be something inanimate or a sunny day.
Therapeutic action	The provision of interpretation in a therapeutic milieu leads to insight management/manipulation of the transference. Coping is enhanced through the ego's use of more developmentally appropriate defences and regression is in service of the ego.	The provision of empathic attunement leads to better use of self-objects, which strengthen cohesion of the self-structure. The cohesive self becomes less fragmentation prone, more resilient and more available to use self-objects to maintain narcissistic balance.
Modes of transference	Only when self and object constancy has been achieved can it be said that feelings, attitudes, and behaviour first experienced with a primary object can be transferred. These transferences are interpretable. Depending on the degree of differentiation, with less structured personalities the subject seeks to replicate early object experience or to fulfil early object need. The narcissistic solutions are pegged at the developmental level the needed partner in the dyad failed in her/his function. Traditional organisation of transference follows libidinal framework and characterisations about the ego's ties with the object world.	The three self-object transferences derive from three sets of overlapping self-objects needs. The mirror transference recreates the patient's need for confirming and validating responses from the therapist. The idealising transference recreates the patient's need to merge in the calmness and facilitating presence of the therapist. The twinship or alter-ego transference recreates the need to be like another in the range of human experience.
Root metaphor(s)	Mechanistic (topographical, economic, dynamic, structural), organismic, or biological (ingestion) contextual.	Organismic or biological (ingestion, translocation).

Modern and postmodern philosophical paradigms in clinical social work from a developmental model perspective

Dimensions	Modern	Postmodern
Texts representative of types of developmental model thinking	Colarusso (1992) *Child and Adult Development: A Psychoanalytic Introduction for Clinicians*	Galatzer-Levy and Cohler (1993) *The Essential Other— A Developmental Psychology of the Self*
Underpinnings and forerunners— psychodynamic/ developmental models	Philosophy: John Locke (empiricism, *a priori* vs. *a posteriori*, all knowledge is based on experience gathered by sensory data; mind is a *tabula rasa*), David Hume (inductive reasoning). Sociology: August Comte. Science: Tycho Brahe (start of the scientific revolution with empirical measurements of the planets—1572), Francis Bacon, Isaac Newton, Charles Darwin. Psychology: Rene Spitz, Heinz Hartmann. Psychosexual: Sigmund Freud, Karl Abraham, and the search for a *Weltanschauung*. Psychosocial: Erik Erikson. Moral: Lawrence Kohlberg. Child development: Margaret Mahler, Stanley Greenspan. Adult development: Daniel Levinson, George Vaillant, Nancy Chodorow. Narcissistic development: Heinz Kohut, Otto Kernberg. Cognition: Jean Piaget ("the view from above").	Philosophy: Friedrich Nietzsche, Emmanuel Levinas, Jean-Francois Lyotard, Jacque Derrida, Richard Rorty, Michel Foucault. Science/physics:Max Planck, Albert Einstein, Werner Heisenberg (uncertainty principle, 1927). Psychology: (Interpersonal) Harry Stack Sullivan, Donald W. Winnicott (social constructivism) Merton Gill, Irving Hoffman, Kenneth Gergen (narrative) Roy Schafer (intersubjectivity) George Atwood, Robert Stolorow, Jessica Benjamin, Christopher Bollas, Thomas H. Ogden, Stephen A. Mitchell. Development: Carol Gilligan, Daniel Stern. Cognition: Jean Piaget ("the view from below").

Dimensions	Modern	Postmodern
Influences	white/Eurocentrism, privileged status, male/masculinity, competitiveness, binaries (tension of opposites), hierarchies, patriarchy, pathology/deviance/conflict/deficits based	the Holocaust (1945), minorities, feminism, complementarity and Africentrism; ecology model, strengths, competencies/abilities and resilience based
Theoretical frameworks	drive theory, structural theory, ego psychology, object relations, self psychology	interpersonal theory, intersubjectivity theory, relational theory
Examples of each paradigm	philosophy of nature/natural philosophy = science (the microscope was considered aphilosophical instrument) "classical psychoanalysis" "psychodynamic psychotherapy" "Child–Parent Psychotherapy"	second-order cybernetics personal construct theory "narrative therapy" "relational theory" "solution focused therapy" "Emotionally-Focused Couple Therapy"
Epistemology—paradigms	modern, traditional, dominant cosmos centred positivism logical positivism, linguistic positivism neo positivism	postmodern, post structuralism non-traditional, alternative, hu(man) centred social constructionism (used more in sociology) constructivism, social constructivism (used more in psychology)
Reality/truth	single, objective quantifiable, quantitative mirror reflection reliability and validity are empirically supported reality—testing and processing	multiple, subjective relative, goodness of fit qualitative, intuitive, integrative intersubjective, interpersonal meaning making, mind-sharing reality—socially constructed
Laws of nature	universal symmetry processes reversible and static reductionism	asymmetry, dynamic, plurality, temporality, complexity, constantly evolving

Dimensions	Modern	Postmodern
Main purpose	prediction	understanding, emancipation, deconstruction
Manner generally expressed with many exceptions	conservative tradition authoritarian certainty, uniform language	liberal tradition laissez-faire uncertainty, ambiguity
Discovery (how knowledge is acquired)	eight step scientific method (ask a scientific question, make observations, gather information form a hypothesis, experiment, collect data, analyse data and draw a conclusion) systematic trial and error problem solving hypothesis formulation and testing research study replicability "correspondence criterion," Joseph Palombo (1991)	heuristic research (Herbert Simon): common sense, "rule of thumb," informal trial and error decision making naturalistic inquiry hermeneutic approach (Wilhelm Dilthey, Martin Heidegger, Paul Ricoeur) "coherence criterion," Joseph Palombo (1991)
Alignment of variables	linear, sequential, complete causality, epigenesis investment in conceptualising "normality" linear determinism, non-linear determinism ("lawless behavior governed by law", "Chaos is stochastic behavior occurring in a deterministic system") non-linear dynamic systems theory / catastrophe theory / chaos theory / complexity theory In physics (e.g., Galatzer-Levy, 2004): By using non-linear differential equations, the nature of prediction shifts to involve mathematical probabilities of stable configurations and patterns of change in the evolution of complex adaptive systems. Precise predictions of variables such as velocity, time, position, and direction in the measurement of these systems are not possible.	field, non-sequential, contextualism, pluralism, multiplicity of perspectives, incomplete causality infinite possibilities, speculative change is discontinuous (surgent, dormant or unpredictable) non-linear dynamic systems theory / catastrophe theory / chaos theory / complexity theory In psychology (Feinberg, 2009; Harter, 2012; Bendicsen, current volume): The neural self, as a complex adaptive system, is in an ongoing process of social and cognitive construction and reconstruction.

Dimensions	Modern	Postmodern
Data collection and extrapolation	distortion free, experience distant observer OR participant/subject "one-person" psychology nomothetical (law like generalisations) role of the therapist: to interpret (Kurt Eissler) more deductive reasoning (from the general to the particular)	distortion expected, experience near observer JOINS participant/subject "two-person" psychology idiographic (in terms of the particulars of the case) role of the therapist: to witness (Donnel Stern) more inductive reasoning (from the particular to the general)
Research ethics	peripheral, value free exogenous (all parameters of research are researcher determined) etic (research carried out from an outside perspective) ex. *Hospitalism* (discoveries about wasting away due to maternal deprivation), Rene A. Spitz (1945)	central, value bound endogenous (respondents have equal rights to determine research parameters) emic (research carried out from an inside perspective) ex. *The Girl Within* (discoveries about the development of female identity), Emily Hancock (1989)

We must remember that, conceptually, there is no one postmodern approach. From a heuristic standpoint the referenced texts should serve as exemplars illustrating how these philosophical paradigms can manifest in the study of human development. It is recognised that attempts to draw exact conceptual boundaries may run the risk of reductionism. Some content may not fit precisely in the category in which I have placed it. Additionally, this data array is intended to be a guide; no claim is made to either comprehensiveness or authoritativeness.

REFERENCES

Abraham, K. (1925). Character formation on the genital level of the libido. In: E. Jones (Ed.), *Selected Papers of Karl Abraham* (pp. 407–417). New York: Basic Books.

Abraham, K. (1927). A short study of the development of the libido, viewed in the light of mental illness. In: E. Jones (Ed.), *Selected Papers of Karl Abraham* (pp. 418–501). New York: Basic Books.

Ainsworth, M. D. S., Blehar, M., Waters, E., & Wall, S. (1978). *Patterns of Attachment: A Psychological Study of the Strange Situation*. New Jersey: Lawrence Erlbaum.

Almond, B. A. (1990). The secret garden: a therapeutic metaphor. *The Psychoanalytic Study of the Child, 45*: 477–494.

Altman, N., Briggs, R., Frankel, J., Gensler, D., & Pantone, P. (2002). *Relational Child Psychotherapy*. New York: Other Press.

Amini, F., Lewis, T., Cannon, R., Louie, A., Baumbacher, G., McGuiness, T., & Shiff, E. Z. (1996). Affect, attachment, memory: contributions toward psychobiological integration. *Psychiatry, 59*: 213–239.

Anderson, R. E., Carter, I., & Lowe, G. R. (1999). *Human Behavior in the Social Environment: A Social Systems Approach* (5th edn). Hawthorn, NY: Aldine De Gruyter.

Applegate, J. (1989). Mahler and Stern: irreconcilable differences? *Child and Adolescent Social Work, 6*(3): 163–173.

Arnett, J. (1991). Adolescent storm and stress reconsidered. *American Psychologist, 54*(5): 317–326.

Arnett, J. (2004). *Emerging Adulthood: The Winding Road from the Late Teens to Through the Twenties.* Oxford: Oxford University Press.

Aron, L. (1996). *A Meeting of Minds: Mutuality in Psychoanalysis.* Hillsdale, NJ: Analytic Press.

Atwood, G. E., & Stolorow, R. D. (1993). *Faces in a Cloud: Intersubjectivity in a Personality Perspective.* Lanham, MD: Jason Aronson/Rowman & Littlefield.

Austrian, S. (2002). *Developmental Theories Through the Life Cycle.* New York: Columbia University Press.

Badenoch, B. (2008). *Being a Brain-Wise Therapist: A Practical Guide to Interpersonal Neurobiology.* New York: Norton.

Bartlett's Familiar Quotations (1980). Boston: Little, Brown and Company.

Basseches, M. A. (1984). Dialectical thinking as a metasystematic form of cognitive organization. In: M. Commons, F. Richards, & C. Armon (Eds.), *Beyond Formal Operations: Late Adolescence and Adult Cognitive Development* (pp. 216–238). New York: Praeger.

Beebe, B., & Lachmann, F. M. (1988). Mother–infant mutual influence and precursors of psychic structure. In: A. Goldberd (Ed.), *Frontiers in Self Psychology: Progress in Self-Psychology, Vol. 3* (pp. 3–25). Hillsdale, NJ: Analytic Press.

Bendicsen, H. (1992). Achieving the capacity to tolerate ambiguity: the role played by literature in the psychotherapies of three late adolescents. *The Association of Child Psychotherapists Bulletin, 9*: 21–32.

Benjamin, J. (1988). *The Bonds of Love: Psychoanalysis, Feminism, and the Problem of Domination.* New York: Pantheon.

Benjamin, J. (1998). *The Shadow of the Other: Intersubjectivity and Gender in Psychoanalysis.* New York: Routledge.

Benveniste, D. (1998). Play and the metaphors of the body. *Psychoanalytic Study of the Child. 53*: 65–83.

Bernfeld, S. (1938). Types of adolescents. *Psychoanalytic Quarterly, 7*: 243–253.

Berzoff, J., Flanagan, L. M., & Hertz, P. (2008). *Inside Out and Outside In: Psychodynamic Clinical Theory and Psychopathology in Contemporary Multicultural Contexts* (2nd edn). New York: Jason Aronson.

Bettelheim, B. (1983). *Freud and Man's Soul.* New York: Alfred A. Knopf.

Blake, W. (1794/2009). *The Marriage of Heaven and Hell.* Mineola, NY: Dover.

Blos, P. (1962). *On Adolescence: A Psychoanalytic Interpretation.* New York: Free Press.

Blos, P. (1967). The second individuation process of adolescence. *Psychoanalytic Study of the Child*, 22: 162–186.

Blos, P. (1976). When and how does adolescence end? Structural criteria for adolescent closure. In: S. C. Feinstein & P. Giovacchini (Eds.), *Adolescent Psychiatry, Vol. V* (pp. 5–17). New York: Jason Aronson.

Bollas, C. (1987). *The Shadow of the Object: Psychoanalysis and the Unthought Known*. New York: Columbia University Press.

Boldrini, M., Placidi, G. P. A., & Marazziti, D. (1998). Applications of chaos theories to psychiatry: a review and future perspectives. *International Journal of Neuropsychiatric Medicine*, 3: 22–29.

Bowlby, J. (1969). *Attachment and Loss. Vol. I: Attachment*. New York: Basic Books.

Bowlby, J. (1973). *Attachment and Loss. Vol. II: Separation, Anxiety and Danger*. New York: Basic Books.

Bowlby, J. (1980). *Attachment and Loss. Vol. III: Loss*. New York: Basic Books.

Bowlby, J. (1988). *A Secure Base: Parent–Child Attachment and Healthy Human Development*. New York: Basic Books.

Brems, C. (2002). *A Comprehensive Guide to Child Psychotherapy* (2nd edn). Boston: Allyn and Bacon.

Browning, M. M. (2006). Neuroscience and imagination: the relevance of Susanne Langer's work to psychoanalytic theory. *The Psychoanalytic Quarterly*, 75: 1131–1159.

Buck, R. (1999). The biological affects: a topography. *Psychological Review*, 106: 301-336.

Bullock, M., Gelman, R., & Baillargeon, R. (1982). The development of causal reasoning. In: W. J. Friedman (Ed.), *The Developmental Psychology of Time*. New York: Academic.

Cairns, R. (1988). Spoken comments at the centennial celebration of the Department of Psychology, Indiana University, Bloomington.

Campbell, R. J. (1996). *Psychiatric Dictionary*. New York and Oxford: Oxford University Press.

Cassidy, J., & Shaver, P. R. (Eds.) (1999). *Handbook of Attachment: Theory, Research, and Clinical Applications*. New York and London: Guilford Press.

Chessick, R. (1993). *A Dictionary for Psychotherapists*. Northvale, NJ: Jason Aronson.

Chodorow, N. (1978). *The Reproduction of Mothering: Psychoanalysis and the Sociology of Gender*. Berkeley: University of California Press.

Cholo, A. B. (2003). It's taking a lot longer to reach adulthood, study says. *Chicago Tribune*.9 May.

Colarusso, C. A. (1990). The third individuation: the effect of biological parenthood on separation–individuation processes in young adulthood. *Psychoanalytic Study of the Child, 45*: 170–194.

Colarusso, C. A. (1992). *Child and Adult Development: A Psychoanalytic Introduction for Clinicians*. New York: Plenum.

Common Sense Media (2012). Review of *Failure to Launch*. Available at commonsensemedia.org/movie-reviews/failure-launch; accessed 6 May, 2012.

Commons, M. L., & Richards, F. A. (2007). Postformal stages of cognitive development. *Integral Research Group*. Available at opensourceintegral. blogspot.com/2007/10/four-postformal-stages.html.

Coppolillo, H. P. (1980). The tides of change in adolescence. In: S. J. Greenspan and G. H. Pollock (Eds.), *The Course of Life: Psychoanalytic Contributions Toward Understanding Personality Development, Vol. II. Latency, Adolescence and Youth* (pp. 235–252). Washington, DC: NIMH.

Cozolino, L. (2002). *The Neuroscience of Psychotherapy: Building and Rebuilding the Human Brain*. New York and London: Norton.

Cozolino, L. (2010). *The Neuroscience of Psychotherapy: Healing the Social Brain*. New York and London: Norton.

Damasio, A. R. (1994). *Descartes' Error: Emotion, Reason, and the Human Brain*. New York: Putnam's.

Dana Foundation (2011). *A Decade after The Decade of the Brain*. Available at www.dana.org.

Davies, D. (2004). *Child Development: A Practitioner's Guide* (2nd edn). New York and London: Guilford Press.

Dimen, M. (2003). *Sexuality, Intimacy and Power*. Hillsdale, NJ: Analytic Press.

Doctors, S. (2000). Attachment–individuation: I. Clinical notes toward a reconsideration of adolescent turmoil. *Adolescent Psychiatry, 25*: 3–16.

Donahue, M. J. (1997). An introduction to mathematical chaos theory and fractal geometry. Available at www.fractalfinance.com/chaostheory. html

Duvall, E. M. (1977). *Marriage and Family Development* (5th edn). Philadelphia, PA: Lippincott.

Ebbinghaus, H. (1885/1913). *Memory: A Contribution to Experimental Psychology*. New York: Teachers College, Columbia University.

Edelman, G. (1992). *Bright Air, Brilliant Fire: On the Matter of Mind*. New York: Basic Books.

Eissler, K. (1953). The effect of the structure of the ego on psychoanalytic technique. *American Psychoanalytic Association, 1*: 104–143.

Eliot, T. S. (1943). *Four Quartets*. San Deigo, CA: Harcourt Brace Jovanovich.

Ellis, H. (1890). *The New Spirit*. London: Walter Scott, Ltd.

Erikson, E. H. (1950). *Childhood and Society* (2nd edn). New York: Norton.

Erikson, E. H. (1956). The problem of ego identity. In: R. S. Wallerstein & L. Goldberger (Eds.), *Ideas and Identities: The Life and Work of Erik Erikson* (pp. 173–206). Madison, CT: International Universities Press, 1998.

Erikson, E. H. (1958). *Young Man Luther*. New York: Norton.

Erikson, E. H. (1959a). The concept of ego identity. *Journal of the American Psychoanalytic Association, 4*: 56–121.

Erikson, E. H. (1959b). *Identity and the Life Cycle*. New York and London: Norton.

Esman, A. H. (1993). G. Stanley Hall and the invention of adolescence. *Adolescent Psychiatry, 19*: 6–20.

Feinberg, T. E. (2009). *From Axons to Identity: Neurological Explorations of the Nature of the Self*. New York and London: Norton.

Fenichel, O. (1945). *The Psychoanalytic Theory of the Neuroses*. New York: Norton.

Feynman, R. (1985). *QED*. Princeton, NJ: Princeton University Press.

Flanagan, L. M. (2011). The theory of self psychology. In: J. Berzoff, L. M. Flanagan, & P. Hertz (Eds.), *Inside Out and Outside In: Psychodynamic Clinical Theory and Psychopathology in Contemporary Multicultural Contexts* (3rd edn) (pp. 158–185). New York: Rowman & Littlefield.

Fliess, R. (1942). The metapsychology of the analyst. *Psychoanalytic Quarterly, 11*: 211–227.

Fonagy, P. (2001). *Attachment Theory and Psychoanalysis*. New York: Other Press.

Fonagy, P. (2003). The development of psychopathology from infancy and to adulthood: the mysterious unfolding of disturbance in time. *Infant Mental Health Journal, 24*(3): 212–239.

Fonagy, P., & Target, M. (2002). Early interventions and the development of self-regulation. *Psychoanalytic Inquiry, 22*(3): 307–335.

Fonagy, P., & Target, M. (2006). The mentalization focused approach to self psychology. *Journal of Personality Disorders, 20*(6): 544–576.

Fonagy, P., Gergely, G., Jurist, E. L., & Target, M. (2002). *Affect Regulation, Mentalization and the Development of the Self*. New York: Other Press.

Fosshage, J. L. (2004). The explicit and implicit dance in psychoanalytic change. *Journal of Analytic Psychology, 49*: 49–65.

Fraser, M. W., Kirby, L. D., & Smokowski, P. R. (2004). Risk and resilience in childhood. In: M. W. Fraser (Ed.), *Risk and Resilience in Childhood: An Ecological Perspective* (2nd edn) (pp. 13–66). Washington, DC: National Association of Social Workers.

Freud, A. (1953). Some remarks on infant observation. *Psychoanalytic Study of the Child, 8*: 9–19.

Freud, A. (1958). Adolescence. *Psychoanalytic Study of the Child, 13*: 255–278.

Freud, A. (1965). *Normality and Pathology in Childhood: Assessments of Development.* New York: International Universities Press.

Freud, S. (1895a). *A Project for a Scientific Psychology. S.E., 1*: 283–397. London: Hogarth.

Freud, S. (1900a). *The Interpretation of Dreams. S.E., 4–5.* London: Hogarth.

Freud, S. (1905d). *Three Essays on the Theory of Sexuality. S.E., 7*: 123–243. London: Hogarth.

Freud, S. (1912–1913). *Totem and Taboo, S.E., 13*: 1–161. London: Hogarth.

Freud, S. (1923b). *The Ego and the Id. S.E., 19*: 12–66. London: Hogarth.

Freud, S. (1930a). *Civilization and Its Discontents. S.E., 21.* London: Hogarth.

Freud, S. (1933a). The question of a Weltanschauung. In: *New Introductory Lectures on Psychoanalysis, S.E., 22.* London: Hogarth.

Freud, S. (1974) Indexes and bibliographies. *S.E., 24.* London: Hogarth.

Frick, R. B. (1982). The ego and the vestibulocerebellar system: some theoretical perspectives. *Psychoanalytic Quarterly, 51*: 93–122.

Friedman, L. (1999). *Identity's Architect: A Biography of Erik Erikson.* New York: Scribner.

Fuller, J. (2007). Oliver Sacks looks at the sometimes strange connections between music and the mind. Book review of *Musicophilia: Tales of Music and the Brain. Chicago Tribune*, October, 27.

Gabbard, G. O. (1994). *Psychodynamic Psychiatry in Clinical Practice.* Washington, DC: American Psychiatric Press, 2005.

Galatzer-Levy, R. M. (1995). Psychoanalysis and dynamical systems theory: prediction and self similarity. *Journal of the American Psychoanalytic Association, 43*: 1085–1113.

Galatzer-Levy, R. M. (2004). Chaotic possibilities: toward a new model of development. *International Journal of Psychoanalysis, 85*: 419–441.

Galatzer-Levy, R. M., & Cohler, B. J. (1990). The developmental psychology of the self and the changing world view of psychoanalysis. *Annual of Psychoanalysis, 18*: 1–43.

Galatzer-Levy, R. M., & Cohler, B. J. (1993). *The Essential Other-A Developmental Psychology of the Self.* New York: Basic Books.

Ganz, T. (1993). *Early Greek Myth: A Guide to Literary and Artistic Sources.* Baltimore, MD: Johns Hopkins University Press.

Gibson, M. F. (2012). Opening up: therapist self-disclosure in theory, research, and practice. *Clinical Social Work Journal, 40*(3): 287–296.

Giedd, J. N., Bluementhal, J., Jeffries, N. O., Castellanos, F. X., Liu, H., Zijdenbos, A., Paus, T., Evans, A. C., & Rapoport, J. L. (1999). Brain development during childhood and adolescence: a longitudinal MRI study. *Nature Neuroscience*, 2(10): 861–863.

Gilligan, C. (1982). *In Different Voice: Psychological Theory and Women's Development*. Cambridge, MA: Harvard University Press.

Gilligan, C. (1987). Adolescent development reconsidered. *The Tenth Annual Gisela Konopka Lectures*. May 13, 1987. St Paul, MN: Center for Youth Development and Research, University of Minnesota.

Ginsburg, H. P., & Opper, S. (1988). *Piaget's Theory of Intellectual Development*. Englewood Cliffs, NJ: Prentice Hall.

Gleick, J. (1987). *Chaos: Making a New Science*. New York: Viking.

Gogtay, N., Giedd, J. N., Lusk, L., Hayashi, K. M., Greenstein, D., Vaituzis, A. C., Nugent III, T. F., Herman, D. H., Clasen, L. S., Toga, A. W., Rapoport, J. L., & Thompson, P. M. (2004). Dynamic mapping of human cortical development during childhood through early adulthood. *Proceedings National Academy of Sciences of the USA*, 101(21): 8174–8179.

Grady, J. (1997). Foundations of meaning: primary metaphors and primary scenes. Unpublished doctoral dissertation, University of California, Berkeley.

Graham, E. (2005). When a child returns home. *Wall Street Journal*. September 26.

Green, H. (Joanne Greenberg). (1964). *I Never Promised You a Rose Garden*. New York: Signet.

Greenspan, S. I. (1979). *Intelligence and Adaptation: An Integration of psychoanalytic and Piagetian Developmental Psychology*. New York: International Universities Press.

Greenspan, S. I. (1989). *The Development of the Ego: Implications for Personality Theory, Psychopathology, and the Therapeutic Process*. New York: International Universities Press.

Greenspan, S. I., & Lourie, R. S. (1981). Developmental structuralist approach to the classification of adaptive and pathologic personality organizations: infancy and early childhood. *American Journal of Psychiatry*, 138: 725–735.

Greenspan, S. I., & Porges, S. W. (1984). Psychopathology in infancy and early childhood: clinical perspectives on the organization of sensory and affective-thematic experience. *Child Development*, 55: 49–70.

Greenspan, S. I., & Shanker, S. G. (2004). *The First Idea: How Symbols, Language, and Intelligence Evolved from our Primate Ancestors to Modern Humans*. Cambridge, MA: Da Capo/Perseus.

Grossman, L. (2005). Meet the twixters, young adults who live off their parents, bounce from job to job and hop from mate to mate. They're not just lazy . . . they just won't grow up. *Time*. January 24.

Gutierrez, L. M. (2001). Working with women of color: an empowerment perspective. In: J. Rothman, J. L. Erlich, & J. E. Tropman (Eds.), *Strategies of Community Intervention* (6th edn) (pp. 209–217). Itasca, IL: Peacock.

Haken, H. (1977). *Synergetics: An Introduction*. Heidelberg: Springer-Verlag.

Hall, G. S. (1904). *Adolescence: Its Psychology and Relations to Psysiology, Anthropology, Sociology, Sex, Crime, Religion, and Education* (two volumes). New York: Appleton.

Hall, G. S. (1923). *Life and Times of a Psychologist*. New York: Appleton.

Hancock, E. (1989). *The Girl Within*. New York: Fawcett Columbine.

Harter, S. (1999). *The Construction of the Self: A Developmental Perspective*. New York: Guilford Press.

Harter, S. (2012). *The Construction of the Self: Developmental and Sociocultural Foundations* (2nd edn). New York: Guilford Press.

Hartmann, H. (1939). *Ego Psychology and the Problem of Adaptation*. Princeton, MA: Princeton University Press.

Hartmann, H. (1958). Comments on the scientific aspects of psycho-analysis. *Psychoanalytic Study of the Child, 13*: 127–146.

Hartmann, H. (1964). Comments on the psychoanalytic theory of the ego. In: H. Hartmann, *Essays on Ego Psychology: Selected Problems in Psycho-analytic Theory* (pp. 113–141). New York: International Universities Press.

Henig, R. M. (2010). What is it about 20-somethings: why are so many young people in their 20s taking so long to grow up? *New York Times*. August, 18.

Hill, D. (2010). Fundamentalist faith states: regulation theory as a frame-work for the psychology of religious fundamentalism. In: C. B. Strozier, D. M. Terman, & J. W. Jones, with K. A. Boyd (Eds.), *The Fundamentalist Mindset* (pp. 80–88). New York: Oxford University Press.

Hofer, M. A. (1995). Hidden regulators: implications for a new under-standing of attachment, separation, and loss. In: S. Goldberg, R. Muir, & J. Kerr (Eds.), *Attachment Theory: Social, Developmental and Clinical Perspectives* (pp. 203–230). Hillsdale, NJ: Analytic Press.

Hoffman, I. Z. (1998). Toward a social-constructivist view. In: *Ritual and Spontaneity in the Psychoanalytic Process: A Dialectical-Constructivist View*. Hillsdale, NJ and London: Analytic Press.

Hoffman, I. Z. (2009). Therapeutic passion in the countertransference. *Psychoanalytic Dialogues, 19*: 617–637.

Horney, K. (1950). *Neurosis and Human Growth*. New York: Norton.

Inhelder, B., & Piaget, J. (1958). *The Growth of Logical Thinking from Childhood to Adolescence*. New York: Basic Books.

Jacobson, E. (1954). The self and the object world. *Psychoanalytic Study of the Child, 9*: 75–127.

Jaffe, C. (2000). Organizing adolescents(ce): a dynamic systems perspective on adolescence and adolescent psychotherapy. In: A. H. Esman (Ed.), *Adolescent Psychiatry, Vol. 25* (pp. 17–43). Hillsdale, NJ: Analytic Press.

Johnson, C. (1999). Metaphor vs. conflation in the acquisition of polysemy: the case of SEE. In: M. K. Hiraga, C Sinha, & S. Wilcox. (Eds.), *Cultural, typological and psychological issues in cognitive linguistics. Current Issues in Linguistic Theory, Vol. 152* (pp. 155–169). Amsterdam: John Benjamins.

Johnson, M. (1987). *The Body in the Mind*. Chicago: University of Chicago Press.

Johnson, M. (2001). Functional brain development in humans. *Neuroscience, 2*(7): 475–483.

Jones, E. (1922). Some problems in adolescence. In: *Papers on Psychoanalysis*. London: Bailliere, Tindall, and Cox, 1948.

Kaplan, L. J. (1984). *Adolescence: The Farewell to Childhood*. NewYork: Simon and Schuster.

Kaplan-Solms, K., & Solms, M. (2002). *Clinical Studies in Neuro-Psychoanalysis: An Introduction to a Depth Neuropsychology* (2nd edn). New York and London: Karnac.

Karen, R. (1990). Becoming attached. *The Atlantic Monthly*, February.

Kazdin, A. E. (2011). *Single Case Research Designs: Methods for Clinical and Applied Settings* (3rd edn). New York: Oxford University Press.

Kegan, R. (1982). *The Evolving Self*. Cambridge, MA: Harvard University Press.

Kernberg, O. (1976). *Object Relations Theory and Clinical Psychoanalysis*. New York: Jason Aronson.

Kernberg, O. (1982). Self, ego, affect and drives. *Journal of the American Psychoanalytic Association, 30*: 893–917.

Kestenberg, J. S. (1967). Phases of adolescence, with suggestions for a correlation of psychic and hormonal organization. *Journal of the American Academy of Child Psychiatry, 6*: 426–463, 577–614.

Kestenberg, J. S. (1971). A psychoanalytic model of attention and learning. In: F. Schwartz, & P. H . Schiller (Eds.), *Psychological Issues, Vol. VI, No. 3, Monograph 23*. New York: Universities Press Inc, 1970.

Kestenberg, J. S. (1977). Psychoanalytic observation of children. *Int. R. Psycho-Anal.*, 4: 393–407.

Kent, E. (1981). *The Brains of Men and Machines*. Peterborough, NH: BYTE.

King, M. L. Jr. (1963). I Have A Dream. web66.coled.umn.edu./new/MLK.html

Klein, M. (1946). Notes on some schizoid mechanisms. In: *Envy and Gratitude and Other Works*. New York: Delacorte, 1957.

Klerman, G. L. (1990). The psychiatric patient's right to effective treatment: implications of Osheroff v. Chestnut Lodge. *American Journal of Psychiatry*, 147(4): 409–418.

Koestler, A. (1967). *The Act of Creation*. New York: Dell.

Koestler, A. (1971). *Janus: A Summing Up*. New York: Random House.

Koestler, A., & Smythies, J. R. (Eds.) (1979). *Beyond Reductionism: New Perspectives in the Life Sciences*. Boston: Beacon.

Kohut, H. (1966). Forms and transformations of narcissism. *Journal of the American Psychoanalytic Association*, 14: 243–272.

Kohut, H. (1971). *The Analysis of the Self*. New York: International Universities Press.

Kohut, H. (1977). *The Restoration of the Self*. New York: International Universities Press.

Kohut, H. (1984). *How Does Analysis Cure?* Chicago and London: University of Chicago Press.

Kohut, H. (1991). Four basic concepts in self psychology. In: P. H. Ornstein (Ed.), *The Search for the Self: Selected Writings of Heinz Kohut: 1978-1981*, *Vol. 4*. (pp. 447–470). Madison, CT: International Universities Press.

Kuhn, T. S. (1962). *The Structure of Scientific Revolutions*. Chicago, IL: University of Chicago Press.

Kurzweil, R. (2005). *The Singularity is Near*. London: Penguin.

Labouvie-Vief, G. (1984). Logic and self regulation from youth to maturity: a model. In: M. Commons, F. Richards, & C. Armon (Eds.), *Beyond Formal Operations: Late Adolescence and Adult Cognitive Development* (pp. 158–179). New York: Praeger.

Lakoff, G. (1987). *Women, Fire and Dangerous Things*. Chicago: University of Chicago Press.

Lakoff, G. (2009). The neural theory of metaphor. In: R. Gibbs (Ed.) *The Metaphor Handbook*. Cambridge, MA: Cambridge University Press.

Lakoff, G., & Johnson, M. (1980/2003). *Metaphors We Live By*. Chicago and London: The University of Chicago Press.

Lakoff, G., & Johnson, M. (1999). *Philosophy In the Flesh: The Embodied Mind And Its Challenge to Western Thought*. New York: Basic Books.

Langer, S. K. (1967). *Philosophy in a New Key*. Cambridge, MA: Harvard University Press.

Laplanche, J., & Pontalis, J.-B. (1973). *The Language of Psychoanalysis*. New York: Norton.

Laufer, M. (1965). *Assessment of Adolescent Disturbances: The Application of Anna Freud's Diagnostic Profile* (pp. 57–81). New Haven and London: Yale University Press, 1977.

Lasser, C. J., & Bathory, D. S. (1999). Reciprocal causality and childhood trauma: an application of chaos theory. In: F. Masterpasqua & P. A. Perna (Eds.), *The Psychological Meaning of Chaos: Translating Theory into Practice* (pp. 1–19). Washington, DC: American Psychological Press.

Lee, D. (2010). Recession's effects haunt a Generation. *Chicago Tribune*. October 27.

Lemche, E. (1998). The development of the body image in the first three years of life. *Psychoanalysis and Contemporary Thought, 21*(2): 157–275.

Lemme, B. H. (2006). *Development in Adulthood* (4th edn). Boston, MA: Allyn and Bacon/Pearson.

Levin, F. (1980). Metaphor, affect, and arousal: how interpretations might work. *Annual of Psychoanalysis, 8*: 231–245 [reprinted in *Mapping the Mind: The Intersection of Psychoanalysis and Neuroscience*. London: Karnac, 2003].

Levin, F. (2003). The prefrontal cortex and neural control: the brain's systems for judgement, insight and selective attention. In: *Mapping the Mind: The Intersection of Psychoanalysis and Neuroscience* (pp. 83–104). London: Karnac.

Levin, F., & Kent, E. (2003). The special relationship between psychoanalytic transference, similarity judgement, and the priming of memory. In: *Psyche and Brain: The Biology of Talking Cures* (pp. 57–72). Madison, CT: International Universities Press.

Levine, B. (2005). Back to the nest. Chicago, IL: *Chicago Tribune*, August 25.

Levinson, D. (1978). *The Seasons of a Man's Life*. New York: Knopf.

Levy, A. J. (2011). Neurobiology and the therapeutic action of psychoanalytic play therapy with children. *Clinical Social Work Journal, 39*: 50–60.

Lichtenberg, J. D. (1975). The development of the sense of self. *Journal of the American Psychoanalytic Association, 23*: 459–484.

Lichtenberg, J. D. (1978). Is there a line of development of narcissism? *Int. R. Psycho-Anal., 5*: 435–447.

Lichtenberg, J. D. (1983). *Psychoanalysis and Infant Research*. Hillsdale, NJ: Analytic Press.

Loewald, H. (1962). The superego and time. *International Journal of Psycho-analysis, 43*: 264–268.

Lucente, R. L. (1986). Self-transcending and the adolescent ego. *Child and Adolescent Social Work Journal, 3*(2): 161–176.

Lucente, R. L. (2012). *Character Formation and Identity in Adolescence: Clinical and Developmental Issues.* Chicago, IL: Lyceum.

Lyons-Ruth, K. (1991). Rapprochement or approchement: Mahler's theory reconsidered from the vantage of recent research on early attachment relationships. *Psychoanalytic Psychology, 8*: 1–23.

Mack, K. (2010). In recession, no place like home. *Chicago Tribune,* 4 January.

MacLean, P. D. (1990). *The Triune Brain: Role in Paleocerebral Functions.* New York and London: Plenum.

Mahler, M. S. (1968). On human symbiosis and the vicissitudes of individuation. In: M. Mahler (Ed.), *The Selected Papers of Margaret S. Mahler, Vol. II* (pp. 77–98). New York: Jason Aronson.

Mahler, M. S. (1988). *The Memoirs of Margaret S. Mahler,* P. Stepansky (Ed.). New York: Free Press.

Mahler, M. S., Pine, F., & Bergman, A. (1975). *The Psychological Birth of the Human Infant: Symbiosis and Individuation.* New York: Basic Books.

Mahoney, M. J. (1991). *Human Change Process.* New York: Basic Books.

Main, M., & Goldwyn, R. (1994). *Adult Attachment Scoring and Classification System.* Unpublished manuscript. University of California at Berkeley.

Main, M., & Morgan, H. (1996). Disorganization and disorientation in infant strange situation behavior: phenotypic resemblance to dissociative states? In: L. K. Michelson & W. J. Ray (Eds.), *Handbook of Dissociation: Theoretical, Empirical, and Clinical Perspectives* (pp. 107–138). New York: Plenum.

Main, M., & Solomon, J. (1990). Procedures for identifying infants as disorganized/disoriented during the Ainsworth Strange Situation. In: M. T. Greenberg, D. Cicchetti, & E. M. Cummings (Eds.), *Attachment in the Preschool Years: Theory, Research and Intervention* (pp. 121–160). Chicago, IL: University of Chicago Press.

Main, M., Kaplan, N., & Cassidy, J. (1985). Security in infancy, childhood and adulthood: a move to the level of representation. In: I. Breatherton and E. Waters (Eds.), *Growing Points of Attachment Theory and Research. Monographs of the Society for Research in Child Development, No. 50* (pp. 66–106). Ann Arbor, MI: Society for Research in Child Development.

Makari, G. (2008). *Revolution in Mind: The Creation of Psychoanalysis.* New York: Harper Collins.

Mandelbrot, B. (1977). *Fractals: Form, Chance and Dimension*. San Francisco, CA: Freeman.

Masterpasqua, F., & Perna, P. A. (1999). Introduction and Toward a dynamical developmental understanding of disorder. In: *The Psychological Meaning of Chaos: Translating Theory into Practice* (pp. 1–19 & 23–39. Washington, DC: American Psychological Press.

McGoldrick, M., & Carter, B. (2003). The family life cycle. In: F. Walsh (Ed.), *Normal Family Processes: Growing Diversity and Complexity* (3rd edn). New York and London: The Guilford Press.

Meissner, W. W. (1986). Can psychoanalysis find itself? *Journal of the American Psychoanalytic Association, 34*: 379–400.

Mitchell, S. A. (1988). *Relational Concepts in Psychoanalysis: An Integration*. Cambridge, MA: Harvard University Press.

Mitchell, S. A. (1993). *Hope and Dread in Psychoanalysis*. New York: Basic Books.

Mitchell, S. A. (2000). *Relationality: From Attachment to Intersubjectivity*. Hillsdale, NJ: Analytic Press.

Mitchell, S. A., & Black, M. J. (1995). *Freud and Beyond: A History of Modern Psychoanalytic Thought*. New York: Basic Books.

Modell, A. (1997). Reflections on metaphor and affects. *The Annual of Psychoanalysis, 25*: 219–233.

Modell, A. (2000). The transformation of past experiences. *The Annual of Psychoanalysis, 28*: 137–149.

Moessinger, P. (1978). Paiget on equilibration. *Human Development, 21*: 255–267.

Muuss, R. E. (1996). *Theories of Adolescence* (6th edn). New York: McGraw-Hill.

Narayanan, S. (1997). Embodiment in language understanding: sensorimotor representations for metaphoric reasoning about event descriptions. *Unpublished doctoral dissertation*, University of California, Berkeley.

Nietzsche, F. (1901). *The Will to Power*, W. Kaufmann & R. J. Hollingdale (Trans.). New York: Random House, 1968.

Offer, D. (1980). Adolescent development: a normative perspective. In: S. I. Greenspan and G. H. Pollock (Eds.), *The Course of Life: Psychoanalytic Contributions Toward Understanding Personality Development, Vol. II: Latency, Adolescence and Youth*. Washington, DC: NIMH.

Offer, D., & Offer, J. D. (1975). *From Teenage to Young Manhood: A Psychological Study*. New York: Basic Books.

Offer, D., & Sabshin, M. (1974). *Normality: Theoretical and Clinical Concepts of Mental Health*. New York: Basic Books.

Offer, D., & Sabshin, M. (1984). *Normality and the Life Cycle*. New York: Basic Books.

Offer, D., Ostrov, E., & Howard, K. L. (1981). *The Adolescent: A Psychological Self Portrait*. New York: Basic Books.

Ornston, D. G. (1992). Bruno Bettelheim's "Freud and Man's Soul". *Translating Freud* (pp. 63–74). New Haven, CT and London: Yale University Press.

Ovid (Publius Ovidius Naso) (2004). *Metamorphoses, Book VIII*, D. Raeburn (Trans.). London: Penguin.

Panksepp, J. (1998). Emotions, the higher cerebral processes, and the self. *Affective Neuroscience: The Foundations of Human and Animal Emotions* (Chapter 16). New York: Oxford University Press.

Palombo, J. (1987). Spontaneous self disclosure in psychotherapy. *Clinical Social Work Journal, 15*(2): 107–120.

Palombo, J. (1988). Adolescent development: a view from self psychology. *Child and Adolescent Social Work, 5*(3): 171–186.

Palombo, J. (1991). Bridging the chasm between developmental theory and clinical theory. Part I. The chasm and Part II. The bridge. *The Annual of Psychoanalysis, 19*: 151–193.

Palombo, J. (2006). *Nonverbal Learning Disabilities*. New York and London: Norton.

Palombo, J., Bendicsen, H., & Koch, B. (2009). *Guide to Psychoanalytic Developmental Theories*. New York: Springer.

Paris, B. J. (1999). Karen Horney's Vision of the Self. *The American Journal of Psychoanalysis, 59*: 157–166.

Parker, K. (2012). The boomerang generation: feeling OK about living with mom and dad. *Pew Research Center Publications*. Available at http://pewresearch.org/pubs/2219/boomerang-kids-young-adults-multigenerational-families

Parsons, T. (1960). *Structure and Processes in Modern Society*. New York: Free Press.

Pavlov, I. P. (1927). *Conditioned Reflexes: An Investigation of the Physiological Activity of the Cerebral Cortex*, G. V. Anrep (Trans.). London: Oxford University Press.

Pepper, S. (1942). *World Hypotheses*. Berkeley, CA: University of California Press.

Piaget, J. (1962). The stages of the intellectual development of the child. In: S. I. Harrison and J. F. McDermott (Eds.), *Childhood Psychopathology* (pp. 157–166). New York: International Universities Press, 1972.

Piaget, J. (1975). *The Equilibration of Cognitive Structures: Central Problems in Development*. Paris: The University of France Press.

Piaget, J., & Inhelder, B. (1995). The growth of logical thinking from childhood to adolescence. In: H. E. Gruber & J. J. Voneche (Eds.), *The Essential Piaget: An Interpretive Reference and Guide* (pp. 405–444). New York: Basic Books.

Polan, H. J., & Hofer, M. A. (1999). Psychobiological origins of infant attachment and separation responses. In: J. Cassidy & P. R. Shaver (Eds.), *Handbook of Attachment: Theory, Research, and Clinical Applications* (pp. 162–180). New York and London: Guilford Press.

Pollock, G. H. (1986). Oedipus examined and reconsidered: the myth, the developmental stage, the universal theme, the conflict, and the complex. *The Annual of Psychoanalysis, XIV*: 77–106.

Popper, K. (1965). *Conjectures and Refutations: The Growth of Scientific Knowledge.* New York: Harper.

Prigogine, I., & Stengers, I. (1984). *Order out of Chaos.* New York: Bantam.

Quinodoz, J.-M. (2005). *Reading Freud: A Chronological Exploration of Freud's Writings* (pp. 26–30). New York: Routledge.

Quillman, T. (2012). Neuroscience and self-disclosure: deepening right brain to right brain communication between therapist and patient. *Clinical Social Work Journal, 40*(1): 1–9.

Raines, J. C. (1996). Self-disclosure in clinical social work. *Clinical Social Work Journal, 24*(4): 357–375.

Richards, F. A., & Commons, M. L. (1984). Systematic, metasystematic and cross-paradigmatic reasoning. In: M. L. Commons, F. A. Richards, & C. Armon (Eds.), *Beyond Formal Operations* (pp. 92–119). New York: Praeger.

Richmond, B. M., & Sklansky, M. A. (1984). Structural change in adolescence. In: D. D. Brockman (Ed.), *Late Adolescence: Psychoanalytic Studies* (pp. 97–122). New York: International Universities Press.

Ricoeur, P. (1977). *The Rule of Metaphor: Multi-Disciplinary Studies of the Creation of Meaning in Language*, R. Czerny (Trans.), with K. McLaughlin & J. Costello. Toronto and Buffalo: University of Toronto Press, 1975.

Ross, D. (1972). *G. Stanley Hall: The Psychologist as Prophet.* Chicago and London: University of Chicago Press.

Rothgeb, C. L. (1973). *Abstracts of the Standard Edition of the Complete Psychological Works of Sigmund Freud.* New York: International Universities Press.

Rousseau, J.-J. (1762). *Emile or On Education*, A. Bloom (Trans.). New York: Basic Books, 1979.

Rousseau, J.-J. (1782). *Confessions*, J. M. Cohen (Trans.). New York: Penguin, 1953.

Sadow, L. (2000). About theory. *Annual of Psychoanalysis*, 28: 167–178.

Saari, C. (1993). Identity complexity as an indicator of health. *Clinical Social Work Journal*, 21: 11–24.

Sadock, B. J., & Sadock, V. A. (2007). *Kaplan and Sadock's Synopsis of Psychiatry: Behavioral Sciences and Clinical Psychiatry* (10th edn). Philadelphia, PA: Wolters Kluwer/Lippincott Williams & Wilkins.

Saleebey, D. (2006). *The Strengths Perspective in Social Work* (4th edn). Boston, MA: Allyn and Bacon.

Samuel, C. A. (2008). Responsive teaching: the "response to intervention" framework in Iowa is helping teachers better understand and address students' learning needs. *Education Week*, 2(1): 33–37.

Schafer, R. (1968). *Aspects of Internalization*. New York: International Universities Press.

Schafer, R. (1979). Character, ego syntonicity, and character change. *Journal of the American Psychoanalytic Association*, 27: 867–891.

Schafer, S. (1993). Comets and the world's end. In: L. Howe & A. Wain (Eds.), *Predicting the Future* (pp. 52–76). Cambridge, UK: Cambridge University Press.

Schore, A. N. (1994). *Affect Regulation and the Origin of the Self: The Neurobiology of Emotional Development*. Hillsdale, NJ: Erlbaum.

Schore, A. N. (2000). Attachment and the regulation of the right brain. *Attachment and Human Development*, 2(1): 23–47.

Schore, A. N. (2002). Advances in neuropsychoanalysis, attachment theory, and trauma research: implications for self psychology. *Psychoanalytic Inquiry*, 22(3): 433–484.

Schore, A. N. (2003). *Affect Regulation and the Repair of the Self*. New York: Norton.

Settlage, C. F. (1973). Panel "The experience of separation-individuation through the course of life: adolescence and maturity." J. Marcus, reporter. *Journal of the American Psychoanalytic Association*, 12: 154–167.

Shannon, C., & Weaver, W. (1949). *The Mathematical Theory of Communication*. Urbana, IL: University of Illinois Press.

Sharpe, E. F. (1940). Psycho-physical problems revealed in language: an examination of metaphor. *International Journal of Psychoanalysis*, 21: 201–213.

Sherrington, C. (1947). *The Integrative Action of the Nervous System*. New Haven, CT: Yale University Press.

Siegel, D. J. (1999). *The Developing Mind: Toward a Neurobiology of Personal Experience*. New York: Guilford Press.

Siegel, D. J. (2005). The mindful brain. Paper presented at the *Emotion Meets Spirit conference*, Deep Streams Institute, Watsonville, CA, June 3.

Siegel, D. J. (2006). An interpersonal neurobiology approach to psycho-therapy: how awareness, mirror neurons, and neural plasticity contribute towards the development of well-being. *Psychiatric Annals*, 36(4): 248–258.

Simms, K. (2003). *Paul Ricoeur. Critical Thinkers Series*. London and New York: Routledge.

Sinnott, J. D. (1984). Postformal reasoning: the relativistic stage. In: M. Commons, F. A. Richards, & C. Armon (Eds.), *Beyond Formal Operations: Late Adolescence and Adult Cognitive Development* (pp. 298–325) New York: Praeger.

Sklansky, M. A. (1991). The pubescent years: eleven to fourteen. In: S. I. Greenspan & G. H. Pollock (Eds.), *The Course of Life. Vol. IV* (pp. 63–97). Madison, CT: International Universities Press.

Sklansky, M., & Rabichow, H. (1980). *Effective Counseling of Adolescents*. Chicago, IL: Association Press/Follett.

Spear, L. P. (2000). The adolescent brain and age-related behavioral mani-festations. *Neuroscience and Behavioral Reviews*, 24: 417–463.

Spear, L. P. (2010). *The Behavioral Neuroscience of Adolescence*. New York: Norton.

Spelke, E. S. (1990). Principles of object perception. *Cognitive Science*, 14: 29–56.

Spitz, R. A. (1945a). Hospitalism: an inquiry into the genesis of psychiatric conditions early childhood. *Psychoanalytic Study of the Child*, 1: 53–74.

Spitz, R. A. (1945b). Diacritic and coenesthetic organizations: the psychi-atric significance of a functional division of the nervous system into a somatic and emotive part. *Psychoanalytic Review*, 32: 146–162.

Spitz, R. A. (1965). *The First Year of Life: A Psychoanalytic Study of Normal and Deviant Development of Object Relations*. New York: International Universities Press.

Sroufe, L. A. (1990). An organization perspective on the self. In: D. Cicchetti & M. Beeghly (Eds.). *The Self in Transition: Infancy to Childhood* (pp. 281–307). Chicago, IL: University of Chicago Press.

Sroufe, L. A., & Waters, E. (1977). Attachment as an organizational construct. *Child Development*, 48: 1184–1199.

St Clair, M. (2004). *Object Relations and Self Psychology: An Introduction* (4th edn). Belmont, CA: Brooks/Cole-Thompson Learning.

Steinberg, L. (2005). Cognitive and affective development in adolescence. *Trends in Cognitive Sciences*, 9(2): 69–74.

Stern, D. N. (1985). *The Interpersonal World of the Infant: A View from Psychoanalysis and Developmental Psychology*. New York: Basic Books.

Stern, D. N. (1989). Developmental prerequisites for the sense of narrated self. In: A. M. Cooper, O. F. Kernberg, & E. F. Person (Eds.), *Psychoanalysis: Toward The Second Century* (pp. 168–178). New Haven: Yale University Press.

Stern, D. N. (1993). Why study childrens' narratives? *The Signal: Newsletter of the World Association for Infant Mental Health, I*(3): 1–13.

Stern, D. N. (1995). *The Motherhood Constellation: A Unified View of Parent-Infant Psychotherapy*. Hillsdale, NJ: Analytic Press.

Stevens, J. W. (1997). African American female adolescent identity development: a three dimensional perspective. *Child Welfare Journal, 76*(1): 145–172.

Stevens-Long, J. (1990). Adult development: theories past and future. In: R. Nemiroff & C. Colarusso (Eds.), *New Dimensions in Adult Development* (pp. 125–169). New York: Basic Books.

Stolorow, D. R., & Atwood, G. E. (1979). *Faces in a Cloud: Subjectivity in Personality Theory*. New York: Jason Aronson.

Stolorow, D. R., & Atwood, G. E. (1992). Three realms of the unconscious. In: *Contexts of Being: The Intersubjective Foundations of Psychological Life* (pp. 29–40). Hillsdale, NJ: Analytic Press.

Strozier, C. A. (2001). *Heinz Kohut: The Making of A Psychoanalyst*. New York: Farrar, Straus, and Giroux.

Sullivan, H. S. (1950). The illusion of personal individuality. *Psychiatry, 13*: 317–332.

Sullivan, H. S. (1953). *The Interpersonal Theory of Psychiatry*. New York: Norton.

Sulloway, F. J. (1979). *Freud: Biologist of the Mind*. New York: Basic Books.

Summers, F. (1994). *Object Relations Theories and Psychopathology: A Comprehensive Text*. Hillsdale, NJ and London: Analytic Press.

Thelen, E., & Smith, L. B. (1994). *A Dynamic Systems Approach to the Development of Cognition and Action*. Cambridge, MA and London: Bradford Books/MIT.

Tulving, E. (1985). Memory and consciousness. *Canadian Psychology, 26*: 1–12.

Urdang, E. (2008). *Human Behavior in the Social Environment: Interweaving the Inner and Outer Worlds* (2nd edn). New York and London: Routledge/Taylor & Francis Group.

von Bertalanffy, L. (1967). *Robots: Men and Minds*. New York: Braziller.

van Geert, P. (1993). A dynamic systems model of cognitive growth: competition and support under limited resource conditions. In: L. B.

Smith & E. Thelen (Eds.), *A Dynamic Systems Approach to Development: Applications*. Cambridge, MA and London: Bradford Books/MIT.

van Geert, P. (1994). *Dynamic Systems of Development: Change Between Complexity and Chaos*. New York: Harvester Wheatsheaf.

Wallerstein, R. S., & Goldberger, L. (Eds.) (1999). *Ideas and Identites: The Life and Work of Erik Erikson*. New York: International Universities Press.

Wallin, D. J. (2007). *Attachment in Psychotherapy*. New York and London: Guilford Press.

Webster's Third New International Dictionary of the English Language. (1993). Springfield, MA: Merriam-Webster.

Weinstein, E. A., & Kahn, R. I. (1959). Symbolic reorganization in brain injuries. In: S. Arieti (Ed.), *American Handbook of Psychiatry, Vol. I* (pp. 964–981). New York: Basic Books.

Weiss, S. (1964). Parameters in child analysis. *Journal of the American Psychoanalytic Association, 12*: 587–599.

Werner, E. E., & Smith, R. (1992). *Overcoming the Odds*. Ithaca, NY: Cornell University Press.

White, R. (1959). Motivation reconsidered: the concept of competence. *Psychological Review, 66*: 297–333.

White, R. (1975). *Lives in Progress* (3rd edn). New York: Holt, Rinehart.

Winnicott, D. W. (1941). Observation of infants in a set situation. *Through Paediatrics to Psycho-Analysis*. New York: Basic Books, 1975.

Winnicott, D. W. (1950). Aggression in relation to development. *Through Paediatrics to Psycho-Analysis*. New York: Basic Books, 1975.

Winnicott, D. W. (1960). Ego distortions in terms of true and false self. In: *The Maturational Processes and the Facilitating Environment*. New York: International Universities Press, 1965.

Wolf, E. S. (1980). Tomorrow's self: Heinz Kohut's contribution to adolescent psychiatry. In: S. C. Feinstein (Ed.), *Adolescent Psychiatry, Vol. VIII* (pp. 41–50). Chicago, IL: University of Chicago Press.

Wolf, E. S. (1988). *Treating the Self: Elements of Clinical Self Psychology*. New York and London: Guilford Press.

Wundt, W. M. (1862). *Contributions to the Theory of Sensory Perception*. Leipzig: C. F. Winter.

Wynn, K. (1992). Addition and subtraction by human infants. *Nature, 358*: 749–750.

Youniss, J., & Damon, W. (1992). Social construction in Piaget's theory. In: H. Berlin & P. Pufall (Eds.), *Piaget's Theory: Prospects and Possibilities*. Hillsdale, NJ: Erlbaum.

SELECTED BIBLIOGRAPHY

Anastas, J. W. (2012). From scientism to science: how contemporary episte-
    mology can inform practice research. *Clinical Social Work Journal*, 40(2):
    157–165.

Blos, P. (1974). The genealogy of the ego ideal. *Psychoanalytic Study of the
    Child*, 29: 43–88.

Colarusso, C. A., & Montero, G. J. (2007). Transience during midlife as an
    adult psychic organizer: the midlife transition and crisis continuum.
    Psychoanalytic Study of the Child, 62: 329–358.

Commons, M. L., Richards, F. A., & Armon, C. (1984). *Beyond Formal
    Operations: Late Adolescent and Adult Cognitive Development*. New York:
    Praeger.

Eagleston, R. (2004). *The Holocaust and the Postmodern*. New York: Oxford
    University Press.

Feldman, J. (2006). *From Molecules to Metaphors*. Cambridge, MA: Bradford
    MIT Press.

Feldman, J., & Narayanan, S. (2004). Embodied meaning in a neural theory
    of language. *Brain and Language*, 89(2): 385–392.

Gedo, J. (1986). *Conceptual Issues in Psychoanalysis: Essays in History and
    Method*. Hillsdale, NJ: Analytic Press.

Gergen, K. (1973). Social psychology as history. *Journal of Personality and
    Social Psychology*, 26(2): 309–320.

Gitelson, M. (1948). Character synthesis: the psychotherapeutic problem of adolescence. *American Journal of Orthopsychiatry, 18*: 422–431.

Goethe, J. W. (1774). *Sorrows of Young Werther*, B. Pike (Trans.). New York: Modern Library / Random House, 2004.

Goldstein, E. (1995). *Ego Psychology and Social Work Practice*(2nd edn). New York: Free Press.

Greenspan, S. I. (1997b). *The Growth of the Mind: And the Endangered Origins of Intelligence*. Reading, MA: Addison Wesley Longman.

Kazdin, A. E. (1977). Assessing the clinical or applied significance of behavior change through social validation. *Behavior Modification, 1*: 427–452.

Kazdin, A. E. (1982). *Single Case Research Designs: Methods for Clinical and Applied Settings* (2nd edn). New York: Oxford University Press.

Keller, J. (2012). Wild thing: Maurice Sendak made incomparable art from childhood's monsters. *Chicago Tribune*. May 9.

Lakoff, G. (1992). The contemporary theory of metaphor. In: A. Ortony (Ed.), *Metaphor and Thought* (2nd edn). London / New York: Cambridge University Press.

Lehrer, J. (2010). The truth wears off: is there something wrong with the scientific method? *The New Yorker*. 52–57. December 13.

Lichtenberg, J. D. (1989). *Psychoanalysis and Motivation*. Hillsdale, NJ: Analytic Press.

Lyotard, J. F. (1984). *The Postmodern Condition: A Report on Knowledge*, G. Bennington & B. Massumi (Trans.). Minneapolis, MN: University of Minnesota Press.

Masterson, J. (1985). *The Real Self*. New York: Brunner / Mazel.

Pine, F. (1985). Moments and backgrounds in the developmental process. *Developmental Theory and Clinical Process* (pp. 38–53). New Haven and London: Yale University Press.

Sacks, O. (2007). *Musicophilia: Tales of Music and the Brain*. New York: Alfred Knopf.

Settlage, C. F. (1973). Panel "The experience of separation-individuation in infancy and its reverbetrations through the course of life: infancy and childhood". M. Winestien, reporter. *Journal of the American Psychoanalytic Association, 12*: 135–154.

Siegel, D. J. (2000). Toward an interpersonal neurobiology of the developing mind: attachment relationships, mindsight and neural integration. *Infant Mental Health Journal, 22*(1–2): 67–94.

Slade, A. (2000). The development and organization of attachment: implications for psychoanalysis. *Journal of the American Psychoanalytic Association, 48*(4): 1147–1174.

Solms, M. (2000). An integration of psychoanalysis and neuroscience. *The Annual of Psychoanalysis, 28*: 179–200.

Stern, D. (1985). *Unformulated Experience: From Dissociation to Imagination.* Hillsdale, NJ: Analytic Press.

The Boomerang Generation: Feeling OK about Living with Mom and Dad (15 March 2012), *Pew Research Center Publications.* http://pewresearch.org/pubs/2219/boomerang-kids-young-adults-multigenerational-families

Waelder, R. (1936). The principle of multiple function: observations on overdetermination. *Psychoanalytic Quarterly, 5*: 45–62.

Waelder, R. (1960). *Basic Theory of Psychoanalysis.* New York: International Universities Press.

Wallace, E. R. (1989). Toward a phenomenological and minimally theoretical psychoanalysis. *The Annual of Psychoanalysis, 17*: 17–69.

Winnicott, D. W. (1968). Communication between infant and mother, mother and infant, compared and contrasted. In: *Babies and Their Mothers* (pp. 98–103). Reading, MA: Addison-Wesley.

Wolf, M. M. (1978). Social validity: the case for subjective measurement or how applied behavior analysis is finding its heart. *Journal of Applied Behavior Analysis, 11*: 203–214.

INDEX

Abraham, K., 30, 203, 209
abuse, 94, 112, 126, 134, 154, 160, 162, 166
  alcohol, 163
  drug, 160, 163
  sexual, 94
  verbal, 152, 162
adolescence/adolescent (*passim*)
  behaviour, 113–114
  cognition, 142–144
  conceptualisation of, 42
  constructivist, 41
  development, 14, 25, 40–42, 57, 110, 113, 135, 144, 179
  elongated, 4
  end of, xviii, 3, 6, 8, 43, 48, 130, 134, 175, 188, 195
  girls, xiii, xvi, 130, 176, 189
  identity struggle, 13
  issue, 5–6, 49
  late, xiv, xvi–xviii, 6–9, 14, 19, 35–36, 42, 47, 57, 64, 67–69, 79, 86–87, 109–111, 135, 144, 176, 180, 184, 187, 189, 196

  male, 6, 51
  middle, xvii, 41
  nature of, 6
  normative, 41, 54, 179
  older, 19, 42
  phase, 4, 6, 8, 41, 43, 47, 68, 77, 133–135, 194
  positivist, 47
  psychology, 59, 188
  psychotherapy, 184
  self, 117
  transformation, 134
  turbulence, 48
  turmoil, 170, 179
  world, 41
Adult Attachment Interview, 91–92, 185
affect(ive), 38, 43, 56, 60, 65–66, 69, 79–82, 86, 96, 103, 105, 110, 114, 119, 152, 183–184, 195 *see also*: consciousness
  arousal, 80
  attunement, 35, 86, 90, 95
  changes, 68